Setting Up

in

Dubai

Essam Al Tamimi

Edition 1-1994
Edition 2-2000
Edition 3-2003

ISBN 9948-03-070-2

Printed by
Emirates Printing Press
in the United Arab Emirates

Published by
Cross Border Legal Publishing FZ LLC
Suite 313, Building 8, DMC
PO Box 502129
Dubai, United Arab Emirates.
Phone: 00971 4 390 3520
Fax: 00971 4 390 8219
info@crossborder.ae
www.crossborder.ae

Setting Up

in

Dubai

Essam Al Tamimi

Abu Dhabi
Arab Tower, 5th Floor, Hamdan Street
PO Box 44046, Abu Dhabi, UAE
Tel: 971 2 6744535
Fax: 971 2 6768762

Sharjah
3rd Floor, Suite #306, Al Reem Plaza
PO Box 5099, Sharjah, UAE
Tel: 971 6 5727255
Fax: 971 6 5727258

AL TAMIMI
& COMPANY

Advocates & Legal Consultants

التـميـمـي
و مـشـاركـوه

للمحاماة والاستشارات القانونيه

Dubai Internet City
Building No. 5, #G-08, Sheikh Zayed Road,
PO Box 500188, Dubai, UAE
Tel: 971 4 3912444
Fax: 971 4 3916864

Al Tamimi & Company, originally established in 1989, by Essam Al Tamimi is today one of the leading law firms in the Arabian Gulf region. It is the largest independent law firm in the United Arab Emirates with four offices in Dubai, Abu Dhabi, Sharjah and the Dubai Internet City.

Dubai
29th Floor, Dubai World Trade Centre
PO Box 9275, Dubai, UAE
Tel: 971 4 3317090
Fax: 971 4 3313177

Clients are ably served by an international team of over 43 high-caliber lawyers from the United Kingdom, North America, Europe, South Africa, the United Arab Emirates and several other Arab countries. Each member of its team of professionals and qualified administrative staff is fully committed to providing clients with accurate, creative and cost effective advice. In addition, the firm has the largest and most experienced team of UAE national advocates with rights of audience before the UAE courts. This combination makes the firm unique in being able to offer clients first class representation in both consultancy and advocacy services.

The firm can assist multinational companies to establish operations in the UAE independently, or in association with local partners. Both local clients, many of whom have business interests outside the UAE, and international companies, rely on its global perspective. The firm subscribes to the belief that the world of opportunity does not recognise national boundaries.

Al Tamimi & Company specialises in:
Company / Commercial Law , Litigation, Banking / Securities, Project Finance, Islamic Finance, Construction Law, Insurance, Maritime Law, Aviation Law, Intellectual Property, Information Technology, E-Commerce, Mergers and Acquisitions, Joint Ventures, Alternative Dispute Resolution, Arbitration, Privatisation and Property Law.

Al Tamimi & Company is also the most subscribed to source of information in the region. The firm publishes a monthly newsletter covering the GCC and Middle East region called Law Update. The firm is highly regarded for its opinion on the local legal perspective and is poised to offer clients advice and counsel regarding all regional business operations and concerns.

Contents

Chapter 4   Business in Dubai – Business Structures

Chapter 5   Employment Issues

Application forms are available in PDF format on the CD included with the book. These are indicative only and may not be accepted by the departments as computer printouts.

Directories for the following are listed on individual files in Adobe Acrobat PDF format on the CD included. This is a selective listing only.

- Accountants
- Airlines
- Area Codes
- Banks
- Business Councils
- Car Rentals
- Clinics
- Consulates and Embassies
- Government
- Hotels
- Insurance
- Leisure Activities
- Real Estate Agencies
- Recruitment Consultants
- Restaurants
- Schools
- Serviced Apartments
- Shopping Malls

Sections are marked by ▮ band

Subsections are marked by ▯ band

All procedures are indicated by →

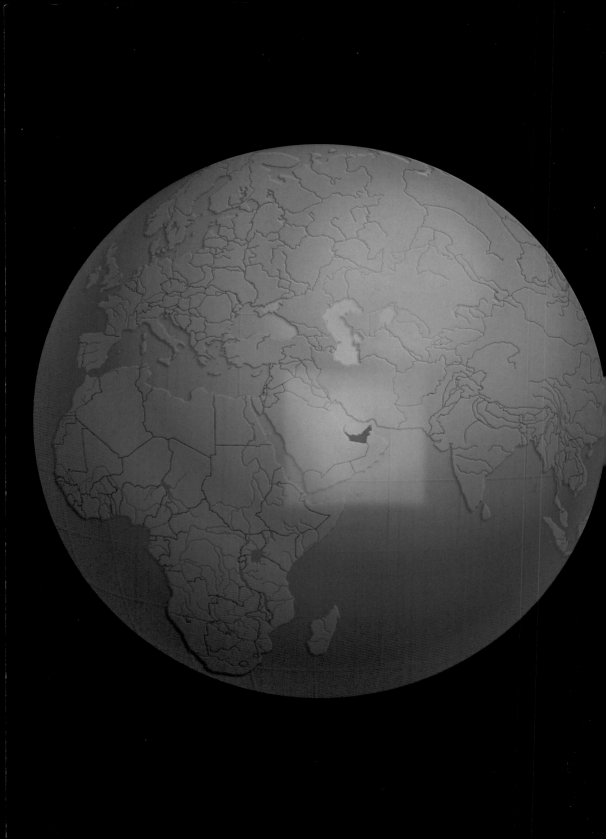

Chapter One

An Introduction to Dubai

The United Arab Emirates

▲ An early picture of H.H. Sheikh Zayed bin Sultan Al Nahyan - President and Founder of the UAE

The United Arab Emirates (UAE), Al Emarat Al Arabiyah Al Mutahidah in Arabic, was established on 2 December 1971 and is a federation of the seven emirates: Abu Dhabi, Dubai, Sharjah, Ras Al Khaimah, Umm Al Quwain, Ajman and Fujairah.

From the 1850s until the union of the emirates in 1971, the British colonial administration maintained influence in the region, and each emirate entered into separate treaties with the British. The emirates were then collectively known as the Trucial States or Sheikhdoms.

The states were each led by a Sheikh who belonged to a particular tribe which was usually the most influential tribe in the area. The tribe often branched into several smaller tribes, and each also had its own leaders who would work closely with the Sheikh in both political and other matters. For instance, the Al Bu Falah tribe from which the current President of the UAE, H.H. Sheikh Zayed bin Sultan Al Nahyan is descended is part of the Bani Yas tribe which consists of over twelve tribes.

Dubai

▲ An early view of the Creek in Dubai

The growth of Dubai began in the early part of the nineteenth century when members of the Bani Yas tribe led by Sheikh Maktoum Bin Butti left Abu Dhabi and migrated north to found an independent Sheikhdom in the area now known as Dubai. When a maritime agreement was later signed with the British, the area became known as the Trucial Coast.

By the early part of the 20th century, Dubai came to be known as the principal port on the Trucial Coast and established itself as the main centre for trade. Dubai attracted traders from India, Europe and neighbouring Arab countries. The souks here became legendary and the city was quickly established as a leading centre for trade in gold and pearls. The British remained in the area mainly to protect the merchant vessels until 1968.

Following the withdrawal of the British, steps were taken (led by Sheikh Zayed bin Sultan Al Nahyan of Abu Dhabi and the late Sheikh Rashid bin Saeed Al Maktoum, former Ruler of Dubai) to bring the individual Sheikhdoms together into a single federation. This resulted in the formation of the UAE in 1971.

On 6 June 1966 oil was first discovered by the Dubai Petroleum Company at Fateh, 58 miles off the coast. Although a high percentage of its revenue is attributed to non-oil trade, Dubai remains a major oil and gas producer and exporter.

Oil revenues have been used to create and develop the considerable economic infrastructure, which has emerged in Dubai in recent years. Abu Dhabi nevertheless has the largest oil reserves in the UAE, making it the richest emirate in the Federation.

▲ Oil is discovered.

Location

Dubai is the second largest emirate in the UAE, after Abu Dhabi, and is situated on the west coast of the United Arab Emirates in the south-western part of the Arabian Gulf. It lies at longitude 55 degrees east and latitude 25 degrees north. It covers an area of 3,885 sq. km. and, except for a tiny enclave in the Hajar Mountains at Hatta, is in one single block of territory. Most of the land in Dubai is sparsely populated as the population tends to be centered in the city, which is divided into two main parts by the Creek. On one side of the Creek lies Deira and on the other side lies Bur Dubai. To the north of Dubai lies the emirate of Sharjah and to the immediate south, Abu Dhabi.

▲ The location of Dubai in the UAE

Role of Dubai Government

"The business of Government is manufacturing opportunity". H.H.General Sheikh Mohammed bin Rashid Al Maktoum, Crown Prince of Dubai and Defence Minister of the UAE.

The Dubai Government is fully committed to maintaining a stable, responsive and pro-business commercial environment. Over the years it has consistently followed policies directed towards instilling market confidence and enhancing the economy by the encouragement of local and foreign investors. To this end it has created a liberal but soundly based regulatory regime and sponsored a large number of imaginative and growth promoting initiatives.

The E-Government Initiative   www.dubai.ae

The Dubai government has placed great importance and urgency on its commitment to the provision of all government services online via a special web portal devoted to this purpose. Each department has been instructed to make online provision of their services a top priority, and to generate the income necessary to cover the costs of going online. Some institutions have progressed faster than others, and there has been some resistance by those not sure about change. Overall expectations from the project are quite high, and it is certainly a positive development to watch for.

Why Invest in Dubai?

Strategically located at the crossroads of trade and commerce between Europe and the Far East, Dubai is uniquely positioned to service a large and diverse regional market that includes the Middle East, North and East Africa, the CIS (Commonwealth of Independent States) and the Indian subcontinent.

▲ The Dubai International Financial Centre   ▲ The Burj Dubai will be the tallest building in the world.

Dubai also benefits immensely from ready access to a pool of talent, ability to sustain competitive rates of remuneration, a highly cosmopolitan environment and an excellent quality of life.

All these factors have already made Dubai a preferred investment location for a host of prime multinational corporations and the emirate has no difficulty in attracting the skilled personnel required for operations right across the commercial and industrial spectrum.

Against this background, it is hardly surprising that the domestic market remains buoyant and prosperous and has not been affected by world recession. There is no question that Dubai's laissez faire economic policy has proved attractive to investors, both domestic and international.

The overall strategy of adopting free market principles has brought about an increasing volume of investment in a large variety of projects and joint ventures, manufacturing and service industries; retail and tourism business have increased. The effect has spilled over in all areas and the general economic benefits are clearly visible.

A further stimulus to growth has been provided by the Free Zones. The Jebel Ali Free Zone set up in 1985, the recently established Dubai Airport Free Zone, Dubai Internet City, Dubai Media City, Knowledge Village, Dubai International Financial Centre, Dubai Cars and Automotive Zone and the Gold and Diamond Park, and Jebel Ali Offshore Companies offer attractive concessions and investment incentives to foreign investors including superb manufacturing and commercial facilities. The Free Zones initiative has played an important part in developing Dubai into a major industrial centre in the region where high quality export products can be produced at competitive prices.

Dubai also maintains seaport and airport facilities which rival any in the world, and are served by all leading international shipping agencies and airlines. Businesses in Dubai also benefit from a first class service sector. Many of the world's top ranking accounting firms, advertising agencies, consultancy firms, banks and hotels have established operations here.

▲ Sheikh Rashid Terminal - Dubai International Airport

▲ The Jebel Ali Free Zone

Dubai, although rich in oil, has made great efforts to reduce its economic dependence on oil revenues.

A deliberately low level of business and market regulation has been adopted in order to encourage overseas investment in the non-oil commercial sector. As a result, Dubai's non-oil economy has achieved a rate of growth rivaling that of any economy in the world.

The statistics alongside illustrate the growth in non-oil foreign trade up to 2001 (inclusive) in the UAE and in Dubai, the gross domestic product (GDP) at factor cost and per capita GDP between the years 1995 and 2001 (inclusive), the import value of certain commodities brought into Dubai between the years 1991 and 2001 (inclusive), the export value of various products exported abroad from Dubai between the years 1994 and 2001 (inclusive), the goods by broad country group which are exported and re-exported from Dubai between the years 1991 and 2001 (inclusive) and the imports by broad category of goods between 1994 and 2001 (inclusive).

▼ The Burj Al Arab, the world's only seven star hotel

Dubai

Value by Type of Commodity

Value : Million Dhs   Quantity : Thousand Tons

Year	Imports		Exports		Re-Exports		Total Trade	
	Value	Quantity	Number	Quantity	Number	Quantity	Number	Quantity
1975	7,115	3,258	9	-	558	-	7,682	-
1976	9,498	4,745	8	-	973	-	10,478	-
1977	12,660	5,645	293	-	1,141	-	14,094	-
1978	12,708	4,322	115	-	1,380	-	14,202	-
1979	16,737	5,172	238	-	2,016	-	18,991	-
1980	19,551	4,962	951	469	3,220	914	23,722	6,344
1981	19,679	5,223	1,594	861	3,250	457	24,523	6,541
1982	18,866	4,548	1,617	930	2,755	335	23,237	5,813
1983	19,558	4,959	1,548	778	5,195	514	26,301	6,250
1984	17,225	5,038	1,797	792	3,835	525	22,856	6,355
1985	16,796	5,180	1,168	438	3,649	589	21,614	6,207
1986	16,450	5,465	1,288	498	4,434	657	22,172	6,620
1987	18,872	5,161	1,319	509	5,240	961	25,431	6,631
1988	22,474	4,588	1,725	662	5,087	595	29,286	5,845
1989	27,046	5,155	2,082	571	6,514	941	35,642	6,667
1990	31,042	5,728	2,296	627	7,603	950	40,940	7,304
1991	38,111	6,113	2,785	660	7,526	852	48,422	7,625
1992	47,547	7,390	3,302	808	9,000	1,051	59,848	9,249
1993	50,532	7,876	3,541	814	10,278	1,178	64,351	9,868
1994	52,230	8,563	3,273	799	10,670	1,185	66,173	10,547
1995	54,638	8,249	4,686	996	13,069	1,486	72,393	10,731
1996	61,795	8,834	4,213	934	16,120	1,932	82,128	11,700
1997	63,726	9,200	5,473	1,245	16,647	1,917	85,846	12,362
1998	67,621	10,685	5,241	1,257	15,817	1,844	88,679	13,786
1999	65,605	11,196	5,128	1,399	15,031	2,155	85,764	14,750
2000	72,392	11,037	5,464	1,347	17,659	2,373	95,515	14,757
2001	83,187	11,428	5,909	1,570	22,575	2,465	111,671	15,463

Source: Ports, Customs and Free Zone Corporation

Dubai

Gross Domestic Product at Factor Cost

Million Dhs at current prices

Economic Sectors	1995	1996	1997*	1998*	1999*	2000*	2001**
Gross Domestic Product	41,250	44,744	47,879	49,876	55,810	62,335	64,290
Non-Oil Gross Domestic Product	34,016	38,170	42,810	46,278	51,068	53,881	58,816
Agriculture	264	286	394	442	464	501	517
Mining & Quarrying	67	69	72	75	77	78	74
Manufacturing	4,677	5,221	6,497	7,500	8,950	10,090	10,348
Electricity & Water	813	861	885	912	981	1,031	1,080
Construction	3,464	3,680	4,097	4,395	4,790	5,066	5,218
Trade	6,802	8,034	9,228	9,573	9,776	10,163	10,517
Restaurants & Hotels	1,095	1,549	1,921	2,182	2,543	2,713	2,870
Transport, Storage and Communication	4,490	4,877	5,279	5,813	6,706	8,047	8,545
Finance & Insurance	3,409	4,104	4,548	5,451	5,728	6,187	7,044
Real Estate	4,389	4,838	4,873	5,082	5,537	6,057	6,290
Government Services	4,452	4,669	4,897	5,138	5,392	5,659	5,939
Other Services	1,189	1,297	1,551	1,696	1,883	2,045	2,193
Less: Imputed Bank Services	-1,095	-1,315	-1,432	-1,981	-1,759	-1,667	-1,819

Source: Ministry of Planning   * Adjusted   ** Preliminary

UAE & Dubai

Gross Domestic Product at Factor Cost and Per Capita GDP

2001

Million Dhs at current prices

Economic Sectors	Dubai *		UAE	
	Mn. Dhs	%	Mn. Dhs	%
Gross Domestic Product	64,290		248,320	
Non-Oil Gross Domestic Product	58,816	100.0	178,670	100.0
Agriculture	517	0.9	9,700	5.4
Mining & Quarrying	74	0.1	697	0.4
Manufacturing	10,348	17.6	34,433	19.3
Electricity & Water	1,080	1.8	4,890	2.7
Construction	5,218	8.9	17,446	9.8
Trade	10,517	17.9	22,838	12.8
Restaurants & Hotels	2,870	4.9	5,418	3.0
Transport, Storage & Communication	8,545	14.5	17,964	10.1
Finance & Insurance	7,044	12.0	16,903	9.5
Real Estate	6,290	10.7	19,663	11.0
Government Service	5,939	10.1	27,504	15.4
Other Services	2,193	3.7	5,781	3.2
Less: Imputed Bank Services	-1,819	-3.1	-4,566	-2.6
Population ('000)	910		3,290	
Per Capita GDP (Dhs) GDP (Total)	70,625		75,477	
Non-Oil Components	64,612		54,307	

Source: Ministry of Planning   * Preliminary

Dubai

Imports Value by Type of Commodity

In million Dhs

Sections	1991	1992	1993	1994	1995	1996	1997	1998	1999	2000	2001
1 • Live animals: animal products	1,012	1,045	1,085	1,160	1,478	1,602	1,514	1,542	1,497	1,509	1,425
2 • Vegetable products	1,687	2,414	2,509	2,395	2,663	3,118	2,999	3,476	3,542	3,444	3,296
3 • Animal & vegetable fats, oils and waxes	163	134	164	200	277	226	235	298	283	243	162
4 • Prepared foodstuffs, beverages, tobacco	1,411	1,551	1,380	1,641	1,609	1,777	1,821	1,819	1,776	1,816	2,048.4
5 • Mineral products	991	880	950	1,041	987	984	1,000	1,427	933	1,017	659
6 • Products of chemicals or allied industries	2,385	2,508	2,671	2,957	3,062	3,452	4,044	4,406	4,243	4,517	4,564
7 • Plastics, rubbers and it articles	1,556	1,752	1,756	1,980	2,237	2,757	2,652	2,748	2,697	2,950	3,041
8 • Raw hides, skins, leather, etc. and articles	280	306	373	388	456	526	584	533	433	439	483
9 • Wood, cork, plating materials and articles	543	692	829	877	854	774	830	859	756	829	837
10 • Pulp of wood: paper products: waste paper	585	600	564	674	936	839	896	906	917	1,155	1,011
11 • Textiles and textile articles	6,829	8,314	9,255	9,247	9,777	10,591	10,983	10,413	9,300	9,766	9,273
12 • Footwear, headgear, umbrellas etc.	606	801	875	1,090	1,174	1,518	1,235	1,084	787	823	878
13 • Articles of stone, cement, asbestos, ceramics, glass	681	920	1,033	1,058	1,097	1,239	1,264	1,507	1,441	1,427	1,640
14 • Pearls, precious stones and metals	1,882	2,378	3,607	2,516	1,949	1,753	2,127	2,253	4,337	6,097	15,974.4
15 • Base metals and articles of base metals	2,593	3,275	3,623	3,797	4,454	4,727	4,971	5,367	4,820	4,967	5,756.4
16 • Machinery:sound recorders, TV etc.	8,892	11,158	11,278	12,594	13,037	14,581	14,225	16,293	15,650	17,034	17,839
17 • Vehicles, aircraft, vessels etc.	3,523	5,727	5,268	4,907	4,907	6,933	7,591	7,914	8,022	9,782	10,257
18 • Optical, medical etc. equipments: watches	1,194	1,431	1,612	1,755	1,844	2,002	2,154	2,240	1,948	2,020	2,242
19 • Arms and ammunition: parts and accessories	7	8	8	8	4	5	8	5	7	7	9
20 • Miscellaneous manufactured articles	1,282	1,638	1,676	1,946	2,033	2,387	2,580	2,526	2,211	2,537	2,274
21 • Art work, collectors' pieces and antiques	3	14	16	3	4	5	9	5	5	13	18
Total	38,111	47,547	50,532	52,230	54,638	61,795	63,722	67,621	65,605	72,392	83,187

Source: Ports, Customs and Free Zone Corporation

Dubai

Exports Value by Type of Commodity

In million Dhs

Sections	1994	1995	1996	1997	1998	1999	2000	2001
1 • Live animals: animal products	62	78	48.9	103	111	71	46	52.4
2 • Vegetable products	26	25	49.2	58	87	99	74	82
3 • Animal & vegetable fats, oils and waxes	38	101	75.3	82	85	86	79	81
4 • Prepared foodstuffs, beverages, tobacco	129	209	237.2	250	197	168	150	251.4
5 • Mineral products	181	228	214.4	291	277	253	191	229
6 • Products of chemicals or allied industries	126	157	171.2	239	285	208	187	320
7 • Plastics, rubbers and articles	59	102	113.3	118	111	86	63	123
8 • Raw hides, skins, leather, etc. and articles	10	9	7.4	9	6	4	6	10
9 • Wood, cork, plating materials & articles	0	1	0.5	2	2	1	16	
10 • Pulp of wood: paper products: waste paper	42	73	75.6	104	106	102	95	150
11 • Textiles and textile articles	629	693	828.1	976	986	902	636	800
12 • Footwear, headgear, umbrellas etc.	1	1	3.4	1	3	4	5	12
13 • Article of stone, cement, asbestos: ceramics: glass	33	39	61.4	106	148	192	192	358
14 • Pearls, precious stones and metals	143	169	270.7	232	263	146	88	61
15 • Base metals and articles of base metals	1,637	2,210	1,949.2	2,791	2,479	2,713	3,574	3,223.4
16 • Machinery: sound recorders, TV etc.	37	53	61.4	64	50	50	37	68
17 • Vehicles, aircraft, vessels etc.	103	504	14.5	9	13	15	11	7.4
18 • Optical, medical etc. equipments, watches	1	2	4.9	2	1	0	4	6.4
19 • Arms and ammunition: parts and accessories	0	0	0	0	0	28	0	0
20 • Miscellaneous manufactured articles	18	32	25.9	33	33	0	24	66
21 • Art work, collectors pieces and antiques	0	0	0.3	0	0	0	0	2
Total	3,273	4,686	4,213	5,470	5,241	5,128	5,464	5,909

Source: Ports, Customs and Free Zone Corporation

Dubai

Exports by Broad Country Groups

In million Dhs

Country Group	1991	1992	1993	1994	1995	1996	1997	1998	1999	2000	2001
GCC Countries	568	720	642	658	769	544	537	480	397	314	394
Other Arab Countries	90	151	164	123	202	270	416	555	503	510	587
Eastern/S.Eastern Asia	1,351	1,181	1,121	1,329	1,650	1,632	2,332	1,488	1,801	1,981	2,024
Southern & West Asia	145	204	338	329	538	470	574	583	470	580	761
Europe (West)	487	840	907	696	743	864	979	1,338	1,185	1,222	1,072
Europe (East)	3	3	7	12	86	140	2	8	101	54	86
North America	103	178	199	108	171	229	337	485	508	677	697
Central/South America	0	0	1	0	1	3	1	11	8	12	15
Africa (Exc. Arab C.)	73	17	159	16	521	52	87	145	123	77	185
Oceania	1	7	2	2	4	8	25	18	31	35	87
Free Zones (UAE)	-	-	-	-	-	-	0	2	1	-	-
C.I. States	-	-	-	-	-	-	183	128	-	-	-
Duty Free Shops (UAE)	-	-	-	-	-	-	-	-	-	-	-
Ship Stores	-	-	-	-	-	-	3	-	-	-	-
Total	**2,785**	**3,302**	**3,541**	**3,273**	**4,686**	**4,213**	**5,473**	**5,241**	**5,128**	**5,464**	**5,909**
Percentage											
GCC Countries	20.4	21.8	18.1	20.1	16.4	12.9	9.8	9.2	7.7	5.7	6.7
Other Arab Countries	3.2	4.6	4.6	3.8	4.3	6.4	7.6	10.6	9.8	9.3	9.9
Eastern/S.Eastern Asia	47.2	35.8	31.7	40.6	35.2	38.7	42.6	28.4	35.1	36.3	34.3
Southern & West Asia	5.2	6.2	9.5	10.0	11.5	11.2	10.5	11.1	9.2	10.6	12.9
Europe (West)	17.5	25.4	25.6	21.3	15.9	20.5	17.9	25.5	23.1	22.4	18.1
Europe (East)	0.1	0.1	0.2	0.4	1.8	3.3	0.0	0.2	2.0	1.0	1.5
North America	3.7	5.4	5.6	3.3	3.6	5.4	6.1	9.3	9.9	12.4	11.8
Central/South America	0.0	0.0	0.0	0.0	0.0	0.1	0.0	0.2	0.2	0.2	0.3
Africa (Exc. Arab C.)	2.6	0.5	4.5	0.5	11.1	1.2	1.6	2.8	2.4	1.4	3.1
Oceania	0.0	0.2	0.1	0.1	0.1	0.2	0.5	0.3	0.6	0.6	1.5
Free Zones (UAE)	-	-	-	-	-	0.0	0.0	0.0	0.0	-	-
C.I. States	-	-	-	-	-	-	3.3	2.4	-	-	-
Duty Free Shops (UAE)	-	-	-	-	-	-	-	-	-	-	-
Ship Stores	-	-	-	-	-	-	-	-	-	-	-
Total	**100**	**100**	**100**	**100**	**100**	**100**	**100**	**100**	**100**	**100**	**100**

Source: Ports, Customs and Free Zone Corporation

Dubai

Re-exports by Broad Country Groups

In million Dhs

Country Group	1991	1992	1993	1994	1995	1996	1997	1998	1999	2000	2001
GCC Countries	2,669	2,362	2,443	1,808	1,928	2,613	2,531	2,318	2,356	2,634	3,067
Other Arab Countries	708	887	731	823	1,258	1,864	1,986	2,548	2,387	3,361	4,032
Eastern/S.Eastern Asia	485	885	1,111	669	1,021	772	739	461	709	1,038	1,419
Southern & West Asia	2,391	3,193	4,323	5,700	5,283	6,056	6,319	5,303	4,836	6,370	8,680
Europe (West)	651	755	724	616	926	1,009	1,030	1,052	1,244	1,461	2,387
Europe (East)	84	157	238	374	1,251	2,127	157	209	1,504	1,098	1,071
North America	119	173	186	164	244	235	451	457	664	700	718
Central/South America	6	15	13	17	19	26	20	23	48	24	25
Africa (Exc. Arab C.)	332	487	421	359	878	1,078	1,098	1,067	1,002	838	6,153
Oceania	8	6	10	15	16	9	20	19	21	22	22
Free Zones (UAE)	0	0	9	40	128	201	306	261	207	99	.7
C.I. States	-	-	-	-	-	-	1,847	1,981	-	-	-
Duty Free Shops (UAE)	51	63	55	61	97	108	119	25	38	7	1
Ship Stores	21	16	17	22	22	24	25	93	15	7	-
Total	**7,526**	**9,000**	**10,278**	**10,670**	**13,069**	**16,120**	**16,647**	**15,817**	**15,031**	**17,659**	**22,575**
Percentage											
GCC Countries	35.5	26.2	23.8	16.9	14.8	16.2	15.2	14.7	15.68	14.9	13.6
Other Arab Countries	9.4	9.9	7.1	7.7	9.6	11.6	11.9	16.1	15.88	19.0	17.9
Eastern/S.Eastern Asia	6.4	9.8	10.8	6.3	7.8	4.8	4.4	2.9	4.7	5.9	6.3
Southern & West Asia	31.8	35.5	42.1	53.4	40.4	37.6	38.0	33.5	32.18	36.1	38.4
Europe (West)	8.7	8.4	7.0	5.8	7.1	6.3	6.2	6.7	8.28	8.3	10.6
Europe (East)	1.1	1.7	2.3	3.5	9.6	13.2	0.9	1.3	10.01	6.2	4.7
North America	1.6	1.9	1.8	1.5	1.9	1.5	2.7	2.9	4.4	4.0	3.2
Central/South America	0.1	0.2	0.1	0.2	0.1	0.2	0.1	0.1	0.32	0.1	0.1
Africa (Exc. Arab C.)	4.4	5.4	4.1	3.4	6.7	6.7	6.6	6.7	6.67	4.7	5.1
Oceania	0.1	0.1	0.1	0.1	0.1	0.1	0.1	0.1	0.14	0.1	0.1
Free Zones (UAE)	0.0	0.0	0.1	0.4	1.0	1.2	1.8	1.7	1.38	0.6	0.0
C.I. States	0.0	0.0	0.0	0.0	0.0	0.0	11.1	12.5	-	0.0	-
Duty Free Shops (UAE)	0.7	0.7	0.5	0.6	0.7	0.7	0.7	0.2	0.26	0.0	0.0
Ship Stores	0.3	0.2	0.2	0.2	0.2	0.1	0.1	0.6	0.1	0.0	-
Total	**100**	**100**	**100**	**100**	**100**	**100**	**100**	**100**	**100**	**100**	**100**

Source: Ports, Customs and Free Zone Corporation

Dubai

Imports by Broad Category of Goods

In million Dhs

Group	1994	1995	1996	1997	1998	1999	2000	2001
Foodstuffs	5,396	6,027	6,723	6,569	7,135	7,098	7,012	6,931.4
Durable consumer groups	23,713	24,625	26,500	27,731	28,209	26,966	29,922	39,516.6
Intermediate goods	5,610	6,235	7,048	7,593	8,060	7,857	8,622	8,616
Capital goods	17,500	17,743	21,514	21,816	24,207	23,672	26,816	28,096
Other goods	10	8	10	17	10	12	20	27
Total	52,230	54,638	61,795	63,726	67,621	65,605	72,392	83,187
Percentage Distribution								
Foodstuffs	10.3	11.0	10.9	10.3	10.6	10.8	9.7	8.3
Durable consumer groups	45.4	45.1	42.9	43.5	41.7	41.1	41.3	47.5
Intermediate goods	10.7	11.4	11.4	11.9	11.9	12.0	11.9	10.4
Capital goods	33.5	32.5	34.8	34.2	35.8	36.1	37.0	33.8
Other goods	0.0	0.0	0.0	0.0	0.0	0.0	0.0	0.0
Total	100.0	100.0	100.0	100.0	100.0	100.0	100.0	100.0

Source: Ports, Customs and Free Zone Corporation

Dubai

Total	Female	Male	Year
183,187	54,366	128,821	1975
276,301	88,587	187,714	1980
370,788	123,609	247,797	1985
610,926	204,797	406,129	1993
689,420	211,211	478,209	1995
862,387	250,588	611,799	(1)2000
910,336	258,097	652,239	(2)2001

(1) By Feb 2000 census   2) Estimated data for end of the year

Source: Ministry of Planning for Censuses (1975, 1980, 1985, 1995) Source: Dubai Municipality for Censuses (1993, 2000)

Collectively, the foregoing statistics illustrate the growth of Dubai's economy and the level of economic activity which has increased steadily over the years.

The growth of commercial businesses in Dubai has also seen a confident increase thus adding to the Emirate's economic prosperity. The number of licences issued by the Dubai Department of Economic Development (DED) to businesses each year is on the rise, thus increasing the rate of commerce in the emirate.

Dubai's easy and tolerant lifestyle has also been a major factor in attracting overseas investment. Alcohol is permitted and a range of first class leisure facilities have emerged and are still emerging. The attitude towards women is fairly liberal and many women, both foreign and local, pursue successful careers in the emirate. Unlike some areas in the Middle East, women here are free to drive and move around town unaccompanied.

Further, Dubai is a very clean city and contains all the facilities modern businessmen or women and their families may require. Its standard of living is relatively high. Accommodation is modern and spacious and all the major hotel chains are represented.

A very important aspect of Dubai's appeal which is instantly noticeable to foreign visitors is the fact that it is virtually a crime-free city with one of the lowest crime rates in the world.

The Political System

The UAE has a federal political system. The Constitution of the UAE effectively unified the seven emirates and laid down the composition of the federal government. Each individual emirate retains its judicial and political power unless otherwise provided for by the Constitution or by agreements transferring the same to the Federal Government. The Federal Government, however, maintains exclusive jurisdiction in a number of areas such as foreign affairs, defence, health and education while the individual emirates have exclusive jurisdiction in matters relating to municipal work and national resources, among other things.

Although the Constitution provides that each emirate may have a legislative body and a cabinet of ministers independent from that of the federal government, none of the emirates does. Instead, the local affairs of each emirate are run by local government departments which are either headed by a chairman or a director general and the law is enacted in the emirate by way of a Ruler's Decree. However, Dubai and Ras Al Khaimah, both retain an independent judicial system.

In 2003, Dubai established an Executive Council, which includes the heads of the different government departments, in an effort to streamline the efficiency of the government and the coordination between different departments. The Executive Council advises the government, with each department operating according to its own priorities while taking into consideration the requirements of the emirate as a whole.

In the international arena, the UAE has ratified several international treaties and is a member of various organisations including the Arab League, the Arab Gulf Cooperation Council (AGCC), the Organisation of Petroleum Exporting Countries (OPEC), the Organisation of Arab Petroleum Exporting Countries (OAPEC), the World Trade Organisation, the World Bank for Reconstruction & Development, the United Nations, the World Bank, the World Heath Organisation, the International Monetary Fund and the International Organisation for Industrial Development. Al Tamimi & Company publishes a comprehensive listing of all the major international treaties which the UAE has ratified. The list can be found at their website - www.tamimi.com.

The Ruling Family of Dubai

▲
H.H. Sheikh Rashid bin
Saeed Al Maktoum
Ruler of Dubai
1912-1990

▲
H.H. Sheikh Maktoum bin
Rashid Al Maktoum
Vice-President and Prime
Minister of UAE,
Ruler of Dubai

▲
H.H. Sheikh Hamdan bin
Rashid Al Maktoum
Minister of Finance and
Industry, UAE,
Deputy Ruler of Dubai

▲
H.H. General Sheikh
Mohammed bin Rashid
Al Maktoum
Minister of Defence, UAE,
Crown Prince of Dubai

The chart below shows the structure of the UAE government in order of ranking and the names of the individuals who hold the various government posts.

The Federal Government

The Supreme Council

Constitution • The Rulers of the seven emirates

Headed by • The President and the Vice President

The President of the UAE and Head of State • Sheikh Zayed bin Sultan Al Nahyan

Vice President • Sheikh Maktoum bin Rashid Al Maktoum

The Members
Dr Sheikh Sultan bin Mohammed Al Qassimi • **Sharjah**
Sheikh Saqr bin Mohammed Al Qassimi • **Ras Al Khaimah**
Sheikh Rashid bin Ahmed Al Mu'alla • **Umm Al Quwain**
Sheikh Humaid bin Rashid Al Nuaimi • **Ajman**
Sheikh Hamad bin Mohammed Al Sharqi • **Fujairah**

The Council of Ministers, Cabinet
Headed by • The Prime Minister and the Deputy Prime Minister
Prime Minister • Sheikh Maktoum bin Rashid Al Maktoum
Deputy Prime Minister • Sheikh Sultan bin Zayed Al Nahyan
Finance & Industry • Sheikh Hamdan bin Rashid Al Maktoum
Defence • General Sheikh Mohammed bin Rashid Al Maktoum
Information & Culture • Sheikh Abdullah bin Zayed Al Nahyan
Planning • Sheikh Humaid bin Ahmad Al Mu'alla
Higher Education & Scientific Research • Sheikh Nahyan bin Mubarak Al Nahyan
Economy & Commerce • Sheikh Fahim bin Sultan Al Qassimi
Foreign Minister • Rashid Abdulla Al Nuaimi
Interior • Lt. General Dr Mohammed Saeed Al Badi
Health • Hamad Abdul Rahman Al Madfa
Electricity & Water • Humaid bin Nasser Al Owais
Agriculture & Fisheries • Saeed Mohammed Al Ragabani
Communications • Ahmed Humaid Al Tayer
Public Works & Housing • Rakad bin Salem bin Rakad
Petroleum & Mineral Resources • Obeid bin Saif Al Nassiri
Education & Youth • Dr Ali Abdul Aziz Al Sharhan
Justice, Islamic Affairs & Awqaf • Mohammed Nakhira Al Dhahiri
Labour & Social Affairs • Matar Humaid Al Tayer

Ministers of State

Foreign Affairs • Sheikh Hamdan bin Zayed Al Nahyan
Finance & Industry • Dr Mohammed Khalfan bin Kharbash
Cabinet Affairs • Saeed Khalfan Al Ghaith
Supreme Council Affairs • Sheikh Majid bin Saeed Al Nuami

The Federal National Council

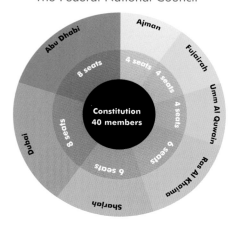

The Judiciary
• An independent body •

Local Government

Each emirate has its own local government structure.

The Rulers of the seven Emirates

	Abu Dhabi Sheikh Zayed bin Sultan Al Nahyan
	Dubai Sheikh Maktoum bin Rashid Al Maktoum
	Sharjah Dr Sheikh Sultan bin Mohammed Al Qassimi
	Ras Al Khaimah Sheikh Saqr bin Mohammed Al Qassimi
	Umm Al Quwain Sheikh Ahmed bin Rashid Al Mu'alla
	Ajman Sheikh Humaid bin Rashid Al Nuaimi
	Fujairah Sheikh Hamad bin Mohammed Al Sharqi

In 1975, Sheikh Hamad bin Mohammed Al Sharqi, Ruler of Fujairah abolished the
previous flag and adopted the federal flag for Fujairah.

The Supreme Council

The United Arab Emirates is governed by the Supreme Council. This is the highest federal governing body and consists of the rulers of the seven emirates. The Supreme Council elects from its own membership the President (which used to be for a five-year term) and the Vice President of the UAE. Now the President is elected permanently. The current President is H.H. Sheikh Zayed bin Sultan Al Nahyan, Ruler of Abu Dhabi, and the Vice President is H.H. Sheikh Maktoum bin Rashid Al Maktoum, Prime Minister of the UAE and Ruler of Dubai. Procedural matters at the Supreme Council are decided by majority vote whereas decisions relating to substantive matters are decided by a majority of five, provided that the Dubai and the Abu Dhabi votes are included in the majority.

The Supreme Council is primarily responsible for the formulation of policy decisions relating to federal matters, which include defence, communications, foreign affairs, finance & industry, public health, economy & commerce, education, agriculture and labour. It also has a legislative arm which sanctions various laws and decrees including the ratification of treaties and international treaties.

The Council of Ministers

Policy decisions of the Supreme Council are implemented by the Federal Council of Ministers, sometimes referred to as the Cabinet or the Executive Authority. Based in Abu Dhabi, the Cabinet of Ministers is headed by the Prime Minister and consists of the Deputy Prime Minister and a number of Ministers who are normally selected (for no fixed terms) by the approval of the Supreme Council on the recommendation of the Prime Minister. The Prime Minister, who is usually selected from the ruling family of the emirate of Dubai, is appointed by the President of the UAE following the approval of the Supreme Council.

Federal matters are regulated through a number of specially created federal ministries which include the Ministry of Interior, the Ministry of Defence, the Ministry of Economy & Commerce, the Ministry of Labour & Social Affairs, the Ministry of Finance & Industry, the Ministry of Justice and the Ministry of Information & Culture. Article 60 of the UAE Constitution defines the responsibilities of the Cabinet which include, but are not limited to, the issuing of regulations, the preparation of draft laws and the drawing up of the annual general budget. Although most of the federal government ministries are based in Abu Dhabi, many maintain offices in Dubai.

The Federal National Council

The Federal National Council is composed of 40 members of the national community who are recommended by the Ruler of each emirate. Each emirate holds a specific number of seats, Abu Dhabi and Dubai having the majority of seats. The members represent the country as a whole rather than their individual emirate.

The Federal National Council is responsible for, among other things, considering and reviewing draft federal laws or bills before they are submitted to the President and the Supreme Council for consideration and subsequent enactment.

The Council also has a Bureau, a Secretary General and is headed by a Speaker. The ordinary sessions of the Council (which are held in Abu Dhabi and last a minimum of six months) are public; decisions or resolutions are taken by a unanimous vote of all the members present.

The Judiciary

The UAE Judiciary is an independent body and consists of the Federal Supreme Court, Primary Tribunals, a Public Prosecutor and Local Courts.

The Supreme Court consists of a President and a maximum of five judges who are appointed by decree issued by the President of the UAE. Based in Abu Dhabi, it is responsible for, among other things, hearing claims between member emirates, determining the constitutionality of federal laws when challenged in general and determining cases against Ministers and other senior public officials, and disputes between emirates and individuals. Judgements passed by the Supreme Court are binding and final.

It has also been provided under the Constitution that the Federal Government may form a special primary tribunal in any of the emirates for special purposes. The jurisdiction of these tribunals is limited to the consideration of the following matters:

- Civil, commercial and administrative disputes between the Union and individuals;
- Crimes committed within Dubai except cases reserved for the Supreme Court under Article 99 of the Constitution;
- Personal status cases, civil, commercial and other cases between individuals which arise in Dubai.

The Public Prosecutor of the Union is appointed by Federal Decree with the approval of the Cabinet as well as members of the Public Prosecutor's office. However, Dubai has its own Public Prosecutor's office as well as Attorney General who is appointed by the Ruler independent of the Federal System.

Under the Constitution, each emirate is permitted to maintain its own legislative body and judicial authority. Accordingly, there are federal and local courts in the UAE. All emirates with the exception of Dubai and Ras Al Khaimah however, have transferred their judicial systems to the UAE Federal Judicial Authority. The Federal Judicial Authority is run and supervised by the Federal Ministry of Justice. Dubai and Ras Al Khaimah maintain their local courts although they have entered into agreements on judicial co-operation. According to the Constitution, where there is a conflict between local and federal law, the federal law will prevail.

The Local Government

The Constitution of the UAE provides that local matters are to be regulated by the governments of the individual emirates through a local decree enacted by the Ruler. In terms of foreign investment, two important departments within the Government of Dubai are the Dubai Department of Economic Development (DED) and the Dubai Municipality. The DED, which is discussed further in Chapter 3, was created in 1992 and is responsible for, among other things, the economic development of the emirate, the regulation of companies incorporated in Dubai, the keeping of a commercial register and the granting of trade licences. The Dubai Municipality is responsible mainly for providing civic services, planning and development.

The Legal System

The UAE is essentially a civil law jurisdiction heavily influenced by French, Roman and Islamic law. In recent years principles of Egyptian law, which are heavily based on French law, have been an additional influence. The increasing presence of international contracts of Common Law nature has resulted in the application of Common Law principles in commercial contracts. This, albeit indirectly, has further influenced the UAE legal system. However, theoretically speaking, Common Law principles, such as adopting previous court judgements as precedents, are not recognised under UAE law. Such precedents may, however, be presented to the Court for persuasion purposes in respect of cases submitted to the Court.

A number of codified federal laws have been passed to regulate matters such as labour relations, maritime affairs, commercial transactions, commercial agencies, civil transactions, intellectual property and commercial companies. A number of local laws have also been passed in various areas by individual emirates.

There are two main types of laws in the UAE, federal and local. The federal laws are applicable to the UAE as a whole and are issued either by the legislative body as explained later, or by the Ministers of each Ministry by virtue of powers conferred upon them. When a Minister passes a law it is known as a Ministerial Order and should be treated as a regulation rather than a law.

Local decrees and orders only apply to a particular emirate. A local decree is passed by the Ruler or Crown Prince of a particular emirate, and a local order is issued by a member of the Royal Family of that emirate. The decree will only be applicable to the emirate concerned. Should there be a conflict between Federal law and local decrees, Federal law will prevail.

The Legal Profession

Since 1997, pursuant to Federal Law No. 23 of 1991 Regarding the Regulation of the Legal Profession (as amended), only UAE nationals may obtain licenses to practise as lawyers or advocates in the UAE, and thus have exclusive rights of audience in the courts. In order to qualify as a UAE lawyer, it is necessary to obtain (a) a law degree from the UAE University in Al Ain (where the medium of instruction is Arabic) or from another approved university (where a law degree requires study for at least four years) and (b) undergo training with a locally approved law firm for at least one year as supervised by the Ministry of Justice. On completion of the training period, the Ministry scrutinises the monthly reports submitted by the law firm on the trainee lawyer's work and performance. A UAE trainee lawyer is only allowed to practise as a lawyer in the UAE after his name is entered into the lawyers' register at the Ministry of Justice, and after he has taken the necessary oath. Registration is renewable annually and is subject to the Ministry's approval.

The above applies to lawyers who wish to practise in the federal judicial system. However, those who wish to practise in the emirates of Dubai and Ras Al Khaimah need to submit separate licensing applications to the Ruler's office in each emirate and/or the Advocates Licensing Department at Dubai Courts which is now in charge of regulation of this matter.

The legal profession in the UAE is supervised by the Ministry of Justice and any complaints concerning UAE lawyers are heard by a committee at the Ministry of Justice.

Arab national lawyers, who obtained their license before 1997, are permitted to continue to practise in the UAE primarily through association with a law firm which is owned by a local advocate. New Arab national lawyers are granted licences provided they have work experience in a locally established law firm, headed or owned by a UAE national lawyer. At the Dubai level, Arab national lawyers may be granted a license to practise and even to open a law firm, but only on an exceptional basis. Non Arab expatriate lawyers may apply for a license to practise as legal consultants usually to work for an international law firm. They may also find opportunities to practise as in-house legal counsel for local and international corporations.

Although there are a few judges who are UAE-nationals, many of the judges in the UAE are Arab expatriates who have either been seconded by their respective governments or directly employed by the Ministry of Justice. Federal court judges are recommended by the Ministry of Justice and appointed by decree of the President of the UAE. However, in Dubai they are appointed by a local decree from the Ruler of Dubai. Judges in the UAE are independent from the Ministry of Justice, subject only to the law. They may only be removed from office for incompetence, resignation or on the termination of their secondment arrangement.

There are three primary sources or types of law in the UAE: federal or union laws and decrees, local laws, and Sharia (Islamic law). The secondary form of law is trade custom or practice.

a• Federal / Union Laws & Decrees

Federal laws, as discussed above, are laws enacted by the UAE Federal Legislative Body. In the event of a conflict between a federal law and a local law, the federal law will prevail.
The chart below illustrates the stages a draft law or bill needs to pass to become a law.

How are Federal Laws Passed ?

❶
The draft law or bill is prepared, submitted by the concerned Ministry in coordination with other Ministers if required, and the Ministry of Justice.

❷
The draft is then forwarded to the Supreme Legislative Committee for review and approval. The Committee consists of legal experts and Ministers from the Cabinet of Ministers.

❸
The draft or bill is then submitted to the Cabinet of Ministers to be discussed and approved for issuance.

❹
The Federal National Council reviews the draft.

❺
The bill is submitted to the President for review and to the Supreme Council for ratification.

❻
The President signs the Bill.

❼
The bill becomes a law three months after being published in the Official Gazette, unless otherwise expressed in the law. It is usually published within two weeks from the date of the President's signature.

It is worth noting that a draft may be referred to a special committee drawn from members of the Cabinet of Ministers or members of the Ministry of Justice or members of the Federal National Council.

On the Federal legislative side there are also what are known as laws issued by decree and ordinary decrees.

Laws issued by decree have the force of law and are passed as a matter of urgency by the President of the UAE and the Cabinet. The Supreme Council must approve the decree, or else it will not have the force of law.

There are, in addition, federal ordinary decrees which also have the force of law and are a form of delegated legislation passed by the President and the Cabinet while the Supreme Council is not in session. Decrees also need to be published in the Official Gazette to be enacted.

b • Local Laws

As discussed above, the UAE Constitution allows individual emirates to maintain their own legislative body. These laws are passed by the Ruler or the Crown Prince of each emirate either in the form of a decree or a law. This law will only be applicable in that emirate.

c • Sharia (Islamic Law)

Sharia is the oldest source of law in the UAE and has its own origins. However, only matters such as inheritance and family issues like divorce and child custody are subject to Sharia.

As a general rule, when a court is determining an issue it gives first consideration to the provisions of any applicable federal law. If the federal law in question does not provide a solution, the court considers the provisions of the emirate's relevant laws. If there is no law on the subject then the usual practice pertaining to that particular trade will apply. If the court is still unable to find a solution, the provisions of Sharia are applied from Al Maliki and Al Hanbali Schools. However, in applying all the above reference has to be made to the UAE Public Order and Policy which will be relevant.

There is yet no official law reporting mechanism in the UAE. Although the UAE legal system is not a common law system with binding precedents, judgements delivered by the higher courts are generally applied by lower courts. There have, however, been exceptions to this. Judgements may be used for persuasive arguments.

The UAE Constitution permits each emirate to have its own legislative body and judicial authority. Accordingly, there are federal courts and local courts in the UAE. All emirates other than Dubai and Ras Al Khaimah have now brought their judicial systems into the UAE Federal Judicial Authority. Dubai and Ras Al Khaimah have retained their own judicial systems which are not part of the UAE Federal Judicial Authority.

Local and federal courts apply UAE federal laws which are enacted by the UAE Federal Legislative Authority as well as laws and regulations enacted by the rulers of the individual emirates.

▼ The Courts in Dubai

Although the legal procedures and the laws applicable to courts in the individual emirates are all fairly similar, there are differences, particularly where a special law has been enacted and applied in a particular emirate. In the event of a conflict between the federal and local laws, the federal law will supercede the local law of the emirate.

Below is a chart illustrating the court structure in Dubai and the number of judges in each court.

Court Structure in Dubai

Court of First Instance	Court of Appeal	Court of Cassation
Civil Court more than Dhs 100,000: 3 judges less than Dhs 100,000: 1 judge	**Civil Court** 3 judges	**Civil Court** 5 judges
Criminal Court 1 judge for misdemeanor 3 judges for felony	**Criminal Court** 3 judges	**Criminal Court** 5 judges
Sharia Court 1 judge	**Sharia Court** 3 judges	**Sharia Court** 5 judges

The court structure in Dubai comprises the Court of First Instance, the Court of Appeal and the Court of Cassation. All three courts have three divisions: the Civil Court, the Criminal Court and the Sharia Court (Islamic Court).

The Civil Court hears all civil claims ranging from all commercial matters including debt recovery cases to maritime disputes. Actions where the claim amount exceeds Dhs 100,000 are heard before a bench of three judges, whereas those for claims below Dhs 100,000 are heard before a single judge. After judgment has been delivered, the parties have the right to appeal to the Civil Court of Appeal on factual as well as legal grounds within 30 days from the date of judgment. It is possible to adduce fresh evidence or request new witnesses at the Court of Appeal. Thereafter the parties may only appeal to the Court of Cassation, the highest court in Dubai, on points of law alone, usually before five judges. All decisions of the Court of Cassation are final and are not subject to appeal.

The Criminal Court in Dubai deals with most criminal cases committed in the emirate. These cases are initiated by a complaint to the local police in Dubai who then usually refer the matter to the Public Prosecutor. Upon considering and investigating the case, the Public Prosecutor decides whether or not to refer the matter to the Criminal Court of First Instance. If he decides to refer the matter to Court, the Public Prosecutor will assume the role of the plaintiff in the case against the defendant, the accused. Cases involving a misdemeanor, i.e. a crime involving a sentence of a fine or imprisonment of one to three years, are tried before a single judge, whereas cases involving a felony, i.e. a crime involving a sentence in excess of three years to life imprisonment or execution are tried before three judges. If a case contains a civil as well as a criminal element, it is at the criminal court's discretion whether or not to join the two or refer the civil point(s) to the Civil Court. Once judgment is passed, the parties have the right of appeal on factual and/or legal points to the Criminal Court of Appeal within 15 days of the judgment. The Attorney General may also appeal the judgment, and must do so within 30 days of the Criminal Court of First Instance's judgment. The accused may be released on bail until the Court of Appeal's decision is made, subject to the Court's approval. The parties then have the right of appeal against the Court of Appeal's judgment to the Court of Cassation (on legal grounds alone) within 30 days of the judgment. Appeal to the Court of Cassation does not suspend the sentence, and thus no bail can be granted on the accused's behalf.

The Sharia courts are responsible for civil matters in the UAE for Muslims. Non-Muslims do not generally appear before the Sharia court in any matter. The Sharia courts hear mostly matters of family law relating to issues such as divorce, inheritance and succession, alimony and custody of children. The Sharia courts will apply the codified provisions of the law and in the absence of any specific provision, the Islamic Sharia will be applied. There is no law governing inheritance, succession, divorce or custody of children in the UAE and so the Sharia Courts apply the Islamic Sharia to such cases.

Filing an Action

Civil proceedings in the Dubai Courts are regulated by Federal Law No. 11 of 1992 (the UAE Law of Civil Procedure). The Law lays down a number of detailed rules relating to litigation such as jurisdiction, the service of documents, pleadings, the attachment of assets, the execution of judgments, the enforcement of foreign judgments and appeals.

→ Procedure for filing an action

Before filing a claim, a potential litigant should ensure that the UAE courts and the courts of the emirate concerned have jurisdiction to hear the dispute according to the provisions of the UAE Law of Civil Procedure. (The claimant must determine not only whether the UAE courts have jurisdiction, but also whether the courts of the emirate in which the action is to be filed have jurisdiction to hear the dispute.)

An action or suit is filed by lodging a Statement of Claim with the court clerk of the appropriate court, according to the jurisdiction provisions referred to in the above-mentioned Law.

The Statement of Claim will normally contain a brief summary of the facts of the case and end with a request to the judge to deliver a judgment against the defendant for the amount claimed (or any other relief required) together with interest and costs. The Statement of Claim must be drafted in Arabic and be accompanied by supporting documents together with Arabic translations thereof if the documents are in a language other than Arabic.

With the Statement of Claim and supporting documents, a power of attorney drawn in favour of the attorney acting on behalf of the claimant must also be filed with the court clerk. The court clerk then assesses the court fees and requests the claimant's attorney to pay the court fees. Upon payment of the court fees, the court clerk opens a court file for the matter, allots a case number and schedules a hearing date for hearing the case. The claimant or his attorney is immediately notified of the date of the hearing. The court clerk then hands the matter over to the court bailiff who is required to effect service of the summons on the defendants not later than 10 days from the date the Statement of Claim was filed. Service of the summons is affected by the court bailiff on the defendant at the address shown in the Statement of Claim. If the defendant fails to attend before the court at the scheduled hearing despite having been personally served, the case may be reserved for delivering judgment ex parte. However, if the defendant was not personally served (unless in summary matters), then the Court should adjourn the hearing for a second notification.

If the defendant has not been properly served, the court will adjourn the case at the first hearing to enable further attempts to be made to effect service on the defendant in accordance with the legal procedures set out by the Law of Civil Procedure.

If the defendant's place of domicile is outside the UAE, service of the summons is effected through diplomatic channels (Ministry of Justice and/ or Ministry of Foreign Affairs).

If the defendant has no place of domicile or known address in the UAE, an application can be made to the court for service of summons by publication in local newspapers.

The defendant may appear personally or through his attorney (who must hold a duly notarised power of attorney). Failure by the defendant or his attorney to attend a hearing may result in the defendant being pronounced absent and judgment being delivered against the defendant in absentia.

The fees for filing a case in the Dubai Courts are laid down by Dubai Emirate Law No. 1 of 1994 and are set out below in accordance with the amount of the claim.

Court Fees

The Court of First Instance

7.5% for first and second Dhs 100,000
6% for third Dhs 100,000
5% for any amount over Dhs 300,000
max Dhs 30,000
Legal Attorney Fees Dhs 10

The Court of Appeal

1.5% for first and second Dhs 100,000
1.2% for third Dhs 100,000
1% for any amount over Dhs 300,000
max Dhs 6,000
Legal Attorney Fees Dhs 10

The Court of Cassation

Dhs 500/- plus a refundable deposit of Dhs 1,000
Stay in Proceedings - Dhs 200
Fees For the Execution of Judgements
1% - max Dhs 5,000
Legal Attorney Fees Dhs 10

Court fees are payable by the plaintiff. However, in the event of a counter claim, the defendant also has to pay such fees. Once court fees are paid to the court it is not possible to get a refund even in the event that the action is withdrawn or a settlement is reached between the parties.

It is worth noting that unlike many jurisdictions, professional legal fees are not recoverable where a case is won. However, court fees are recoverable from the plaintiff if the proceedings are successfully defended or a counter claim is successfully pursued.

Normally the court upon delivering judgment will order as to who should bear the court fees, the general rule being that the losing party will be ordered to pay the court fees.

It is unlikely that the court will give an exemption from payment of court fees or a deferral of the court fees. However, in very limited cases, particularly where personal injuries are involved, the chairman of the court may grant the person who has been injured an exemption from court fees provided he is not capable of paying the same.

Advocacy fees are normally negotiated between clients and advocates on a case by case basis. An arrangement whereby advocates have a retainership agreement with some clients to act generally on their behalf is also quite common. There is no hard and fast rule for charges and fees payable to advocates in the UAE.

Advocacy fees are normally charged as a lump sum (percentage of the claim in suit) or on a time-spent basis computed on an hourly rate. Advocacy fees usually do not include disbursements or court fees. Normally, half the advocacy fee in lump sum matters is payable in advance, the balance being payable on delivery of the judgement by the Court of First Instance. In contentious matters where litigation is involved advocacy fees are usually charged as a flat fee, normally calculated at 10% of the claim.

Advocacy fees for litigation work are rarely charged on a time-spent basis. In the UAE it is illegal to charge contingency fees on a 'no win/no pay' basis.

Advocacy fees are not recoverable. Courts in the UAE normally order the judgment debtor to pay a nominal sum towards the judgment holder's advocacy fees.

In addition to advocacy fees and the court fees, there may be other charges. As Arabic is the official language in court, it is likely that both the claimant and defendant will incur translation expenses. The court will only accept translations from a duly licensed translator. The prevailing charges for a stamped translation are between Dhs 70 and Dhs 100 per page. Translation charges are not recoverable, even if the substantive claim succeeds.

If an expert is appointed, it is likely that the court will order both parties to share his fees, the amount of which depends on the complexity of the issue and on the expert himself. However, the judgment debtor will eventually bear the fees paid to the expert.

Various legal remedies are available to an aggrieved party under the law. One of these is the provision to attach or seize another party's assets. The fees for an application to attach assets are an additional 50% of the Court of First Instance fee payable, subject to a maximum of Dhs 15,000.

Labour Disputes & Tenant/Landlord Disputes

Unlike many jurisdictions, there are separate forums, other than the courts, for disputes concerning labour matters and disputes between tenants and landlords in the UAE.

Under Federal Law No.(8) of 1980 Regulating Labour Relations as amended (the Labour Laws) all disputes between employees and employers must first be filed at the Ministry of Labour & Social Affairs (the Ministry) as opposed to the Court. The Ministry does not act in a judicial capacity but will make its recommendations. If the matter is not settled within two weeks from the date the complaint is filed with the Ministry, either party may refer the dispute to the Civil Court of First Instance. In such circumstances, the case will follow the same path as any other civil claim in the courts.

Similarly, in certain emirates such as Dubai, Sharjah and Abu Dhabi, disputes between landlord and tenant related to rent, fall within the jurisdiction of what is known as the Rent Committee (at the Dubai Municipality) and not the Court. The Rent Committee in Dubai consists of ordinary businessmen from Dubai in addition to a legal advisor. The Rent Committee follows no formal or written procedure in determining disputes and the sessions are more 'ad hoc.' Unlike matters heard before the Ministry, decisions passed by the Dubai Rent Committee are final and may not be appealed in Court. This however varies in the other emirates. The Rent Committee in Sharjah, for example, allows the parties to appeal against its decision to the Sharjah Civil Court of First Instance within 15 days of making its decision.

The Dubai Rent Committee is further discussed in Chapter 3.

Other Forms of Dispute Resolution

There is no law which deals exclusively with arbitration or alternative dispute resolution in the UAE. However, the UAE Civil Procedures Law contains a number of articles which deal with arbitration. Please see the section on the Dubai International Arbitration Centre in Chapter 3.

For instance, parties to an agreement may decide to refer any dispute arising between them to arbitration. The Civil Procedure Law does not object to this provided certain conditions are fulfilled, such as, that the agreement between the parties to refer a dispute to arbitration is clear and in writing. Alternatively, the parties to an agreement may refer their disputes to the Arbitration and Conciliation body at the Dubai Chamber of Commerce & Industry (DCCI) or any other arbitration body for arbitration. Arbitration proceedings need not be institutional and may instead be ad hoc. There is nothing in the law which stipulates that the arbitrators must be Muslims or that the proceedings need to be conducted in Arabic. These aspects will therefore depend on the agreement entered into between the parties.

If the parties agree to arbitration, an action may not be filed in court. However, if an action is filed, the agreement for arbitration must be brought to the court's attention at the first hearing date of the case, otherwise the court will assume jurisdiction.

The parties may agree on the appointment of an arbitrator. In the event of a dispute, the parties may apply to the court to appoint an arbitrator. The arbitrator must, upon his acceptance to arbitrate, give notice of the arbitration 30 days prior to the first hearing.

The arbitrator must deliver the award within six months from the date of the first hearing, otherwise the parties may ask the court to deal with the dispute. However, it is open to the parties to extend the six-month period.

The arbitration award should be delivered by a majority (if there is more than one arbitrator) in Arabic or any other language agreed between the parties.

The arbitration award once it is passed will become binding on the parties and will not be subject to any appeal. However, the arbitration award must be validated by the court before implementation, if a party is to apply to the court to enforce the arbitration award legally. This normally will be made by an application to the court by way of an action requesting the court to validate the award for the purpose of enforcing the same.

Another form of dispute resolution is Alternative Dispute Resolution (ADR), which is different from arbitration or expert determination and is not widely used in the UAE. It essentially involves applying one of the following processes in resolving a dispute: (a) direct negotiation (b) partnering (c) expert evaluation (d) mediation (e) mini trial or (f) dispute review board. These forms of resolving disputes are favoured where the parties in a dispute wish to reach settlement by negotiations or through the use of neutral third parties. The applicable ADR mechanism will depend on the nature of the dispute and the intentions of the parties. For the success of any ADR, it is imperative that the parties act in good faith and have the will to reach a settlement without proceeding to arbitration or litigation. Where the parties reach an agreement through ADR, the agreement needs to be in writing to be legally binding. The only requirement, therefore, when using ADR to resolve a dispute is to ensure that the parties have entered into a valid and binding agreement under the UAE laws. If ADR fails there is nothing to stop the parties from proceeding to arbitration or litigation.

The procedure for ADR can be agreed between the parties as the law does not set down a specific procedure. Certain ADR bodies however have devised procedures which the parties may adopt.

The mention of ADR clauses in an agreement, however, does not preclude the parties from proceeding to arbitration or litigation.

Climate

Dubai has a sub-tropical and arid climate. Between the months of September and March the climate tends to be warm, but pleasant, although the evenings may be chilly. In the summer, between the months of June and September, the weather tends to be very hot and humid; and the temperature may reach 120 F -(47 C) during July and August. Most buildings and cars do, however, have air-conditioning. Dubai receives rain showers during the winter months. The average rainfall is around 110 mm. Dubai also has the occasional sand storm. Below are the average yearly temperatures in Dubai for the years 1998 to 2000 (inclusive) in degrees Centigrade.

▲ Whatever the weather, the date palm flourishes.

Average Climate in Dubai

	1999	2000	2001
Minimum Temperature/ Centigrade	11.2	11.7	9.3
Maximum Temperature/ Centigrade	47.5	47.1	46.4
Minimum Relative Humidity	23%	24%	21%
Maximum Relative Humidity	86%	85%	89%
Rainfall / millimeters	44.5	24.2	8.8
Rain days / 0.2mm or more	5	4	3

Source: Dept. of Civil Aviation - Meteorological Office

▼ An Arabian sunset

Population

▲ An international cross section of the population

     The population of Dubai is approximately 1 million persons. Expatriates make up the majority of the population and are mainly drawn from the Indian subcontinent, Europe and neighbouring Arab countries. The majority of the population lives in the city itself and its suburbs. Below is a chart illustrating the total population in Dubai and the UAE as a whole, including the male and female ratios for the years 1995 to 2000 (inclusive).

Population of Dubai						
	2000	1999	1998	1997	1996	1995
Female	250,600	255,000	241,600	228,900	216,900	211,200
Male	611,800	602,000	563,900	527,900	494,300	478,200
Total	862,400	857,000	805,500	756,800	711,200	689,400

Source: Government of Dubai, Department of Economic Development, 'Dubai Development Statistics'

Population of the UAE						
	2000	1999	1998	1997	1996	1995
Female	1,013,000	963,000	915,000	849,000	825,000	804,200
Male	2,095,000	1,975,000	1,861,000	1,775,000	1,654,000	1,606,800
Total	3,108,000	2,938,000	2,776,000	2,624,000	2,479,000	2,411,000

Source: Government of Dubai, Department of Economic Development, 'Dubai Development Statistics'.

Language

     The official language of Dubai is Arabic. However, English is widely spoken and is the main language used in business. Almost all road/street signs and notices are written in both English and Arabic.

Banking

Many international banks are represented in Dubai (see directory listings on the enclosed CD). International financial transfers are relatively simple and there are no exchange controls. Banking hours are from 8.00 am to 1.00 pm Saturday through Thursday. Some banks also open in the afternoons between 4.00 pm and 5.30 pm. The various money exchange centres are open from 8.30 am to 1.00 pm and from 4.30 pm to 8.30 pm.

Opening a bank account in Dubai is relatively easy. Although requirements vary from bank to bank, after the enactment of Federal Law No. (4) of 2002 in relation to the incrimination of Money Laundering, a prospective individual account holder will be asked to produce the original passport (for a physical check)

▲ Bank Street in Bur Dubai

together with a copy of his passport (including the residence visa page) and a letter of no-objection from his employer/sponsor to open a bank account. Cheque books are not normally issued to non-UAE residents. However, most banks allow non-UAE residents to open savings accounts as opposed to current accounts on the recommendation of a current UAE resident account holder. The purpose of this is to enable the bank to maintain a contact for the non-resident in Dubai.

A prospective company/corporate account holder wishing to open a bank account is normally required to produce the following: a valid trade licence, a letter confirming its membership of the Dubai Chamber of Commerce & Industry, a board resolution authorising the opening of the account, certified copies of the memorandum and articles of association, a list of directors, name and address of the shareholders in such company/corporation and a registration certificate from the Ministry of Economy & Commerce. However, where new business entities are concerned, many of the above documents will not have been issued. In such cases, such businesses should, once they have submitted an application for a trade licence at the Dubai Department of Economic Development (DED) (as discussed in Chapter 4), request a letter from the DED confirming that such an application has been made and that it has no objection to the opening of an account. Most banks will allow the prospective business to open a bank account on the presentation of such a letter. As one will see in Chapter 3, one of the prerequisites for establishing a limited liability company (LLC) is that its share capital must be at least Dhs 300,000 (in Dubai). In such cases, most banks will allow a prospective LLC to open a fixed deposit account on the presentation of the above letter for the purposes of establishing to the DED that it has met the minimum capital requirement. It should be noted that to do so, most banks will require all the intended shareholders of the LLC or the authorised signatory of the company to sign the account opening forms at the bank itself.

E-Dirham

In support of the E-government drive, the Ministry of Finance & Industry has introduced the E-Dirham card to replace the use of cash payment for procedures done with various federal government ministries. Currently, the following ministries require E-Dirham usage: Ministry of Labour & Social

Affairs, Ministry of Health, Ministry of Economy, Ministry of Interior, and the Ministry of Finance & Industry.

Two types of E-Dirham cards are available: the **Fixed Value Card** which is non-rechargeable and purchased at face value, and the **Government Client Card** which is intended for frequent users of government services.

→ Procedure to obtain an E-Dirham Card

The procedure to obtain a **Fixed Value E-Dirham Card** is to purchase the card at any E-Dirham member bank. This card can be purchased in the amounts of Dhs 100, 200, 300, 500, 1000, 3000, or 5000. You will need to bring one passport photo and complete a cash or bank transfer for the amount required.

For the **Government Client Card** you will be required to complete the Government Client Card application form available at the Ministry of Finance & Industry or at any E-Dirham member bank and submit the application at the Ministry of Finance & Industry. Once the application is approved, a card will be issued and personalised. Collect the card, which will have a value of zero. The PIN number will be sent in a secure envelope to you. Go to any E-Dirham member bank to charge the card. Pay any amount, either in cash or through an account transfer. To personalise and e-enable the card, enter a PIN code at the bank at the time of purchase.

Cheques

A cheque book is not given to a customer unless he has a valid residence visa. The account holder should always bear in mind the following when operating the chequing account:

1 • It is a criminal offence to write a cheque if there are insufficient funds in the account to enable the bank to honour payment. The holder of a dishonoured cheque is entitled to complain to the police. In the event of such a complaint, the drawer and/or the signatory of the cheque will be arrested regardless of the fact that he has issued a cheque in his personal capacity or in his capacity as the authorised signatory of the company. If payment is subsequently not made, the matter will be referred to the Public Prosecutor. It is of course open to the Public Prosecutor to order that the drawer's and/or signatory's passport be attached or seized to prevent him from leaving the jurisdiction. Persons convicted of writing cheques which are subsequently dishonoured are usually sent to prison.

2 • It is not possible to countermand payment of a cheque unless (i) it has been lost or stolen or (ii) the bearer of the cheque has become bankrupt. Banks in Dubai will not refrain from honouring a cheque unless they are satisfied that one of these conditions exists. In any event, there are provisions in the law which allow the bearer of a cheque to object to the countermanding of payment. If such an objection is found to be valid, the bank will be required to honour the cheque.

3 • The UAE Central Bank has ruled that if an account holder issues three or more cheques which are dishonoured, he shall be prohibited from obtaining a cheque book and operating a cheque account.

4 • In the UAE, it is possible for post dated cheques to be issued. Accordingly, a person may issue a cheque now but due and payable after a period of time, thereby being similar to a promissory note. However, it must be noted that cheques carry one date, while promissory notes carry two dates.

Postal, Courier Services and Telecommunications

www.emiratespost.com

Postal Services

Postal services in Dubai used to be operated by the General Postal Authority which was established under Federal Law No. 4 of 1985. Its successor, the Emirates Postal Service (Empost) was established pursuant to Federal Law No. 8 of 2001. Letters take an average of one to two days to reach destinations in Dubai and two to three days to reach destinations in other emirates. Mail takes 7 – 10 days to reach the USA and Europe, 8 – 10 days to reach Australia and 5 – 10 days to reach India.

▲ The newly branded post office facade

There is no house address based postal service; all incoming mail is delivered to a PO Box at a central location and has to be collected from there. It is essential therefore for any business setting up in Dubai to obtain a post office box at the earliest opportunity.

→ Procedure to obtain a post office box

The application form (which is available at any post office) should be completed and signed by the applicant's sponsor. Where the sponsor is a company, the company stamp should appear on the form. The application form should then be submitted to the post office together with the appropriate fee and the following documents:

If the applicant is a business - Two copies of the business's trade licence and the original for presentation only or a letter from the Dubai Department of Economic Development stating that an application for a trade licence has been made and that it has no objection to a post office box being opened for the applicant. The application is renewable annually for a fee (currently Dhs 150).

If the applicant is an individual - Two copies of the applicant's passport (including the page containing the residence visa), 2 passport photographs and the appropriate fee (currently Dhs 110). The application is renewable annually for a fee (currently Dhs 150).

Empost provides a range of services as described below:

Electronic Document Centre

Empost has recently developed a sophisticated Electronic Document Centre (EDC) to manage printing, sorting and dispatching documents on the client's behalf. Emirates Post, being a mail management specialist, is implementing strict security procedures at various levels to ensure client's data confidentiality, and hence providing services from its premises at the same standards maintained at client's in-house facilities.

International Express

A cross-branded product recently launched as a result of Empost and DHL's (UAE) strategic business alliance. Consignors can utilise the DHL worldwide network that links 120,000 destinations in over 228 countries. International Express is an alternative offering which has the added-value of DHL's hallmark values of speedy and reliable deliveries plus the ability to track and trace shipments. The service is available at Emirates Post Main Branches.

Instant Money Transfer in Association with Western Union

Money transfer transactions occur via a direct link between Emirates Post's nationwide systems and Western Union's World-Wide network that covers 186 countries and territories across the globe at over 110,000 locations.

Special Services Related to Government Departments:

Ministry of Labour & Social Affairs

This service saves the time of individuals and businesses by making it possible for them to apply for labour licences, labour card renewals and UAE work visa sanctions without having to visit the Ministry of Labour themselves.

Emirates University Registration

Empost receives admission applications to Emirates University in Al Ain for students throughout its Post Office branches across the UAE.

E-Sha'ar Service

Emirates Postal Service notifies you by email when you receive registered mail or parcels in your PO Box. There is no charge for this service, but you do have to register your email address.

▲ The General Post Office, located in Bur Dubai.

▲ The post being collected at a Post Office Box.

Mumtaz Post (EMS)

Mumtaz Post (EMS) is the quick and efficient way to send urgent business documents and general items. Mumtaz Post delivers locally and internationally to 85 countries around the world and (unlike private courier companies) accepts both documents and parcels. Insurance fees are inclusive and the consignor is protected by a money back guarantee.

Business Reply Service (BRS)

Using the Business Reply Service (BRS), a company can offer its customers the opportunity to reply to its correspondence free of charge. Respondents simply place their letters in the pre-paid envelope provided and drop it in the nearest post box. This service is available locally and internationally to over 90 countries.

Ad by Post

Ad by post provides companies with direct access to all households and business post boxes in the UAE. An extremely cost-effective and flexible mass advertising medium, letter box promotion of this kind constitutes an important element in today's marketing mix.

Stamp-Ads

Using stamp cancellation imprints, advertisers and organisations can reach their targeted groups in a novel, measurable and cost-effective fashion. A specially designed stamp cancellation imprint can be designed with any given company's logo or message. This will then be imprinted on mail destined for delivery to hundreds of thousands of households across the UAE and around the world.

Furthermore, other services are available such as Postal Agency Service, Private Boxes Complexes, Insured Items Service for Letters and Parcels, Pick-up and Delivery Service, Franking Machine Service, Postage Paid Service and Empost Courier. Also, a model Emirates Philatelic has been established to provide philatelists with all the required services placed in the premises of the Emirates Post in Dubai.

Courier Services

All the major courier services operate fast, inexpensive and efficient services in Dubai and are used by many businesses for the delivery of letters and packages within the emirate and the UAE. Expatriates moving to Dubai should always bear in mind that packages sent by mail to Dubai from overseas are opened and searched by the authorities (magazines and videos are checked by the censors). Such packages are not always repackaged properly and so the use of courier services (particularly for valuable items) should always be considered. The main courier companies are listed in the directory on the CD included with this book.

Telecommunications in Dubai is operated by the Emirates Telecommunications Corporation (Etisalat) which was founded in September 1976.

Etisalat provides a range of services relating to Voice Communication, Wireless Communication and Data Communication.

On the following page are listed a short description of services provided under each of the ranges that have been mentioned above.

Voice Communication

Besides a comprehensive range of readily available standard telephones and feature phones, Etisalat offers businesses sophisticated Keyphone and PABX Systems incorporating the very best in telecommunications technology to meet their communication needs.

Etisalat's Calling (ECC) and Prepaid Cards (PPC) enable customers not only to make calls from the UAE to a host of countries worldwide but also to make calls from these countries to the UAE while travelling. ECC cards are available free on application to Standard and GSM Telephone Service. Smart Payphone Cards are disposable Prepaid Calling Cards which have an electronic chip.

▲ The distinctive Etisalat buildings can be instantly identified.

Etisalat's Maysour Prepaid Telephone Service enables subscribers to receive incoming calls for a full year, while making outgoing calls on a prepaid basis to match budget needs.

Supplementary Services for Standard Telephone Lines

Home Country Direct Service enables you to make calls to your home (using Etisalat Calling Card /Etisalat Prepaid Card), reverse charge, operator assisted telephone calls to any telephone subscriber.

Service 800 is a nationwide, toll-free service which provides businesses with a valuable tool to effectively market their products and services by dialing one easy to remember, dedicated number.

Service 900 is offered to businesses who wish to provide information in the form of Interactive Voice Response to callers.

Calling Line Identification Presentation Service - CLIP gives customers the ability to see the telephone number of the calling party along with the date and time of the call. A CLIP integrated standard telephone or feature phone enables easy hook up to this service.

Wireless Communication

GSM International Roaming Service is a facility which allows you to use your mobile phone when you travel outside your home country. International Roaming offers the convenience of keeping in touch - anytime, anywhere. This is possible because of roaming agreements between Etisalat and countries around the world.

GSM Supplementary Services offered by Etisalat are value added services providing enhanced levels of convenience to GSM Subscribers.

GSM Ishaar Package is a combination of three GSM Value Added Services - GSM Call Waiting Facility, GSM Call Conference and Email Notification on GSM handsets via SMS Text.

Etisalat's GSM Fax and Data Service allows GSM Customers (excluding WASEL and Speak Easy) to send and receive fax and data using their mobile phones over the GSM Network at speeds of up to 9600 bps within the UAE or while roaming.

RISALA - SMS Mail is a service that allows GSM, WASEL and SPEAK EASY customers to send a short text message of up to 160 characters from their GSM handsets to other GSM subscribers within the UAE.

SMS Breaking News Service provides the latest breaking news in politics, business, sport or entertainment as it happens around the world.

EWAP Service WAP enabled handset customers can have a more organised life. They can have the latest news, sports scores or stock positions.

GPRS or General Packet Radio Service is an innovative mobile data technology utilised for accessing information via GPRS enabled mobile phones.

Data Communication

Telex is a tried and tested, text communication system which remains the largest and most widespread, confirmed messaging system.

Leased Circuits are a permanent, dedicated communication channel between two or more points, available at a monthly rental and reserved exclusively for use by the organisation that leases it.

Service 500 is a Dial Up Data Access Service provided on the Etisalat Public Switched Telephone

Network over either standard analogue telephone lines or digital ISDN lines.

Fax Plus provides you with a Virtual Fax Number (VFN) and a fax mailbox that gives you the flexibility of 'anywhere communication'.

Packet Switched Data Network - EMDAN, enables data from one communications system to be transmitted in a series of 'packets' to a receiving system.

Integrated Services Digital Network - ISDN is a digital transmission standard that has radically changed the approach to communications around the world.

The Roll-about Video Conferencing service from ETISALAT allows for face-to-face meetings over any distance by allowing groups of people to participate in live audio-visual conferences, linked via a digital line, to any video conferencing site in the world.

Etisalat's Frame Relay Service is a packet switching protocol service designed for WAN Connectivity, but uses smaller packets and less error checking than traditional forms of packet switching (such as X.25) - an international standard for efficiently handling high-speed data bursts over Wide Area Networks.

Asynchronous Transfer Mode - ATM is a new form of broadband communications technology. It provides a way of transporting data from a wide range of applications using one seamless network and supports many types of traffic - data, image, voice and video - over common facilities, enabling users to consolidate current diverse networks. ATM can be used as a basis for both LAN and WAN technologies, and is the only standards based technology which has been created to accommodate the simultaneous transmission of diverse customer applications.

Very Small Aperture Terminals - VSATs are small, software driven earth stations used for the reliable transmission of data or voice via satellite.

A telephone will be installed within one week if a junction box is available. Installations normally take 15-30 days if cables need to be laid. Line rentals are charged at Dhs 45 per quarter, payable in advance. Telephone bills are issued monthly and must be paid within fourteen days. If a line is disconnected for failure to pay on time, a fee of Dhs 50 must be paid to restore the service.

All local telephone calls and faxes within Dubai are free except for those made from public phone booths. The cheap rate periods for international calls are between 9pm and 7am; and from 2pm to 4 pm Saturdays to Thursdays. Cheap rates also apply throughout Fridays and national/public holidays declared by the federal government but not on holidays declared by the local government.

Etisalat offers all the services a modern business may need including mobile phones, paging services and Internet. Those who have GSM (Global System for Mobile Communications) handsets and are visiting the UAE or are UAE residents and want to control their phone bills can benefit from Etisalat's prepaid GSM SIM Card 'Speak Easy' service. For Dhs 300, Etisalat provides a SIM card which can be inserted into a GSM handset or mobile phone allowing both international and local calls to be made for up to Dhs 300. The SIM card is valid for one month from the date of issue but can be recharged for a further month and is available from the Etisalat sales counter, or through authorised Rent-A-Car companies at the Dubai and Abu Dhabi International Airports.

Normal mobile telephone rates within the country are currently 60 fils per minute from 7am to 2pm and 4pm to 12am and 30 fils per minute during other hours. International calls made from mobile phones are charged at the normal tariffs applicable to normal telephones.

Further information on telecommunication services available in Dubai can be obtained from Emirates Telecommunications Corporation, PO Box 1150, Dubai, UAE or on 04-2228111. Directory enquiries in English can be made by dialling 181.

Newspapers, Radio and Television

▲ The Gulf News premises off Sheikh Zayed Road

There are three main English language newspapers available in Dubai, namely Gulf News, Gulf Today and Khaleej Times (all Dhs 2 and Dhs 3 on Fridays). These newspapers provide full coverage of events within the UAE and devote many pages to international news. Most international newspapers and magazines are available in Dubai, although they tend to be expensive. Many other weekly and monthly magazines are also issued in Dubai taking interest in the educational, economic, sports and social affairs. Since the opening of the Dubai Media City, a number of new magazines have emerged focusing on political, economic and social affairs. Dubai bookshops are rich in books, printed matters, periodicals and Arabic and foreign newspapers in different languages. All publications entering Dubai are checked by censors to ensure they do not offend public decency.

United Arab Emirates Radio & TV – Dubai TV & Radio Station was inaugurated in 1971 and it has gained a prominent place on the media map locally and abroad. The Dubai Information Department now operates three radio stations and four TV Channels, which transmit their programs round the clock attracting millions of listeners and viewers worldwide.

Operating 24 hours a day, everyday, the English language stations, Dubai FM (92 FM) and Ajman's Channel 4 FM (104.8 FM), play modern music. Broadcast throughout the UAE, EFM1 (99.3, 100.5 FM) plays modern music for a 'younger' audience, while EFM2 (90.5, 98.7 FM) broadcasts a mixture of news, talk shows and modern music.

Ras Al Khaimah's Radio Asia (1152 khz) has programmes in Hindi, Urdu and Malayalam, while Umm Al Quwain's Hum FM (106.2 FM) broadcasts mainly in Hindi with a bit of English.

Emirates Dubai Television (EDTV) Dubai Satellite Channel commenced transmission in 1974. It was the first colour television channel in the Gulf. Many factors contribute to the success of this channel:

decent programs, modern studios and facilities, elite engineers, technicians and staff, which enable the channel to provide viewers with distinctive services. In addition to Dubai TV, there is also the Dubai Sports Channel, Channel 33 and the Dubai Business Channel.

Channel 33 is a comprehensive channel aiming to serve viewers who speak English. It presents news, current affairs, drama, documentaries and entertainment programs. The Dubai Business Channel aims to furnish investors, businessmen, executives, decision makers, local and international bankers with the latest business information.

Many people prefer to watch satellite television. The Star Cannels are available via satellite in Dubai and include Star Sports, BBC World, Star World, Star Plus, Star Movies and Channel V music station. Most hotels and apartment blocks are equipped to provide satellite television facilities. Dubai Cable Vision offers a number of channels, including CNN, a sports channel, Dubai Satellite Channel and an English movie channel to subscribers.

In April 2000 Emirates Cable TV & Multimedia LLC (E-Vision), a subsidiary of the Emirates Telecommunications Corporation (Etisalat), was created. E-Vision offers entertainment, information, education and interactive multimedia services that are transmitted digitally across the UAE. E-Vision is prepared to offer pay-per-view programming and interactive services to subscribers in Dubai, and plans to extend the reach of their network to the entire UAE in future.

Currency

The unit of currency in Dubai is the UAE Dirham (Dhs) or the Arab Emirates Dirham (AED) as it is termed in international markets. The dirham is divided into units of 100 fils. Currency notes are issued in denominations of 5, 10, 20, 50, 100, 200, 500 and 1000 dirhams. Coin denominations are 25 and 50 fils and 1 dirham. Coins with a denomination below 25 fils are rarely used.

The value of the dirham has been fixed to the US dollar since 1980 at the rate of 1 USD to Dhs 3.678. Below is a summarised chart of the Middle East currencies against the US dollar, the Pound Sterling and the Japanese yen as they stood at August 2003.

▲ The UAE Dirham Currency notes

Dirham per Unit of Various Currencies.			
Sterling Pound	5.966	Bahraini Dinar	9.748
US Dollar	3.678	Kuwaiti Dinar	12.328
Japanese Yen	0.0308	Omani Riyal	9.548
Euro	4.151	Qatari Riyal	1.010
Jordanian Dinar	5.214	Saudi Riyal	0.979
Yemeni Riyal	0.222	Indian Rupees	0.080
Moroccan Dirham	0.3862		

Local Time

Dubai is four hours ahead of GMT and there are no adjustments for daylight saving time.

Holidays and Festivals

▲ The city celebrates

▲ A typical holiday

Dubai is an Islamic state, therefore Muslim holidays and festivals are very important. The dates of many Islamic holidays and festivals tend to vary from year to year, but are usually announced in the newspapers a few days before they occur. The most important events in the Islamic calendar are the following:

Ramadan

Ramadan lasts for one lunar month. During this time Muslims are required to abstain from food, drink, tobacco and all other pleasurable pursuits between sunrise and sunset. Non-Muslims should show consideration and refrain from eating or drinking in public during daylight hours. Failure to comply is a criminal offence. Most of the hotels in Dubai do, however, serve food and drink to non-Muslims during Ramadan. It is also important that men and women dress conservatively in public during this holy month.

Eid Al Fitr

This festival marks the end of Ramadan and is a feast which lasts for three days. It is regarded as a time for great celebration when cards and gifts are exchanged.

Eid Al Adha

This is a very important event in the Islamic calendar. It commemorates the occasion when the Prophet Ibrahim was willing to sacrifice his son Ismael as an act of devotion to God. A sheep was ultimately sacrificed instead and the practice of sacrificing a domestic animal continues as a demonstration of willingness to sacrifice everything in the name of God. Again, this festival is a time of great celebration. It is also customary to send cards which should arrive a day or two in advance.

Lailat Al Qadr

This holy event falls on one of the odd numbered nights during the last ten days of Ramadan and commemorates the night on which the revelations of the Quran were made to the Prophet Mohammed. However, no official or public holiday is declared on this day.

Lailat Al Isra' Wa Al Miraj

This holy event commemorates the vision of the Prophet Mohammed during which he was received by God and saw the glory of Heaven. Again, no official holiday is declared on this day.

Mawlid Al Nabi (Birth of Prophet Mohammed)

This holiday is in celebration of the Prophet Mohammed's birthday. Observance is traditional rather than Islamic as Islam does not centre on any human being.

▲ Holidays are for prayer and thought as well.

Ras Al Sana (Islamic New Year)

This holiday falls on 1 Muharram, the first day of the Islamic calendar year, and marks the time of Prophet Mohammed's migration from Mecca to Medina which is regarded as the beginning of Islam.

Dates of Holidays up to 2006			
Hijrah New Year	1 Muharram 1424 4 Mar 2003	1 Muharram 1425 21 Feb 2004	1 Muharram 1426 10 Feb 2005	1 Muharram 1427 30 Jan 2006
Prophet's Birthday	12 Rabi'A. 1424 13 May 2003	12 Rabi'A. 1425 1 May 2004	12 Rabi'A. 1426 21 April 2005	12 Rabi'A. 1427 10 Apr 2006
Al Isra'wa Al Miraj	27 Rajab 1424 23 Sept 2003	27 Rajab 1425 11 Sept 2004	27 Rajab 1426 1 Sept 2005	27 Rajab 1427 21 Aug 2006
Ramadan	1 Ramadan 1424 26 Oct 2003	1Ramadan 1425 14 Oct 2004	1Ramadan 1426 4 Oct 2005	1 Ramadan 1427 23 Sept 2006
Eid Al Fitr	1 Shawwal 1424 25 Nov 2003	1 Shawwal 1425 13 Nov 2004	1 Shawwal 1426 3 Nov 2005	1 Shawwal 1427 23 Oct 2006
Arafat Day	9 Thu Hijah 1424 31 Jan 2004	9 Thu Hijah 1425 19 Jan 2005	9 Thu Hijah 1426 9 Jan 2006	9 Thu Hijah 1427 29 Dec 2006
Eid Al Adha	10 Thu Hijah 1424 1 Feb 2004	10 Thu Hijah 1425 20 Jan 2005	10 Thu Hijah 1426 10 Jan 2006	10 Thu Hijah 1427 30 Dec 2006

Religion

The official religion in Dubai is Islam. Other religions are respected. There are six Christian churches in Dubai: St. Mary's (Roman Catholic), St. Thomas (Orthodox), Evangelical Community Church, International Christian Church, St Francis de Assissi and Holy Trinity Churches. There are two Hindu temples (the Shiva temple and the Krishna temple) which are situated near the Dubai Museum in Bur Dubai. There is also a Sikh temple (the Gurudwara) which is also located near the Dubai Museum.

Trade Fairs, Exhibitions and Conferences

▲ The World Trade Centre Exhibition Halls

Over the past decade, Dubai has matured significantly and its infrastructure has embraced the Meetings, Incentives, Conferences and Exhibitions (MICE) tourism sector to Dubai. There are now a number of large state-of-the-art exhibition spaces showcasing a variety of exhibitions each year including the Dubai Airport Expo, The Dubai International Convention Centre and the Grand Hyatt Dubai.

International trade fairs and exhibitions held in Dubai each year include the International Spring Trade Fair, the Industrial Service, Plant Maintenance & Environment Technology exhibition, the Arab Oil and Gas Show, Arab Lab, the Middle East International Boat Show, the Middle East International Motor Show and the Index, Gitex and Motexha Exhibitions, Gulf Education & Training Expo and the Arabian Travel Market.

Covering every kind of professional and academic interest, exhibitions are now a regular feature of Dubai life and conference organisers are happy to provide a list of events they stage.

Dubai International Convention Centre (DICC) was opened in March 2003 and is big enough to accommodate events for up to 11,000 delegates. In addition, its main multipurpose hall has the capacity to hold up to 6,000 people when set as an auditorium. Adjustable walls and retractable seating can be configured in an endless array to accommodate any event – from an opera, ballet or theatrical production, to a lecture or plenary session, or world-class sporting championship game, for example, tennis or basketball and a range of entertainment options including specialised concerts, be they jazz, classical or pop. The DICC features a 6,860 square metre multipurpose hall and 44 breakout rooms that can hold from 60 - 600 delegates.

▲ The Grand Hyatt with the Middle East's largest conference facility

The Grand Hyatt Dubai is one of the Middle East's largest and most sophisticated conference hotels with world-class facilities set in a resort environment. With over 4340 square meters of conference and meeting space, the hotel has two magnificent pillar-free conference ballrooms which are divisible, a cutting-edge Media Room and 9 meeting rooms.

▼ Dubai International Convention Centre (DICC), next to the Dubai World Trade Centre

Chapter Two

Immigration and Customs

Introduction

The laws governing immigration requirements are mainly contained in Federal Law No. 6 of 1973 regarding the Entry & Residence of Expatriates as amended by Federal Law No. 13 of 1996, the Immigration Law. Other immigration regulations have been issued in various Ministerial Decrees and Orders, the most relevant of which in terms of procedure is Ministerial Decree No. 360 of 1997 to Issue the Executive Bylaw of Federal Law No. 6 of 1973 (the Decree).

The general rule regarding foreign visitors to the UAE is that all visitors, except transit passengers who do not leave the airport and citizens of GCC countries (Qatar, Kuwait, Saudi Arabia, Bahrain and Oman) and citizens of 33 exempted countries, require a visa for entry.

The 33 Exempted Countries

Andorra	Greece	Monaco	Australia
Hong Kong	New Zealand	Austria	Iceland
Belgium	Norway	Brunei	Canada
Ireland	Portugal	Cyprus	Italy
San Marino	Denmark	Japan	Singapore
The Netherlands	Liechtenstein	Spain	Finland
Sweden	Luxembourg	Switzerland	France
Malaysia	USA	Germany	Malta
Vatican	UK		

Citizens of the above countries can obtain visas at the port of entrance, in exchange for a fee of Dhs 100. This entitles the visitor to stay in the country for 60 days, extendable for another 30 days. UK citizens receive an automatic 28-day visa on arrival in the UAE.

In order to apply for any visa or permit, it is necessary to obtain the sponsorship of either a UAE resident (who may be a foreigner) or other legal entities in Dubai such as companies or hotels. If the visa or permit is being arranged by a hotel or a local sponsor, it is usually deposited at the airport for collection by the visitor on arrival.

The UAE bodies which are responsible for issuing visas and permits to foreigners wishing to enter the UAE are the Naturalisation & Residency Administration in the concerned authority such as the Department of Naturalisation & Residency (the DNR) where Dubai is concerned, the International Airport Authority of any member emirate and any other body designated for this purpose by the Ministry of Interior. Entry permits as distinct from visas, however, may only be obtained from within the UAE from the Headquarters of Naturalisation & Residency, the DNR in the case of Dubai.

Although only some of the immigration laws and regulations are applicable to a business person, it is useful to grasp a basic understanding of these for both business and personal purposes. In the sections that follow, we have outlined the immigration requirements new businesses will need to fulfill in order to employ staff in the UAE, the different types of visas and permits which would be useful to foreigners, what they are, to whom and when they may be useful, and the procedures for obtaining them.

Tourist Visa
Transit Visas (96 hours and 14 days)
Visit Visa (Renewable after 60 days)
Multiple Entry Visa
Residence Visa

Employment Permit
Residence Permit
Residence for Employees
Residence Without Work

There are several types of visas and permits one may apply for. The type that a person needs will primarily depend on the individual's purpose of entry into the UAE. As discussed before, the procedures for obtaining these are governed by the Immigration Law and the regulations and decrees issued by the Ministry of Interior. As the Immigration Law is a federal one, the procedures will be applicable to all of the emirates. This book, however, considers the procedures taken only in Dubai.

It is worth noting that the immigration requirements change frequently. It is therefore advisable to ensure that the requirements mentioned below have not been revised.

Each permit or visa has its own requirements and procedures. However, there are general conditions which all applicants must satisfy in order to obtain a visa or permit regardless of who they are, as listed below:

❶
The applicant must hold a valid passport or document allowing him to enter the country and return to his country of residence, or the country where the passport was issued.
❷
The official authorities should have approved his entry for the purpose sought.
❸
The applicant should have a foreign or local sponsor who is resident in the UAE.
❹
The applicant is not banned from entering the UAE. Applicants with Israeli stamps on their passport are banned from entering the UAE.
❺
The applicant has not previously been deported from the UAE, unless special permission has been obtained for his entry.

Visas

An entry visa is legally defined under the Decree as:

"...a permission to be fixed on the passport or on the travel document of a foreigner which allows him to enter the territory of the country, accompanied by all persons included in such passport or document, unless the visa specifies the names of the beneficiaries of the visa."

Visas, as opposed to permits, allow entry into the UAE for short or temporary periods although some of these periods are renewable. Therefore, those wishing to visit the UAE will need to apply for one of the visas explained below depending on the purpose of entry.

Transit Visas

There are two forms of transit visas, the 96-hour transit visa and the entry visa for a mission, which is commonly known as simply a transit visa.

96-hour Transit Visa

The 96-hour transit visa which is issued at the Dubai International Airport (DIA) allows a foreign passenger (in transit) to enter the UAE for a maximum period of 96 hours at the request of the airline which has flown him, and the flight conditions oblige the passenger to enter the country. This form of transit visa requires the passenger to hold a valid passport and have a valid continuing, as opposed to return, air ticket. Only airlines as distinct from businesses, may apply for this type of transit visa.

→ To obtain a 96-hour transit visa, the airline carrying the foreign passenger is required to submit a list of its transit passengers for whom it assumes responsibility in accordance with the law. The concerned authority at the airport will then stamp the passenger's passport and state the period of stay permitted.

Entry Visa for a Mission: 14-Day Transit Visa

This type of visa as the name suggests is issued to those who need to enter the country for a commercial mission relating to a licensed company or an establishment, public or private, operating in the UAE for a total unrenewable period of 14 days, commencing on the day following the date of arrival in the country.

The 14-day transit visa is therefore useful for those who wish to enter the UAE for business purposes for periods of not more than two weeks. In order to apply for this visa on someone's behalf, the following conditions need to be fulfilled:

Changing the Status of a Visitor to a Resident

If a person enters the UAE on a visit visa he is normally not allowed to work. **However, it is** possible to change a visit visa (which was obtained for purposes other than tourism) into an employment visa if the following conditions are fulfilled:

The applicant falls under one of the following categories:

- Engineer
- Doctor, Chemist, Nurse and Medical Technician
- Teacher
- Agricultural Advisor
- Qualified Accountant and Auditor
- Technicians in electronic, scientific equipment and labs
- Driver licensed to drive heavy vehicles and buses
- Employee in private oil companies

In practice, however, persons who do not fall within one of the above categories but hold jobs of a professional nature, rather than jobs of an unskilled nature can change their visit visas into employment visas.

Obtain the Ministry of Labour & Social Affair's approval for residency.
The sponsor will be the same who obtained the visit visa.

Pay a fee of Dhs 500 for obtaining exemption from the requirement of leaving the country, as is usually required for visit visa entrants.

Submit an application for an employment visa as explained below.

→ Procedure for Changing a Visit Visa into an Employment Visa

In order to change a visit visa into an employment visa, it is first necessary to apply for an employment visa to the DNR. Once the employment visa has been issued, it will need to be submitted to the DNR together with the applicant's original passport and copy, the applicant's original visit visa and the appropriate fee (currently Dhs 500). There is no specific form for changing a visit visa into an employment visa.

Once the employment visa has been obtained, the applicant will need to obtain a residence permit, as explained later, within 60 days.

Changing a visit visa into an employment visa takes an average of two days to complete.

Visas for Tourists

Tourists may enter the country on a visit visa, a transit visa or a tourist visa. The most appropriate visa will primarily depend on three factors: the visitor's nationality, who the sponsor is and the intended period of stay.

If the sponsor is a business operating in the UAE or an individual residing in the UAE, the visitor may enter the country either on a visit visa or on a transit visa, depending on how long he intends to stay. If, on the other hand, the sponsor is a tour operator or a hotel then an application for a transit visa or a tourist visa would be applicable, with the exception of citizens of the 33 exempted countries and GCC countries who do not require visas to enter the country.

In practice, some hotels and tour operators submit different applications depending on the nationality of the visitor. With regard to visitors from Arab countries (other than GCC state nationals) and Africa (except South Africa) the hotel or tour operator will normally apply for transit visas on their behalf rather than tourist visas. As mentioned above, transit visas allow the holder to remain in the country for a total unrenewable period of 14 days from the date of entry.

For guests of other nationalities, hotels usually apply for tourist visas. A tourist visa allows the visitor to remain in the country for a total unrenewable period of 30 days from the date of entry into the UAE.

→ Procedure for obtaining a Tourist Visa

When a visa is being obtained through a hotel in Dubai, the procedures are the same vis a vis the visitor, regardless of the type of visa that is being applied for, as the hotel will handle the necessary requirements.

The intending visitor has only to fill out an application form, provided by the hotel including details of his credit card (which is normally also on a form provided by the hotel) and send a copy of his passport either by fax or mail to the hotel. The credit card details are used to deduct the visa charge (currently Dhs 300) by the hotel.

The hotel will then submit the necessary documents to the DNR and send a copy of the visa to the visitor. The original visa is placed at the immigration desk at the airport before the visitor's arrival for collection. The visa may take seven to ten days to finalise from the date of submission of documents to the hotel although this period may be less. However, for an additional Dhs 100, the visa will be processed within 24 hours.

Children who are on their parents' passports are exempt from paying the Dhs 300 fee. They also need no separate immigration application.

③
The original medical certificate
④
The employee's original passport
⑤
The original employment visa issued to the employee
⑥
A copy of the sponsor's passport (if the sponsor is an individual)
⑦
A copy of the Business's trade licence
⑧
A copy of the Immigration Card of the Business
⑨
Two passport size photographs of the employee
⑩
The appropriate fee (currently Dhs 300 or Dhs 400 if the application is urgent).

The above requirements should be satisfied within 60 days of the employee's entry into the UAE on his employment visa. There is no specific time limit for completing each of the above steps under the law. However, it is advisable to complete these requirements within 30 days of the employee's entry into the UAE.

If these requirements are not completed within the time limit stated, a fine of Dhs 100 will be payable for each day until the procedures are completed.

Residence Visas & Permits

Once a non-UAE national enters the UAE and intends to live in the UAE indefinitely for whatever purposes, he should obtain a residence permit as distinct from a residence visa. This will be stamped on the applicant's passport.

A residence visa allows a person to enter the UAE only once within two months of its date of issue. Therefore, if after getting a residence visa the applicant does not use it within two months, he will have to apply for a new one. The period of permissible stay in the country is sixty days from the date of entry into the UAE. Therefore applications for a residence permit should be submitted before the expiry of this time. The visa is converted to a permit and stamped in the passport.

A Residence Visa is required for those who wish to enter the UAE with the intention of living indefinitely with, say, their husbands who are already resident in the country. Those entering the UAE for employment and intending to reside in the country do not require a residence visa as in most instances the intending employer will act as sponsor and their entry into the country will be on an employment visa. A Residence Permit, on the other hand, allows the applicant to live in the country for three years. This is the normal period granted in practice. However, legally speaking, the DNR may issue residence permits for shorter periods but not shorter than one year. As stated above, it is necessary for everyone intending to live in the UAE indefinitely to apply for a residence permit upon entry into the country.

There are two types of residence permits: the residence permit for or with employment and the residence permit without employment. The former, as stated above, is normally granted for a period of three years. The latter is applicable for instance to a foreign resident sponsoring his family. The period of residence granted varies depending on who the sponsor is. For instance, the period of residence granted to those who are sponsored by non-UAE nationals (not in the capacity of an employer) such as a relative or spouse is limited to that person's period of residence, after which the person must leave the country.

It should be noted that whichever residence permit one obtains, if the holder spends more than six months out of the country the permit becomes invalid. However, the following are some of the persons exempted from this rule (their residence permit will expire at the end of the period originally granted):

---

❶

Foreign wives of UAE-nationals

❷

Those traveling for medical reasons. In this case a medical report
is required which must be attested and certified by the Ministry of Health.

❸

Those studying in universities and other educational institutions abroad

❹

Those working for public authorities or other public sector establishments who have been
sent abroad for training/ professional courses or to work in their branches.
The families of such persons are also exempt.

As we shall see below, once a person obtains a residence permit and provided he satisfies certain other conditions, he can sponsor other individuals who wish to visit the country, such as members of his family.

The law limits persons who may apply for a residence permit. They are basically those who can seek sponsorship by either an individual who is resident in the UAE or other legal entities in the UAE, such as a company for employment purposes. Article 28 of the Decree lists the persons who may reside in the UAE (provided they are sponsored) as follows:

• Persons joining their family supporter or guardian such as the children of a foreign resident, in which case the latter will act as the sponsor. However, foreign residents may only act as sponsors on their children's behalf if, in the case of sons, they are under the age of 18 years and in the case of daughters, if they are not married. In the case of married daughters the husband will normally act as sponsor. Males who are over the age of 18 may obtain sponsorship for residence purposes either through an educational establishment they are studying at or through their employer.

- Persons studying in a college/ university or institution in the UAE.

- Persons attending or intending to attend a training course in a public establishment or department.

- Foreign women who are divorced from their UAE national husbands provided they have one or more sons from them.

- Parents and sons of UAE nationals who hold foreign passports.

- Husbands and sons of UAE nationals who hold foreign passports.

- Foreign wives of nationals of GCC countries residing in the GCC states of their husbands.

- Family members of foreign women who are employed (for a period of at least one year) in one of the following professions: teaching, medicine, engineering or other similar professions which require a university degree or a specialised course.

In addition to the above, the sponsoring foreign resident must meet the minimum salary requirements as stipulated under Article 31 of the Decree: receive a minimum monthly salary of Dhs 3,000 plus accommodation provided by his employer or at least Dhs 4,000 without accommodation. Teachers, leaders of mosques and bus drivers who transport students to school, university or other educational establishments are exempt from this requirement.

Domestic helpers and labourers are not allowed to sponsor persons for entering the country even if they meet the salary requirements.

Residence Permits for Persons other than Employees

→ Procedure for obtaining Non Employment Residence Permit

Residence permit applications for persons living abroad are made either at the DNR or at the UAE Embassy/Consulate abroad:

The documents required for such applications depend on who the applicant is. Below is a list of these documents according to the category of the applicant which must be submitted, in addition to the relevant prescribed form provided by the DNR (typed in English and Arabic), the applicant's passport (and copy), a medical report, two passport size photographs of the applicant and the appropriate fee (currently Dhs 300).

Wives of Foreign Residents

The duly attested marriage certificate certified by the UAE Embassy/Consulate abroad or the embassy of the country in which the marriage certificate was issued. In the latter instance the certificate has also to be attested by the Ministry of Foreign Affairs.

A copy of the labour contract of the husband (and the original for verification) showing a monthly salary of at least Dhs 3,000 (with accommodation) or at least Dhs 4,000 (without accommodation). This requirement only applies to the sponsor who is not a teacher, leader of a mosque or a bus driver.

The husband's passport with the residence visa (and a copy).

Wives (or Divorcees) or Widows of UAE Nationals

A duly certified marriage certificate attested by the UAE Embassy/Consulate or by the embassy of the country in which the marriage certificate was issued. It should also be attested by the Ministry of Foreign Affairs. In the case of a divorced wife or widow, the eldest son should act as sponsor and submit the application. If there are no sons, the eldest daughter assumes this role.

Children of Foreigners

The same documents as required for the sponsorship of wives of foreign residents need to be submitted to the DNR (except for the marriage certificate) in the case of applicants who are the sponsor's children. Daughters may only be sponsored by their fathers if they are single. A son cannot be sponsored by his father unless he is below the age of 18.

Parents or Sons of UAE Nationals (holding foreign passports)

An attested certificate of support regarding parents and a duly attested birth certificate regarding sons.

Persons Joining a University or College or Attending Training Courses

The application for residence in this case is handled by the concerned college or university in the UAE which deals directly with the Naturalisation & Residency Department and assumes responsibility for the student during his period of residence in the UAE.

Similarly, the public authority or establishment concerned with persons attending training courses with them is responsible for their sponsorship.

Unlike many jurisdictions, businesses in the UAE are required to fulfill certain requirements with both the immigration authorities and the Ministry of Labour & Social Affairs (the Ministry) if they wish to employ staff in the UAE or if they wish to submit visa applications on behalf of their employees or other persons. Below are details of these requirements.

Business Registration with the DNR:
The Immigration Card of the Business

➜ Procedure to Register a Business with the DNR

When a business intends to recruit staff from overseas, it needs to register the business by opening a file at the Immigration Department (as well as at the Ministry of Labour & Social Affairs) as soon as it obtains its trade licence. Without this the business will not be able to recruit staff. An immigration file can be opened by submitting two copies of the prescribed application form (which must be typed in Arabic and English, stamped with the company stamp and signed by the local partner or national agent) together with the following documents:

---

❶
Copies of the passports of the authorised signatories and the owners of the Business. (The DNR requires all the relevant pages of the passport to be printed on one side of a single sheet of A4 paper.)

❷
Original trade licence (and copy),

❸
Power of attorney of authorised signatories

❹
The appropriate fee (currently Dhs 300).

❺
Copy of the telephone bill

❻
Map of the location of the Business

Upon satisfaction of the above, the new business will be issued an Immigration Card which is renewable every 3 years. Such renewals are conducted by submitting the same documents and fee to the immigration authorities as outlined above.

Business Registration with the Ministry of Labour & Social Affairs:
The Establishment / Labour Card (the Labour Card)

➜ Procedure to Register a Business with the Ministry

All businesses who wish to employ staff and submit visa applications on their behalf must register with the Ministry by opening a file for the business with the Ministry. Where a business is employing an individual, it will first need to obtain the Ministry's approval to do so before it can apply for any visas on the individual's behalf, where applicable. Such applications therefore cannot be made without first registering with the Ministry. Once the business has been registered with the Ministry, it will be issued with a Labour Card.

Representative Cards: Immigration & Labour

All businesses need to appoint a representative to deal on their behalf with the immigration and labour departments, as individuals will not be allowed to deal on the business's behalf at the immigration or labour authorities without first obtaining representative cards from each respective authority. Such representatives will be required to be employed by the business itself.

→ **Procedure for obtaining a Representative Card**

A representative card, renewable annually, can be obtained by filing two copies of the prescribed application form (which must be typed in English and Arabic) at both the immigration authorities and the Ministry along with the following:

> ❶
> Copy of the business's valid trade licence
> ❷
> Copy of the intended representative's passport and residence visa
> ❸
> Two colour passport size photographs of the intended representative
> ❹
> The appropriate fee (currently Dhs 410)
> ❺
> Representative Cards are renewable every 2 years
> ❻
> Copy of the Establishment Card at the Labour Office

Transit Visa Cards

It is advisable for all businesses to obtain a transit visa option in their Immigration Card. This allows a business to obtain 14-day transit visas for clients and other contacts who may be visiting Dubai. Applications are made by submitting to the Inspection Section at the DNR the following:

This option can be added only to the card after at least three months from the date the Business commences operations.

> ❶
> A letter to the head of the inspection Section explaining the requirement for such option
> ❷
> Copies of authorised signatories' passports and copies of their residence permits (for expatriates)
> ❸
> Copies of the telephone bills for the last three months (original for verification)
> ❹
> Evidence of the level of the business including copies of the sale and purchase bills
> ❺
> The application fee of Dhs 100

Upon receiving the above documents the Inspection Section at the DNR will set a date for the applicant's business premises to be inspected. When the office inspection has been carried out and provided the inspectors are satisfied that the application is in order, the approval fee, amounting to Dhs 300 will have to be paid; the transit visa option is then added to the Immigration Card.

Visit Visa Cards

A business may obtain a visit visa option to allow it to obtain regular visit visa for any person visiting the business in Dubai. Application for visit visa option is made by submitting the following to the Inspection Section at the DNR:

This option can be added only to the card after at least three months from the date the business commences operations.

---

❶

A letter to the head of the Inspection Section explaining the requirement for such an option

❷

Copies of authorised signatories' passports and copies of their residence permits (for expatriates)

❸

Copies of the telephone bills for the last three months (original for verification)

❹

Evidence of the level of the business including copies of the sale and purchase bills

❺

The application fee of Dhs 100

If the application is accepted, the approval fee will then be due, amounting to Dhs 600 and then the visit visa option will be added to the Immigration Card.

Other Sponsorships

New Born Babies

If a foreign woman residing in the UAE gives birth, an application for a residence permit must be made on the baby's behalf within four months of the baby's date of birth, failing which the father or legal guardian of the child must pay a fine of Dhs 100 for each day after that period until a residence permit is obtained. The same rules apply to foreign women resident in the UAE who give birth outside the UAE. In such cases, it is necessary to apply for a residence visa on the baby's behalf. Applications are made to the DNR. The documents which need to be submitted include copies of both the father's and the mother's passports and a copy of the baby's birth certificate attested by the Ministry of Foreign Affairs.

Domestic Help

Maids or domestic help may be obtained either through agencies in Dubai or directly from abroad. The agency will only provide the maid's passport copy and the employing individual will need to complete the procedures necessary for employment.

As domestic helpers are exempt from the provisions of Federal Law No. 8 of 1980 on the Regulation of Labour Relations (the Labour Law), they do not have to obtain a labour card in order to be employed nor does the employer need to seek the approval of the Ministry for their employment. Therefore applications for the employment of domestic help are made directly to the immigration authorities on the prescribed application forms provided that the necessary requirements for obtaining an employment visa as discussed above are met. Unlike normal residence permits, residence permits for maids or domestic help are for periods of one year rather than three years. It should be noted that maids or domestic help can be employed only by individuals resident in Dubai and not businesses. Such individuals will assume the role of the domestic help's sponsor for immigration purposes provided they satisfy the conditions stipulated under Article 23 of the Decree, namely:

Have a monthly salary of at least Dhs 6,000.

Pay an annual amount to the state treasury equal to the annual salary of the help. The help's monthly salary must be at least Dhs 400 in which case the amount payable is Dhs 4,800.

The sponsor should not have sponsored a domestic help or a housemaid for one year ending on the date the application is submitted.

The help should not be related to the sponsor.

The sponsor resides in the country with his family.

The fees are Dhs 5000 annually.

There are additional requirements regarding women who practise certain professions such as in the fields of medicine and engineering.

It is illegal to employ a domestic help who is on someone else's sponsorship. It is not permitted to transfer the sponsorship of a domestic help to a new employer, unless a period of at least one year has lapsed from the date the help last left the country. This is pursuant to Article 63 of the Decree which states that when an employment is terminated, the residence permit for employment is considered void and that "no entry permit or new visa can be issued unless after the lapse of six months from the last date of departure from the country, and for one year for house servants."

Transferring Employment Sponsorship

Those who are already employed in the UAE may only seek new employment by transferring their sponsorship from their current or previous employer to their new employer or alternatively cancelling their original sponsorship and undergoing the same process as if they were employed for the first time, that is, re-entering the country on an employment visa. There are certain conditions associated with the transfer of sponsorship from one employer to another in the private sector. These include the following:

- The employee must have been employed by the original employer for at least one year.
- The previous employer approves the new employment.
- The new employment is in the same profession as the previous one.
- The employee holds a valid residence visa.
- The employee's title should be from the categories for which visa transfer is permitted.
- The Ministry approves the transfer, unless the employee is not subject to the labour law such as domestic help.

→ Procedure for Transferring Employment Sponsorship

The documents required for transferring one's employment sponsorship to a new employer:

❶
The duly completed prescribed application form
❷
Copy of the labour card
❸
A copy of the business' trade licence and the Establishment Card at Labour & Immigration
❹
A copy of the employee's passport and residence visa (stamped on the passport)
❺
Copy of the employee's degree and/or professional certificates attested by
the Ministry of Foreign Affairs
❻
The appropriate fee (currently Dhs 200 on submitting the application and Dhs 1,500 when approved)

Once the application is approved the Ministry of Labour issues three letters to the new sponsor; the first contains a list of all the documents required to proceed with the transfer; the second is an undertaking from the previous sponsor that he has paid all the employee's dues, signed by him and the employee to confirm the same; the third contains the approval and payment codes.

Once the approval fee of Dhs 1500 is paid, and the requirements stated above are met, the procedures to obtain the labour card and visa can be commenced.

The employee will also need to obtain a new residence visa as explained above and within the 60-day prescribed time limit starting from the date the transfer was effected.

Lost/ Damaged Passports

If one has lost or damaged his passport, the Director of Naturalization & Residency should be informed within three days from the date of the incident.

Health Requirements & Health Service

No health certificates are needed for entering Dubai. This may, however, change from time to time and so it is recommended that all visitors check this before their departure. It is advisable for all persons travelling to Dubai to ensure that they have inoculations against the following diseases:

• Typhoid
• Hepatitis
• Tetanus
• Polio

Malaria tablets are optional. Most people in Dubai do not take malaria tablets, because it is generally believed that the dry climate eliminates the risk of the disease. All visitors should, however, obtain specific medical advice before departure.

The UAE has a highly advanced and efficient medical health service. All residents in the UAE are entitled to receive medical treatment from the government hospitals, as discussed in Chapter 7, for a fee.

In order to receive such treatment, it is necessary to apply for a medical card. This involves completing the prescribed application form provided, attaching a copy of one's passport including the residence permit page and paying a fee of Dhs 300. Medical cards are renewable annually for a fee of Dhs 300. The medical services available range from general consultations to child birth and dental care.

Emergency health treatment is nevertheless free of charge for everyone in Dubai, be they visitors or residents, although follow-up treatment is chargeable.

In order to get an exemption for goods under category. It is necessary to obtain a letter from the Ministry of Finance & Industry confirming that the goods are going to be used for industrial purposes.

Category II
Products of member states of the Arab Gulf Cooperative Council
Goods for transit/transhipment
Commercial samples which are supplied free of charge and marked "not for sale" or "free sample"
Advertising materials and catalogues which are not for sale
35 mm cinematography film for public exhibitions
The Holy Quran, books and other printed matter imported by non-profit making schools
Goods imported for temporary exhibitions which will later be re-exported
Supplies, equipment and spares for ocean going vessels of international shipping lines
Marine lubricants supplied to local shipping agents on an "on consignment" basis and free of charge
Aircraft operating equipment and parts imported by or on behalf of international airlines for use in their aircraft
Aviation fuel and aviation functional fluids
All personal effects (accompanied or unaccompanied)
Medical and pharmaceutical products
Veterinary medicines

Category III
Live animals and honey bees
Meat
Fish and crustaceans
Dairy products
Dates, fruits, vegetables, edible seeds and sowing seeds
Coffee, tea, spices, rice, wheat, maize, barley and flour
Animal and vegetable oil for human consumption
Sugar, salt and infant milk powder
Animal food

Category III (contd.)
Fertilisers and insecticides certified by the Ministry of Agriculture & Fisheries
Timber, saw wood and plywood
Newspapers, journals, periodicals, plans, drawings, unused postage stamps, cheque books, bank notes, stock and share certificates
Fishing nets
Natural pearls
Silver and gold (unworked or in powder form)
Iron and steel bars, rods, angles, channels and beams for use in buildings.Corrugated iron or aluminium sheets for use in roofing
Re-usable containers for compressed or liquefied gas and the transport of goods
Agricultural machinery and equipment

Cargo may be cleared through customs at Dubai's ports or airport by either consignees who hold either a UAE Federal, Department of Economic Development (DED) or Jebel Ali Free Zone licence or by an agent who holds a DED clearing and forwarding licence.

Customs Procedures

There are various procedures which need to be followed regarding the import and export of goods into and from Dubai. As a general rule, goods exported from Dubai are exempt from customs duties. Import of goods into Dubai for the purpose of re-export is permitted but exemption of customs duties can be claimed only if the goods are re-exported within six months from the date of their import, provided that the necessary procedures are satisfied. In such cases, a payment is normally deposited with the relevant customs authorities in lieu of the duty applicable, which is forfeited if the goods remain in the country for more than six months.

Below are the various customs mechanisms used for importing or exporting goods from Dubai, which would be of particular interest to those contemplating export/ import business.

Deposits

For the purposes of making the customs system efficient and flexible, Dubai has introduced the practice of paying deposits equal to the duty payable on a consignment. This deposit is returned upon the fulfilment of certain conditions. Deposits are paid to customs in the following cases:

- Duty Deposits
  These are deposits paid in lieu of duty payable where, for instance, there is a doubt as to whether duty is payable or not.
- Missing Document Deposits
  Here, the Customs allow a consignment to be cleared upon payment of a deposit if the Certificate of Origin of the goods is missing in order to avoid delays.
- Temporary Import Deposits
  These deposits are required on goods which are intended for re-export within 6 months of being imported as discussed above.
- Transit Deposits
- Free Zone Overland Exports
  Deposits are paid in respect of the customs duty chargeable on goods being imported into Dubai from the Free Zones, unless they are being transported by Dubai Port Authority vehicles, in which case no deposit is required.

In order to pay a deposit an application has to be submitted on the prescribed forms before clearing a Customs Bill. The deposit payable is determined by Customs on a case by case basis and such decisions are final.

Deposit reclaims are made by submitting the white copy of the deposit receipt and the relevant documents (these depend on each case) to the Customs office where payment was initially made. Reclaims must be made within the prescribed time limits, depending on the type of deposit made. These are listed in the following chart:

Type of Deposit	Time Limit for Claim
Duty Deposits & Missing Document Deposits	60 days
Temporary Imports	210 days (NB. Goods must be re-exported within 180 days of bill date)
Transit Deposits	45 days (NB. Goods must leave the country within 30 days)
JAFZA, DAFZ and DFSA	45 days (NB. Goods must leave the country within 30 days)

Provided the necessary documents have been submitted, deposit refunds normally take two weeks to be obtained.

Bank Guarantees

To help businesses run smoothly, the Customs allow them the use of bank guarantees. These must be issued by a bank in Dubai and are used in three circumstances:

(a) "Customs Duty Guarantee" is used in lieu of a Customs Duty Receipt - Banks. The consignee presents it to Customs upon clearance of the customs bill if the documents required for the collection of customs duty are incomplete, instead of a Customs Duty Receipt.

Upon receipt of the missing document, the consignee obtains either a "Customs Duty Receipt - Bank" from the bank or a "Customs Duty Receipt - Cash" from Customs and hands it over to the Guarantee Section in the Customs main office. Failure to produce the Customs Duty Receipt within 120 days allows Customs to demand the guarantee from the bank.

(b) "Standing Guarantees" are used in lieu of cash deposits by clearing and forwarding agents involved in cash deposit transactions. Applications are made to Customs for such guarantees for the movement of transit cargo, overland exports from the free zones or the DFSA and temporary imports. Applications are made on a Standing Guarantee Information Sheet. Upon approval, a bank guarantee and an undertaking on a standard form are required.

The clearance of a consignment with the above guarantee is done by completing an "Application to clear under a Standing Guarantee". This is available with the Customs and must be presented upon clearance of the bill.

(c) "Special Guarantees" are used on a case by case basis regarding special Customs control arrangements as security for duty payments or compliance of the relevant regulations, such as when the clearance of a bill is delayed.

Temporary Imports

As discussed above, goods imported into the UAE can benefit from customs duty exemption if they are re-exported within six months of their arrival into the UAE. In order to do so, the person importing the goods must provide Customs with a deposit or a standing bank guarantee. In addition, the following documents should be presented to Customs when importing the goods:

• Delivery Order
• Invoice
• Certificate of Origin
• Deposit Receipt (or "Application to clear on the standing guarantee")
• Copy of the Business's Trade or Professional Licence

In re-exporting the goods, the shipper is required to request the customs office which cleared the Import Bill to inspect them and supervise their packaging. The inspector then seals the package with the endorsement "Customs Exit-Entry Certificate" prepared by the shipper. The shipper must then obtain proof of export of the consignment which should be on the Exit/ Entry Certificate. Such proof is obtainable from one of the following authorities:

• Customs officers in the UAE (port or airport)
• Customs authorities in foreign countries

• Certification from UAE border post
• Vessel's stamp and master's signature for ships' spares

The refund of the deposit may be claimed within 210 days of the date of the Import Bill by the shipper. This process takes about two weeks to complete.

Goods entering Dubai for the purposes of exhibitions may also be cleared as temporary imports upon payment of a deposit. If such goods are sold during the exhibition, they will be subject to customs duties.

Inter-Port Transfers (IPTA)

Agents who wish to move consignments before clearing a Customs Bill may do so by obtaining an Inter-Port Transfer Authority from Customs. This is acceptable to port authorities for the release of such consignments, which are sealed before they are despatched and are inspected on arrival. It should be noted that an IPTA cannot be obtained for consignments which have already been cleared on a Customs Bill.

Bonded Storage and Transport

"Bonded storage" is a term used for goods which are stored in an area controlled by Customs. For example, Port Rashid contains agents' bonded warehouses. In such cases, it is possible to move the goods without clearing them on a Customs Bill, in which case the consignee is not regarded as the owner of such goods. Other bonded storage facilities are located at Al Awir and the Dubai Airport.

It should be noted that in order to handle goods stored in bonded storage in any way it is necessary to obtain the prior consent of Customs.

Duty Free Storage Area

Dubai Ports Authority offers Duty Free Storage Area (DFSA) facility to UAE importers for long term storage of goods at concessionary rates subject to prior approval. Goods can be declared for DFSA entry by presenting to Customs:

1. The DFSA Bill of Entry prepared by the consignee
2. The Shipping Agent's Delivery Order
3. The original Invoice and Packing List
4. Bill of Lading second original
5. The original Certificate of Origin

▲ The Customs Authority at Al Aweer. One of the many Duty Free Storage areas is here.

Movement of goods out of the DFSA is controlled by DFSA Import or Export Bills which are prepared by the consignee or agent. Duty is payable for imports. Deposit or guarantee will be required for overland exports. Goods cleared for export must be shipped out within 30 days of the DFSA Export Bill date, if not, they are liable for duty payment. Ownership of goods may be transferred within the DFSA provided Customs are notified. However, repacking is not, normally, permitted.

Manifests

SMS (Sea Manifest System) is a computerised Manifest system to electronically record all incoming Sea Manifests for Port Rashid, Jebel Ali and Aweer Terminals. SMS Messages will be printed on the New Customs Bill of Entry stationary in which goods will be released. Also, Electronic Manifests will be accepted in a Structure Format (Check SMS Message Format).

Manifests are submitted by shipping agents to Customs Port Rashid Office for annual entry, in addition, all supplement, amendment and cancellation are done at the same office.

Electronic Manifest can be accepted on floppy disk 3.5" using DPA manifest format. Agents who cannot produce DPA manifest format use the customs' sea manifest format temporarily until it can be replaced with DPA manifest format.

Vehicles

In order to import a vehicle into Dubai, it is necessary to obtain a "Vehicle Clearance Certificate" without which the vehicle cannot be registered. In order to obtain this certificate, it is necessary to provide Customs with the original Bill of Entry and the details of the vehicle. The vehicle may be inspected by Customs if it is second hand or some information is missing. When all the necessary documents are submitted and the Customs have conducted the inspection, where applicable, they issue the Vehicle Clearance Certificate, which currently costs Dhs 5. This certificate is then presented to the Dubai Police when registering the vehicle.

▼ Cargo awaits clearance at the Cargo Village Customs Centre.

DCCI Conciliation Procedures

❶

The party seeking conciliation submits a written request to the secretariat of the Dubai International Arbitration Centre (DIAC). The application should contain a summary of the dispute and supporting documents.

❷

The secretariat of the DIAC notifies the other party of the request within, not more than 7 days of the date of submission of the request. The other party should reply to the request within, not more than 15 days of receiving the request. The request and the reply are then submitted to the committee.

❸

The committee appoints a conciliation panel according to article 17 of the Rules. The parties concerned have the right to object to the body within two weeks of being notified of the name or names of the conciliator or conciliators. Conciliation procedures should begin as soon as this period is over.

❹

The committee has the right to ask for an advance payment against the conciliation costs. The committee sets the fees for the conciliators, before giving them the file on the dispute. The Chamber collects an administrative fee, commensurate with the value of the dispute, as shown at the end of Chapter 4.

❺

The conciliation panel studies the dispute and hears the statements of the parties concerned or their representatives. If the panel arrives at a solution which the parties agree to, this is recorded and ratified by the panel.

❻

Conciliation should be concluded within two months. The period can be extended for another two months by the committee.

❼

The file is not submitted to the conciliation committee until the administrative fees and the advance payment decided by the committee are paid. If the parties concerned fail to pay one of the advance payment installments (if payment is by installments), the conciliation process is halted and the secretariat notifies the body and the committee of this development.

DCCI Arbitration Procedures

Those requesting arbitration are required to submit a written application to the Secretariat at DIAC, attaching the arbitration agreement, if any and other supporting documents.
The application should contain:
- The name of the plaintiff, his title, nationality and address
- The name of the defendant, his title, nationality and address
- The subject of the dispute and the plaintiff's requests
- The name of the arbitrator and his address, or a mandate authorising the committee to choose an arbitrator.

The request for arbitration and the documents attached must be in triplicate if there is to be one arbitrator. Five or more copies are required if more arbitrators are to be involved, because there should be two extra copies. A non-refundable registration fee is collected by the Chamber at the time of submission of the request.

The secretariat of DIAC sends a copy of the request for arbitration and the attached copies to the defendant within 7 days of its submission by registered letter with an acknowledgement of receipt.

If there is no agreement on arbitration and if the defendant does not reply to the request within 30 days of receiving it, this will be taken as rejection on his part.
If he agrees, the defendant must reply and attach the documents required, according to the number of arbitrators (as mentioned above).
The reply should be sent within 30 days of receipt of the request. It should contain:
- The name and address of the arbitrator he chooses
- His reply to the claims made by the plaintiff
- Counter claims, if any

DIAC's secretariat sends the defendant's reply with the documents attached and a counter reply, if any, to the plaintiff within 3 days. Arbitration procedures continue, even if the defendant does not send his reply within this period as long as there is an arbitration agreement.

The secretariat presents to the committee chairman the request for arbitration together with a summary of what has been submitted by the parties to the conflict.
The committee meets within 30 days of sending the replies in order to:
- Approve the arbitrators appointed by the parties concerned according to the standards set out in the Conciliation and Arbitration System

- Appoint the remainder of arbitrators
- Choose a venue for the arbitration if the parties have not agreed on a location
- Decide on an advance payment against the costs of arbitration. The committee also makes a preliminary assessment of the fees to be paid to the arbitrators.
  The committee can give the parties 21 days in which to appoint a chairman for the panel. Failing that, the committee will undertake the task itself. The Chamber collects an administrative fee commensurate with the disputed amount (refer to end of Chapter 4).

DIAC's secretariat informs the arbitration panel of their appointment by registered letter with an acknowledgement of receipt. The letter also contains a summary of the dispute. Each appointed arbitrator should send a written reply within 2 weeks of receiving notice of his appointment. Otherwise he will be deemed to have rejected the request and another person will be appointed, in accordance with the same procedures.

When the arbitration panel accepts its mandate, the secretariat sends the arbitration file to them and a ruling is issued within six months if the parties do not agree to a longer period. The panel can grant a six month period of grace which can be extended further with the approval of the parties or, if the parties cannot reach an agreement through a decision of the committee.

The case file is given to the arbitration panel only after payment of the administrative fee and the advance payment set by the committee. If the parties do not pay any installment of the advance payment, (if it is being paid in installments), arbitration proceedings are stopped and the secretariat notifies the panel and thecommittee of its decision.

The start of arbitration does not prevent the parties from going to the courts to take temporary or preventive measures. The party taking such measures should immediately notify DIAC's secretariat and arbitration panel.

The arbitration award signed by the panel,
with the costs set by the committee and any clarifications or amendments made are deposited with DIAC's secretariat. The secretariat then gives a copy to each party after arbitration costs and arbitrator's fees are paid.

The Dubai Department of Economic Development (DED)   www.dubaided.gov.ae

▲ The offices of DED on the Creek in Deira

The DED, previously called the Economic Department, is a governmental organisation established on 18 March 1992 by H.H. Sheikh Maktoum bin Rashid Al Maktoum, Vice President and Prime Minister of the UAE and Ruler of Dubai, by virtue of Law No. 1 of 1992. Chaired by H.H. General Sheikh Mohammed bin Rashid Al Maktoum, Crown Prince of Dubai and UAE Minister of Defence, it was primarily established for developing trade and industry both within Dubai and outside it.

Structure

The DED consists of four departments or divisions: (1) Finance and Administrative Affairs (2) Business Registration (3) Compliance Division and (4) Studies and Planning Division. There are two other offices affiliated to the Director-General of the DED, namely, the Legal Affairs Office and the Internal Audit and Performance Control Office.

The Department of Finance and Administrative Affairs has a number of functions. These include the carrying out of financial transactions related to the DED's expenditure and revenue and preparing and implementing mass media plans to improve Dubai's image.

The Department of Business Registration is the most relevant to investors in terms of the necessary procedures involved in setting up a business. It deals with nearly every aspect relating to the registration and licensing of companies and sole proprietorships which are discussed below. The Department also deals with the processing of transactions and their follow-up at the federal and local government level on behalf of the business community.

The Compliance Division ensures that companies and establishments in Dubai comply with the relevant rules and regulations. The procedures include random inspections by the Department of such parties. The DED has played and continues to play an important role in the protection of intellectual property rights and has carried out many raids against businesses dealing in fake products. The Compliance Department is also responsible for the implementation of tasks involving advertising campaigns, trade exhibitions and entertainment events.

The Studies and Planning Division, as the name suggests, is mainly concerned with research and project planning of matters relating to the commercial aspects of Dubai. It also, among other things, provides commercial information to those interested, and conducts feasibility studies of investment and industrial projects. The library at the DED is supervised and maintained by the Studies and Planning Division.

The Legal Affairs Office provides legal advice both internally and to the public who deal with the DED. It also prepares draft laws, regulations and orders relating to the DED's working.

The Internal Audit and Performance Control Office is mainly involved in the internal audit of the Department of Economic Development.

Functions and Responsibilities

According to Article 4 of Law No 1 of 1992, the DED's functions and responsibilities are:

a • Preparing, maintaining and supervising a commercial registry

b • Registering and protecting industrial trade rights

c • Considering applications relating to the construction of plants and factories

d • Regulating the affairs of commercial agents, brokers and commercial advertising offices

e • Regulating and encouraging marketing of Dubai's industrial products

f • Encouraging the investment of national and foreign capital in commercial and industrial projects

g • Organising exhibitions

h • Controlling and supervising insurance companies in Dubai

i • Supervising the incorporation of companies, registering and controlling national and foreign companies, studying government participation in companies and development projects and representing the government in companies in which the government has an interest

j • Regulating and controlling the auditing profession

k • Working with the federal government in the implementation of federal laws on trade and industry and other economic activities

l • Performing any other business related to the DED's jurisdiction listed in the first paragraph of this article.

A key role played by the DED in establishing businesses is the issuing of trade licences to new businesses. The DED also accepts the fees which are payable to the various other government departments such as the Ministry of Economy & Commerce.

In the field of industrial projects, the DED ensures that the pre-feasibility study of a proposed industrial project complies with the relevant laws and regulations. The procedure for establishing industrial projects is discussed in Chapter 4.

Drive Towards Quality

▲ The Dubai Quality Award is a prestigious award.

As a means of achieving higher standards in the delivery of goods and services throughout the public and private sectors, and in the interests of promoting economic development within the emirate, the DED has taken a number of initiatives, which have proved highly successful. These include the introduction of the Dubai Quality Award and the Dubai Service Excellency Scheme and the Invest in People Standard, and the setting up of the Industrial Development Centre.

The Dubai Quality Award (DQA) Scheme was launched in 1994 by H.H. General Sheikh Mohamed bin Rashid Al Maktoum and the Government of Dubai with the specific aim of developing the emirate's existing reputation for reliability and expertise, by encouraging the business community as a whole to strive for a culture of raising quality standards in all areas of industrial and commercial life and also within the public administration itself. The Award Scheme is divided into a number of categories (professional, financial, trade, manufacture/production, service, business and construction).

An associated programme, the Dubai Quality Appreciation Programme, imposes fewer criteria than the DQA and is primarily aimed at small businesses.

Investors in People (IIP) is an internationally recognised set of principles applying to the development of human resources. The aim of IIP is to bring about improved personnel management within the organisation, thereby enhancing its performance. Interested businesses can apply to the DED for an assessment.

"Promoting Dubai to become an International Centre for knowledge-based, high-tech, value added manufacturing industries". This is the vision of Industrial Development Centre (IDC). Central to the mission of the IDC is the selective attraction of foreign direct investment by multinational corporations with the aim of strengthening and supporting the local manufacturing base, encouraging technology transfer and increasing levels of investment in Dubai. Alongside these objectives, the IDC seeks in particular to encourage UAE nationals to participate in the industrial development process as investors and employees in the private industrial sector, and to strengthen regional cooperation by the establishment of industrial joint ventures between Dubai and neighbouring emirates.

The Service Excellence Scheme (SES) focuses on Dubai as a retail centre in a competitive global market. The Scheme, which is monitored by a special SES Department within the DED, aims at promoting this idea of excellence in customer service, and the application of sound business ethics. No awards are given, but approved members are issued with certificates and entitled to display the SES logo.

Shopping and Tourism Festivals   www.mydsf.com

▲ It's fun, fun, fun for the whole family during the Dubai Shopping Festival.

The Dubai Shopping Festival (DSF) was staged for the first time on February 25, 1996. Months of preparation go into staging the DSF every year, and today DSF lives up to its reputation for conducting the most exciting activities for the whole family, inspired by the theme One World, One Family, One Festival. The DSF is held for 30 days, and is synonymous with 'Special Offers', spectacular fireworks and hosts of events and promotions

Also sponsored by the DED, the Dubai Summer Surprises (DSS) is a three-month summer festival of colourful events and 'surprises', aimed primarily at families with children. DSS, which began life in 1998, represents yet another part of the Dubai

tourism service providers. The DTCM also monitors and analyses the information contained in the regular reports, which it receives from its Overseas Offices.

Other DTCM responsibilities include the issue of various kinds of licences to service providers within the tourism industry and the application of licensing byelaws and regulations.

The Operations and Marketing Division promotes Dubai's Heritage sites and the many events which are now held in the emirate.

The Media Information Section focuses on DTCM's overall global marketing strategy for the development of Dubai as a major centre for tourism and business. As part of its remit, this section is required to plan and implement international advertising in selected publications worldwide, and to publicise Dubai's special events and attractions through TV and press advertisements, especially within the AGCC market.

In addition to its other functions the DTCM hosts numerous media and commercial missions throughout the year, organising itineraries, preparing tour programmes within the emirate, making visa arrangements (when necessary) and providing general assistance to mission guests.

www.uaecb.gov.ae   **The UAE Central Bank**

Established in 1980, the UAE Central Bank is the main regulatory and supervisory body in the banking industry. It has the power to implement banking policy with regard to directing monetary credits taking into account the UAE's general policy. Article 5 of Law No. 10 of 1980 (the 1980 Law) states that the Central Bank will achieve its objectives by:

▲ The Cental Bank in Bur Dubai.

a • Exercising the privilege of issuing currency in accordance with the 1980 Law

b • Supporting the currency, maintaining its stability, both internally and externally, and ensuring its free convertibility into foreign currencies

c • Directing the credit policy in order to help achieve a steady growth of the national economy

d • Organising and promoting banking and supervising the effectiveness of the banking system in accordance with the 1980 Law

e • Undertaking the functions of the bank of the UAE government within the limits set by the 1980 Law

f • Advising the UAE government on financial and monetary issues

g • Maintaining the UAE government's gold reserve and foreign currencies

h • Acting as the bank for banks operating within the UAE

i • Monitoring money laundering

The Central Bank has been granted substantial powers to enable it to carry out the above objectives particularly the organisation, promotion and supervision of the banking and financial system in the emirate.

There are different types of banks and financial institutions. Each is subject to specific requirements and conditions. All commercial, Islamic and investment banks, Islamic financial institutions and Islamic investment companies, for instance, are required to take the form of public joint-stock companies. However, this does not apply to branches of foreign banks in the UAE who have a commercial bank licence and representative offices of foreign banks whose activities are limited to the promotion and marketing of the activities of their mother bank. The following types of banks and financial institutions are regulated by the Central Bank:

A commercial bank is any institution which, customarily, receives funds from the public in the form of demand, under notice or time deposits, or which carries on the placement of debt instruments or deposit certificates to be used, in whole or in part, for its account and its risk and for the granting of loans and advances.

Commercial banks may also carry on operations relating to the issue and collection of cheques, the placing of public or private bonds, trade in foreign exchange and precious metals, or any other operations allowed for commercial banks either by law or by customary banking practice.

Investment banks are those banks which may also be referred to as merchant, investment, development, medium term, or long term banks, or any such expression or name distinguishing them from commercial banks principally in that they do not accept deposits for less than two years.

Financial Institutions are those institutions whose principal functions are to extend credit, to carry out financial transactions, to take part in the financing of existing or planned projects, to invest in moveable properties, and such other functions as may be specified by the Central Bank. Further, they may not accept funds in the form of deposits but may borrow from their head offices, from local and foreign banks or from financial markets.

Financial and Monetary Intermediaries are any physical or juridical person, other than Financial Institutions who:

practice the profession of foreign exchange dealing based on the purchase and sale of currencies, currency notes, coins of all kinds and travellers' cheques;

act as a stock-broker or agent who sells and purchase domestic as well as foreign stocks and bonds, in local capacity or as agent of a foreign institution.

Representative offices are offices which represent foreign banks and financial institutions in the United Arab Emirates. Such representative offices may not commence operations in the United Arab Emirates without being first licensed by the Central Bank.

Islamic banks, financial institutions and investment companies are "those companies whose Articles and Memorandum of Association include obligations to apply the Islamic Sharia Law and whose operations are conducted pursuant to Islamic Sharia Law".

Nevertheless, nearly all forms of banks and institutions dealing in financial services including financial and monetary brokers, financial and investment consultancy, branch and representative offices of foreign banks and financial institutions are required to obtain a licence from the Central Bank in order to operate.

The establishment or announcement of investment funds, with the exception of governmental development funds and private savings and pensions, are also prohibited unless a licence from the Central Bank is obtained. In addition, only licensed financial investment companies or licensed banks are allowed to create investment funds.

It is therefore advisable for any investor interested in the banking industry to first refer to the Central Bank's rules and regulations.

Anti-Money Laundering Law

The UAE has lately enacted Federal Law No. (4) for the year 2002 in relation to the incrimination of money laundering ("Money Laundering Law"). Under the said Law, all money derived from drugs, piracy, terrorism, illegal arms trade, violations of environmental laws, theft, bribe, fraud and embezzlement will be considered derived from money laundering activities. In addition, any further activities that are deemed, in any treaty to which the UAE is a party to, an activity of money laundering, will be incriminated.

The Money Laundering Law provides severe penalties for assisting in money laundering operations and failing to report the same intentionally. The penalty may be imprisonment for a number of years. Under the said law, there is an obligation on financial, commercial and economic institutions in the UAE to report any suspicious transactions to the financial information unit (the unit set up by the Central Bank for monitoring money laundering activities in the UAE). The said law gives the Central Bank, the Civil Court and the Public Prosecution the right to freeze any accounts that may concern suspicious transactions.

The Central Bank issued circular 24/2002 (amended by notice No. 1045/2001 and Notice No. 2371/2000) that provided for implementing regulations for banks and financial institutions in the country in relation to the incrimination of money laundering. The said circular gives examples of suspicious transactions which have to be reported by bank staff and further, there is an obligation on bank staff to report every transaction above Dhs 40,000 to the financial information unit at the Central Bank.

The Dubai Land Department

www.dubailand.gov.ae

▲ The Land Department Building shares premises with the DED on the Creek.

The Land Department, which is located next to the Dubai Department of Economic Development, is the municipal authority in Dubai responsible for land registration and the issuance of title deeds. The Department may also note any restrictive conditions against titles.

Transfer transactions, such as sales, donations and inheritances along with mortgages are registered at the Land Department.

The two categories of title capable of registration at the Land Department are Granted Land title and Freehold title. Except in respect of one recent specific real estate project, it is not possible to obtain registration of a Leasehold title. Leases remain unregistered commercial contracts.

Transfer of title is effected by the attendance of the parties, or their representatives appointed by Power of Attorney, at the Disposal Section of the Land Department. Even if the parties have previously signed a sale and purchase agreement, they will be required to sign the Department's standard form of Sale and Purchase Agreement at the Land Department. A transfer fee of 2% of the purchase price is payable to the Land Department, of which the purchaser usually pays 1.5% and the seller pays 0.5%. The parties are, however, permitted to agree on the allocation between themselves. Upon completion of the formalities, the Land Department will immediately register the transfer and issue title to the buyer.

The above transfer procedures are applicable in respect of the transfer of the whole of the land comprised in a registered title, transfer of part of the land only and for adding or deleting owners from the title.

Transfers of title pursuant to a donation or grant take place in much the same manner as other transfers at the Land Department. The Land Department also notes orders withdrawing residential donations if the donee does not build on the land donated to him within five (5) years from the date of the donation. The Land Department attends to the issuing of deeds of title to heirs where the owner of the land has died. The transfer of the land in these cases is effected in terms of the Sharia Law and the deceased's will.

Real estate property in Dubai can only be mortgaged to financial institutions and banks which are licensed to operate in the United Arab Emirates. The mortgage will only be effected if and when both parties sign the specimen of the mortgage application at the Land Department and pay the mortgage registration fee. It is possible to attach agreed special conditions to the standard specimen at the Land Department relating to the validity, sale and release of the mortgage. Second or third mortgages can be registered as well as amendments to any mortgage from time to time upon payment of the specified fee. A mortgage can only be cancelled if both parties apply to the Land Department confirming their agreement and consent to the same. Enforcement of a mortgage, however, can only be effected through the court and not through the Land Department.

If the mortgagor is a minor, permission to register the mortgage at the Land Department will first have to be obtained from the Public Prosecutor's Office. The Land Department will only register mortgage bonds on residential land for the purpose of building upon the land; commercial land cannot be mortgaged unless there is a building constructed upon it.

www.difc.ae   **The Dubai International Financial Centre (DIFC)**

The origin of the idea of establishing the Dubai International Financial Centre (DIFC) was the perception that a significant gap lay between the great financial centres of Europe on the one hand, and those of the Far East on the other. It was felt that Dubai had the potential to fill this vacuum, if an appropriate regulatory structure could be put in place and well-directed incentives devised. International standards of transparency and accountability would need to be maintained and at the same time the requirements of international financial institutions and investors would have to be catered for with a flexible and positive approach.

▲ The Gate - a rendering of the lofty structure that will house the Dubai International Financial Centre.

The function of the DIFC, which is located on a site on the eastern side of Sheikh Zayed Road (adjacent to the Emirates Towers), is twofold. The regulatory division is responsible for the legal framework within which banks and finance houses conduct their operations. Institutions, which seek to take advantage of DIFC facilities are still subject to the jurisdiction of the UAE Central Bank so far as local Dubai business is concerned.

The other function of the DIFC is to act as a service company. The brief of the Service Division is to attract prime international institutions in the financial sector and at the same time to encourage corporate investors and high net worth individuals to invest in the regional market that the DIFC is bringing to maturity. As part of its proactive role in the development of Dubai as an acknowledged hub of international finance, the DIFC also provides, through the Service Division, a full range of reliable and professional back office services.

In its initial stage, the DIFC is focusing on five particular areas:

• Asset management
• Islamic finance
• Regional financial exchange
• Reinsurance activity
• Back office operations

The Dubai Electricity & Water Authority (DEWA)

www.dewa.gov.ae

▲ The DEWA building is located in the Oud Metha area.

Founded in 1992, the DEWA is the governmental body in Dubai responsible for all aspects of fresh water and electricity production and consumption in the emirate. Installation of water and electricity services for both business and private use is exclusively carried out by DEWA.

DEWA is continually upgrading and extending its supply network, installations and contracting companies interested in participating in DEWA renovation and construction programmes can obtain tender details relating to forthcoming contracts from the DEWA website (http:/eservices.dewa.gov.ae/dws/tenders/TenderList.asp).

In line with its mission, DEWA already provides reliable, clean and safe supplies of water and electricity, and is fully committed to environmental management systems and environment protection. As a new departure, DEWA has recently launched a campaign to heighten awareness of the importance of thermal insulation. Reduction by means of thermal insulation in the level of electricity consumptions required to maintain conventional air-conditioning systems in operation will have a dramatic effect in decreasing electricity supply requirements, so benefiting individual customers financially, and in the conservation of valuable energy resources.

The Dubai Development & Investment Authority (DDIA)

www.ddia.ae

▲ The DDIA offices are at the Emirates Towers.

The Dubai Development & Investment Authority (DDIA) was set up with the specific aim of developing and enhancing Dubai's economy.

The central purpose of the DDIA is to foster an investor-friendly regulatory climate by the centralisation of procedures. Applicants for registration now only need to deal with a single agency, on the "one stop shop" principle. Multiple clearances that were originally an inevitable aspect of commercial investment in the emirate are now followed up by DDIA still on an intra-government basis, with consequential benefits for the applicant in terms of time and effort saved.

Additional functions of the DDIA includes:

The attraction to Dubai of major international corporations and leading-edge technological investment at all levels.

Match-making between inward investors and internationally recognised local enterprises

❸

Where indicated by policy developments and practical experience, proposing changes to applicable laws and regulations for consideration by H.H. General Sheikh Mohammed bin Rashid Al Maktoum.

❹

Managing the Mohammed bin Rashid Establishment for Young Business Leaders.

The (MBREF) Young Business Leaders Programme is designed to encourage entrepreneurship and investment among the young business community in Dubai and the UAE as a whole by the award of grants from the 700 million Dirham resources. Eligible businesses will benefit not only financially, during their start-up and initial operational stages, but also from the availability of professional advice and practical support, including linkage with local service providers. By Dubai Government Order (issued in October 2002) all government departments are required to allocate not less than 5% of their procurement budget to purchases from entities registered with the Young Business Leaders Programme.

The Dubai Technology, E-Commerce and Media Free Zone Authority

In recognition of the huge commercial potential of the world-wide web, the Dubai Technology, E-Commerce and Media Free Zone (TECOM) was incorporated in 2000 under the guidance of H.H. General Sheikh Mohammed bin Rashid Al Maktoum, Crown Prince of Dubai and UAE Defence Minister. On its site within the TECOM Zone, Dubai Internet City operates as the world's first free trade zone for e-commerce. Among its many facilities the Internet City offers licensed businesses, 100 per cent foreign ownership, tax exemptions, full protection of intellectual property rights, exhibition facilities, state-of-the-art networks and connectivity, and a science and technology park. It is also the designated home of the planned Internet University.

▲ TECOM is spread out over acres of lanscaped terrain beyond Umm Sequeim.

Also located within the TECOM zone, Dubai Media City provides a highly convenient base from which international media organisations can conduct their regional and global operations.

A proven success from the outset, having as many as 50 media units at the time of its opening in 2001, Media City has been able to attract some of the biggest corporate names in the media industry including Reuters, CNN, CNBC and the MBC satellite channel. A key element in the Media City project was the decision to install an advanced infrastructure based on an inclusive network linked by satellites, computers and the Internet. This in turn has facilitated access to audiences through the conventional media of television, radio, cinema and journalism. The City also contains one of the world's largest state-of-the-art production facilities.

Ports, Customs and Free Zone Corporation

The Dubai Customs, Dubai Ports Authority and Jebel Ali Free Zones have been merged into one authority called the Ports, Customs and Free Zone Corporation. The establishment of the corporation was stipulated by Law No. 1/2000 issued by H.H. Sheikh Maktoum bin Rashid Al Maktoum, Vice President and Prime Minister of UAE and Ruler of Dubai.

The Dubai Customs has been previously dicussed in Chapter 2.

▲ The distinctive 'twin-hulled' buildings house the Ports, Customs and Free Zone Corporation.

▲ Part of the 100 square kilometre facilities of the JAFZ.

The Jebel Ali Free Zone

www.jafza.co.ae

In 1985 the Government of Dubai founded the first free zone in the UAE, the Jebel Ali Free Zone (the Free Zone), on the outskirts of Dubai in an area known as Jebel Ali. The Free Zone is principally a designated location spanning approximately 100 square kilometres (38 square miles) and is about 50 kilometres (30 miles) from Dubai city. It facilitates various commercial operations ranging from the lease of pre-fabricated buildings to the use of advanced seaport facilities. Due to its location, it benefits from a potential market and distribution network of 1.4 billion people. Although the Free Zone is located in Dubai, companies established there are legally treated as offshore companies and are therefore subject to the Free Zone's laws and regulations as distinct from Dubai law.

The benefits of investing in the Jebel Ali Free Zone:

- 100% foreign owned ventures possible
- Local sponsor or a local partner not required
- No corporate taxes for at least 15 years (renewable for an additional period of 15 years)
- No restrictions on the repatriation of capital and profits
- No personal income taxes
- No administration problems; but easy and efficient services
- Easy registration procedures with assistance provided by JAFZA
- Recruitment of staff made simple (JAFZA provides a full recruitment service and will, if necessary, provide staff)
- Abundant energy supply
- No currency restrictions
- Modern and efficient communication infrastructure
- Two modern seaport terminals
- Option to lease land and develop it according to one's needs
- A modern road network providing easy access to the Dubai International Airport and to Abu Dhabi.

The Dubai Ports Authority

Formed in May 1991, the Dubai Ports Authority (DPA) handles one of the major ports in the UAE, Port Rashid. Although it is a separate legal entity from the Jebel Ali Free Zone, the Dubai Ports Authority is inextricably linked to it.

The DPA currently has three terminals, Port Rashid, Jebel Ali and Aweer which are collectively regarded as one of the best cargo handling capabilities in the world. Their position allows them to serve traders in several regions covering the Arab world, Africa, Iran and the Indian sub-continent, thus serving a potential consumer market of 1.5 billion people worldwide.

The terminals of the DPA operate 24 hours a day, 7 days a week and offer over 200,000 square metres of warehousing in addition to 50,000 square metres for cargo agents. The Dubai Port open storage space consists of over 1 million square metres in addition to 21,000 square metres of temperature controlled warehouses. It is also geared to handling all kinds of cargo ranging from petroleum-related products to perishable goods. It contains facilities such as tanks for the storage of gasoline and other products and fourth generation double trolley computer control ship-to-shore gantry cranes operating over 40 moves per hour. Some of the DPA's other facilities are:

- 25 gantry cranes
- 2 mobile harbour cranes
- 61 transtainers and straddle carriers
- Modern shore side equipment operating across 102 deep water berths
- Computerised control system enabling immediate tracking and location of containers
- Over 40,000 cubic metres of temperature and humidity controlled storage space for semi-perishable goods
- A 43,000 cubic metres Lloyds-approved cold store with nine chambers and a 24-hour controlled system for perishable cargo
- A 50-truck fleet fitted with two-way radios
- Modern navigational guidance systems and the latest tugs and pilot boats (fitted with multi-channel VHF radios)

www.dafza.gov.ae

The Dubai Airport Free Zone (DAFZ)

The Dubai Airport Free Zone (DAFZ) was formed recently in accordance with Law No. 2 of 1996 for the Establishment of a Free Zone in Dubai International Airport by the Ruler of Dubai, H.H. Sheikh Maktoum bin Rashid Al Maktoum. Complementing rather than competing against the Jebel Ali Free Zone, the DAFZ provides similar yet diverse incentives to both the local and foreign investor in view of its location in the Dubai Airport area. Companies or establishments set up in the DAFZ are subject to DAFZ law.

DAFZ offers a number of facilities including pre-fabricated light industrial units, warehouses and offices. Investors are also allowed to develop leased land according to their own specifications and needs.

▲ The DAFZ facilities near the Dubai Airport

DAFZ contains freight handling operations of 140,000 square metres and public facilities which businesses may require, such as parking, restaurants, shopping and so forth.

The benefits of investing in the Dubai Airport Free Zone:

- 100% foreign ownership
- Corporate tax holiday up to 15 years, renewable for a similar period
- Freedom to move capital including dividends and profit
- Exemption from import duties
- Proximity to the Dubai International Airport and Dubai city
- No personal income tax
- A potential market access of over 1.4 billion people
- Streamlined bureaucracy
- Full repatriation of both capital and profits
- Modern efficient communication system
- No recruitment problems
- No currency restrictions
- An attractive working environment
- Fifteen minutes from Port Rashid and 45 minutes from the Jebel Ali Free Zone
- Abundant energy supply
- Ten parking bays capable of handling up to ten Boeing 747 - 400 aircrafts at the same time (currently under construction)
- Excellent support services from Dubai International Airport

The Dubai Cargo Village (DCV)

www.dubaicargovillage.com

▲ The Cargo Village, on the Airport Road

The Dubai Cargo Village is a part of the Dubai Department of Civil Aviation, which is headed by H.H. Sheikh Ahmed bin Saeed Al Maktoum. Located adjacent to the main airport building, the sole handling agency at the Dubai Cargo Village is the Dubai National Air Travel Agency (DNATA). The DCV has a large handling capacity with the built-in capacity to increase without extension. There are separate building facilities within the DCV for cargo agents and freight forwarders. The DCV also maintains other public facilities such as conference facilities and banking. As discussed in Chapter 8, the Department of Civil Aviation has, as a result of increased cargo operations, commenced an expansion programme intended to meet this increase both now and in the coming decade (see page 242).

The Dubai World Trade Centre (DWTC)

Established in 1979, the Dubai World Trade Centre continues to be a focal point of commercial activity within the emirate. Its landmark 33-story tower (at the Dubai City end of Sheikh Zayed Road) houses a large number of national and multinational companies, the Dubai Financial Market, several consulates, numerous facilities, a restaurant and on the top floor, the World Trade Centre Club. Adjacent to the tower the five-star World Trade Centre Hotel and the popular DIH Apartments are convenient amenities. From its offices in the tower, the Dubai World Trade Centre Management promotes the WTO objectives of fostering international business activity, the removal of trade barriers and adherence to high standards in all branches of commerce. In line with these objectives, the DWTC stages a large number of fairs and exhibitions throughout the year in its recently modernised and extended Exhibition Halls which form part of the DWTC complex of buildings.

▲ The World Trade Centre is a commanding presence at the beginning of Sheikh Zayed Road.

The Dubai Investment Park

The Dubai Investment Park (DIP) is a new venture founded in 1995 and owned by a public joint stock company called Dubai Investments (DI). The project involves a 3,180 hectare site which is 9.7 km long and 3.5 km wide and is located near the Jebel Ali Free Zone, 35 kilometres from downtown Dubai and the Dubai International Airport.

The proposed project offers investors a range of services and facilities unique in the Arabian Gulf. Among these facilities are:

▲ The DIP is slated to occupy 3,180 hectares, close to JAFZ.

- Environmentally clean, self-supporting community of light to medium industrial, residential, office, wholesale and retail commercial and recreational facilities
- Land plots of various sizes for a variety of uses available for lease
- Pre-fabricated buildings available for lease
- Gated access with on site security
- State-of-the-art telecommunications system
- Immediate access to major UAE motorways, Jebel Ali Port and the proposed second Dubai Airport
- Possible local sponsorship by DIP
- Possible equity participation by DIP in some private developments
- An 18-hole golf course
- Other recreational facilities for its park residents including a hotel, conference centre, sports club, fire and police protection, health care, postal services and major shopping facilities.

Chapter
Business in Dubai-Business Structures
Four

Introduction

Various legal structures are available for the establishment of businesses in Dubai. These are collectively addressed in the following main laws:

- Federal Law No. 18 of 1981 on the Organisation of Commercial Agencies
- Federal Law No. 8 of 1984 concerning Commercial Companies as amended
- The UAE Commercial Transactions Law, Federal Law No. 18 of 1993
- The UAE Civil Transactions Law, Federal Law No. 5 of 1985
- Local Order No. 63 of 1991 on Service Establishments

Although this chapter discusses all the forms of business entities, it places particular emphasis on those which may be of interest to foreign investors. These are the following:

> - Limited liability companies
> - Branch office of foreign companies
> - Representative offices of foreign companies
> - Public Joint Stock companies
> - Civil Companies
> - Businesses in the Jebel Ali Free Zone
> - Businesses in the Dubai Airport Free Zone
> - Businesses in the Dubai Internet City, Dubai Media City and Knowledge Village
> - Businesses in the Dubai International Financial Centre
> - Businesses at the Dubai Cars and Automotive Zone
> - Businesses at the Gold and Diamond Park
> - Offshore companies

In addition, the procedures for the establishment of industrial projects, engineering consultancies, insurance activities and the hotel, guest house and furnished apartment business have also been discussed.

Commercial Companies

Federal Law No. 8 of 1984 Concerning Commercial Companies as amended by Federal Law No. 1 of 1984, Federal Law No.13 of 1988 and Federal Law No.15 of 1998 (the CCL).

- General Partnership
- Simple Limited Partnership
- Joint Participation
- Public Joint Stock Companies
- Private Joint Stock Companies
- Companies with Limited Liability
- Partnerships Limited with Shares
- Foreign Companies (Branches and Representative offices outside the Free Zones).

Civil Entities

UAE Civil Transactions Law Federal Law No. 5 of 1985 (the Civil Code).

- Service Companies
- Work Companies
- Speculative Venture Partnerships
- Mudaraba Companies

Commercial Agencies

Federal Law No.18 of 1981 on the Organisation of Commercial Agencies as amended by Federal Law No. 14 of 1988 (the Agency Law). The Civil Code and the UAE Commercial Transactions Law, Federal Law No.18 of 1993 (the Commercial Code).

- Registered Commercial Agency
- Unregistered Commercial Agency

Jebel Ali Free Zone Companies

Implementing Regulation No.1 of 1992 pursuant to Law No. 9 of 1992.

- Jebel Ali Free Zone Establishment (FZE)
- Jebel Ali Free Zone Company (FZCO)
- Branch of a Foreign Company

Dubai Local Order No. 63 of 1991

• Service Establishments

The Dubai Airport Free Zone

Implementing Regulation No. 1 of 1998 pursuant to Law No. 2 of 1996.

• Dubai Airport Free Zone Establishment (FZE)
• Dubai Airport Free Zone Company (FZCO)
• Branch Office of a Foreign Company

Dubai Technology E-Commerce and Media Free Zone

Law No. 1 of 2000
The Dubai Technology and Media Free Zone Private Companies Regulations 2003

• Free Zone Limited Liability Company (FZ LLC)
• Branch of a Foreign Company

Dubai International Financial Centre

Law No. 3 of 2002

Jebel Ali Free Zone Authority Offshore Companies

Offshore Companies Regulations 2003

The above list illustrates the legal forms in which a business may be established in Dubai and the laws and regulations applicable to each. As mentioned above, the form the business will take will depend on a number of factors, as more often than not the characteristics or ingredients of the venture will dictate the form of the business entity required in both legal and commercial terms. Every business structure has its advantages and disadvantages. For instance, companies or establishments which are established in any of the free zones in Dubai can benefit from being wholly owned by foreign entities.

The Legal Mechanisms Available for Carrying on Business in Dubai

The various structures for establishing a business in Dubai are discussed below together with the procedures prescribed in cases where the business format is relevant to foreign investors.

Sole Proprietorships or Establishments

A sole proprietorship is a simple business method whereby an individual trades on his own account pursuant to a trade licence issued in his own name. This form of business entity is referred to as an 'establishment' rather than a company and the sole proprietor is personally liable to the full extent of his assets for the liabilities of the business. The establishment will not have an independent legal entity from that of the owner.

Mainly UAE nationals and nationals of GCC countries (subject to certain conditions) are permitted to form sole proprietorships in Dubai. A practice has, however, arisen in recent years whereby a UAE national obtains a trade licence for a sole proprietorship and leases it to expatriates who then take on all the management functions of the business and retain all the profits. However, this type of arrangement is not recommended as it is essentially unlawful and problems can arise if the business relationship between the parties breaks down. Further, the legal holder of the licence will be 100% liable for debts vis-à-vis third party, who may have no knowledge of the private arrangement.

Foreigners may form sole proprietorships if they reside in the UAE. However, the law restricts the activities a foreigner may engage in as a sole proprietor to certain fields. These include the following:

- The provision of medical services
- Engineering consultancies
- Legal consultants
- Computer consultants
- Similar services and non-trading activities

It is worth noting that in order to practise certain professions, it is necessary to fulfill various criteria and conditions. For instance, engineering consultants must be registered in the Register for Engineering Consultancy Practitioners at the Dubai Municipality before they can practise. In addition, special approval is normally required, such as in the area of legal consultancy, where it is necessary to obtain the approval of the Ruler's Office in order to establish a legal consultancy practice.

Nonetheless, a foreign sole proprietor is required to appoint a local services agent. The local service agency contract must be authenticated by the Notary Public and the foreigner's residence should be under the new business sponsorship.

Thus, the procedures for establishing a sole proprietorship vary according to the nationality or identity of the prospective sole proprietor. However, the common and main factor for establishing any type of sole proprietorship is that a licence should be obtained from the Dubai Department of Economic Development (DED) after submitting an application together with all relevant documents.

Below are the main procedures which need to be fulfilled with the DED according to the nationality of the investor.

→ Procedure to set up a Sole Proprietorship in Dubai

UAE Nationals

Submit the following documents to the DED:
1. Completed (typed) prescribed Licence Application Form
2. A completed (typed) prescribed Commercial Names Application Form
3. Copy of the prospective owner's passport (including proof of nationality/naturalisation)
4. Special approval of the activity where applicable (see end of chapter)
5. If the national is originally from an Emirate other than Dubai, a photocopy of the trade licence regarding the activities conducted in the emirate of origin.

Nationals of GCC States

If a GCC national wishes to establish a sole proprietorship establishment in Dubai he must first satisfy certain conditions.

Where the activity of the business is in the retail and wholesale trade and the investor is a natural person, he must be resident in the UAE, practise the activity on his own and hold a licence to practise the activity in his country of origin.

If these conditions are met, a trade licence must be obtained from the DED by submitting the completed prescribed Licence Application Form together with the following documents:

1. Copy of the proprietor's passport
2. Copy of the trade licence issued in the GCC country of origin
3. Certificate of good conduct from the GCC country of origin

There are other conditions which must be fulfilled where the intended activity is outside the retail and wholesale business.

Other Foreign Nationals

If a foreigner (other than a GCC state national) wishes to establish a sole proprietorship, he must appoint a local service agent and reside in the UAE under the sponsorship of the business he is practising. The following documents should be submitted to the DED:

1. Copy of the local service agency agreement as authenticated by the Notary Public
2. Copy of the local service agent's passport
3. Copy of the foreign investor's passport
4. Degree certificate duly notarised, legalised and authenticated and/or
5. Work experience certificate
6. Certificate of good standing from the authorities responsible for registering the profession in question (if applicable), for instance in the case of lawyers, the applicable Bar Association or Law Society
7. Copy of the tenancy contract of the office premises

Once the application is approved, the sole proprietorship (of whichever kind) must be registered in the Commercial Register at the DED after payment of the relevant registration fee.

Commercial Agents

Although it is possible for overseas manufacturers and traders to conduct business in Dubai by dealing directly with importers and traders in Dubai, such arrangements are not particularly well suited to continuous, high volume trading. Overseas manufacturers or traders who wish to import goods into Dubai in large quantities and on a regular basis may want to establish a business presence in Dubai. A common way to do so is to appoint a local trade or commercial agent through the establishment of a commercial agency.

Unlike other jurisdictions, the UAE legal system distinguishes between two forms of commercial agencies, the registered commercial agency and the unregistered commercial agency. The main difference between the two lies in the set of rules and regulations governing each.

Registered Commercial Agencies

The provisions relating to registered commercial agencies are collectively set out in Federal Law No. 18 of 1981 on the Organisation of Commercial Agencies as amended by Federal Law No.14 of 1988 (the Agency Law), Federal Law No. 18 of 1993, (the Commercial Code) and Federal Law No. 5 of 1985, (the Civil Code). As these laws are federal laws, they are applicable to all Emirates.

Article 1 of the Agency Law defines a registered commercial agency as "the representation of a principal by an agent for the purpose of distributing, selling, offering or providing merchandise or services within the state for a commission or profit." Under the same Article a principal is defined as "the producer or manufacturer or the exclusive accredited exporter or representative of the producer."

The Agency Law further stipulates a number of conditions which need to be fulfilled for a registered commercial agency to be valid. These are:

1• It must be duly registered with the Commercial Agencies Registrar at the Ministry of Economy & Commerce. Otherwise it will be deemed void under the Agency Law.
2• The agent must be a UAE national or a wholly owned UAE entity incorporated in the UAE.
3• The subject matter of the agency must be exclusive to the agent within the agency territory. The territory can be any and/or all of the Emirates. (Article 5)
4• The agency agreement must be in writing and include the following provisions (Article 10):
   • The name, nationality and address of the agent and the principal
   • The products, commodities and services covered by the commercial agency
   • The territory the agreement is to cover. It is possible to employ a different trade agent in each or all of the Emirates in the UAE, providing the agency is exclusive to the agent within that territory
   • The date on which the agreement is to commence, its duration and provisions in the event of default

- Where the agent is a commercial company, the company's name, legal form, head office and UAE branch addresses and its capital amount
- The agent is an exclusive agent for the territory defined in the agency agreement
- The rights given for the distribution of the product in question are given directly by the principal.

5• The agency agreement must be notarised, legalised by the Foreign Ministry and authenticated by the UAE Embassy in the country it is executed in (Article 4).

The Agency Law further states that only registered commercial agents may be authorised to engage in commercial agency activities. Although the Agency law does not define what constitutes a commercial activity, these are nevertheless defined under the Commercial Code.

There is, however, no distinction between commercial agency agreements regarding franchises, distributorships, commission arrangements and other forms of sales representative or agency relationships under the Agency Law. Thus, all these may qualify as registered commercial agencies.

Apart from the above requirements, the significant difference between a registered and an unregistered commercial agency agreement is the various protections or safeguards provided to both the principal and the agent under the Agency Law. As we shall see these tend to favour the agent.

For the agent, the Agency Law provides three advantages:

1• Exclusivity

Under Article 23 of the Agency Law, registered commercial agents have the exclusive right to import the goods which are the subject matter of the agency agreement. Any imports of goods, the subject matter of the registered agency, brought into the territory through parties other than the registered agent can be seized by the Customs Department unless the agent or the Ministry of Economy & Commerce consent to their release. This includes any goods which have been imported by the principal.

Further, under Article 8 of the same law, a replacement agent may not be registered at the Ministry's Commercial Agents Register unless the previous agency has been terminated.

However, the courts have indicated in a recent judgement that an individual (other than the registered agent) who imports goods covered by a registered commercial agency will not be subject to prosecution unless he purports to be the agent for such goods. In such cases, it is open to the registered agent to sue for damages through the Civil Courts and to revert to the Ministry of Economy & Commerce to seize the goods. While this is true in Dubai, it may not be the case in other Emirates.

Notwithstanding the above judgement, the advantage of establishing a registered commercial agency over one, which is not registered, is from the agent's point of view, the safeguard offered under the Agency Law for the prevention of parallel imports.

2 • Commissions

Under Article 7 of the Agency Law, agents are entitled to receive commissions on both the sales they make as well as the direct sales made by the principal or other parties, regardless of whether or not the agent has contributed towards these sales. This is clearly advantageous to the agent. The principal should consequently ensure that the agency agreement clearly defines the products which constitute the agreement and the territory concerned.

3 • Non-Termination & Non-Renewal

One of the factors which may be worrying to principals of registered commercial agencies is the fact that the Agency Law does not allow the principal to terminate such agencies without there being a 'justifiable cause.' Although the Agency Law fails to define a justifiable cause, recent judgements have indicated that the following acts or omissions made by the agent may amount to one:

a • Gross negligence and subsequent non-rectification of it after receiving sufficient notice of the negligence
b • Dealing with competitive products in the presence of a clear intention by the parties that the agent would not deal with such products
c • Assigning the agency to third parties under a management agreement
d • Breaching the legal conditions relating to agents, for instance where the agent is no longer a wholly owned UAE entity and
e • Failing to meet the agreed sales target

Further, under Article 8 of the Agency Law, the principal of a fixed term registered commercial agency may not refuse to renew the agency agreement even after its expiry date. In such cases, the termination is considered a violation of the agent's rights and the agent is entitled to claim damages from the principal.

There are no guidelines on the computation of compensation which an agent may be awarded and the amount will primarily depend on each case. However, matters such as the duration of the agency agreement, the extent of the agent's efforts in investing and promoting the product and the net profits received by the agency are generally the influencing factors in calculating compensation.

Although a precautionary measure which a principal may take in a registered commercial agency would be to expressly provide in the agency agreement the maximum compensation payable and what may amount to a justifiable cause for termination or non-renewal of the agency. However, this may not be regarded as sufficient to justify the same in the eyes of the court or the Agency Committee, but may nevertheless mitigate the amount of compensation awarded to the agent.

The Agency Law according to Dubai and Abu Dhabi Court judgements will prevail over the contractual terms agreed by the parties. Certain Articles of law are considered as a matter of public policy.

For the principal, on the other hand, the Agency Law provides the following protections:
Protection of Trade Marks & Protection against Parallel Imports

As discussed above, under Article 23 of the Agency Law only the agent stipulated under a registered commercial agency may import the goods which are the subject matter of the said agency. The customs authorities may be precluded from clearing such goods to persons other than the registered agent unless the Ministry or the agent approves. The customs authorities will only act upon a formal complaint from the registered agent or from the principal.

When there is a dispute regarding the import of goods which are under a registered commercial agency agreement, the agent may request the Ministry to attach the goods or to write to the customs departments and the competent authorities to attach the goods until the dispute is resolved.

These factors are therefore in the principal's benefit in that he can prevent parallel imports. The agent also has a duty to support the agency, provide services and keep adequate stock of spare parts. Assistance may be provided to the principal from the agents in local tenders, where the agent can only be qualified if he has a registration.

Unregistered Commercial Agencies

Unregistered commercial agencies on the other hand are not subject to the Agency Law and are instead governed by the Commercial and the Civil Code. Consequently, they may not benefit from the protections offered by the Agency Law nor are they subject to its requirements. A prospective agent is likely therefore to insist on the establishment of a registered commercial agency as opposed to one that is unregistered, subject to fulfilling the relevant criteria.

Despite the fact that Article 3 of the Agency Law provides that any commercial agency not registered at the Ministry of Economy & Commerce's Register shall be deemed void and no claim shall be recognised with respect thereto, unregistered commercial agencies are nevertheless seen as valid commercial contracts where the parties will be subject to the terms and conditions they have agreed to.

Three types of commercial agencies may be created under the Commercial Code: contract agencies, commission agencies and commercial representations. In addition to the provisions regulating these, the Commercial Code also contains provisions on other matters such as the liability of a replacement agent and the limitation period applicable for instigating legal proceedings concerning commercial agency agreements.

Unlike registered commercial agencies, the Commercial Code and the Civil Code do not require agents to be UAE nationals or commercial entities wholly owned by UAE nationals. What would however be required is a licensed entity to trade in the UAE. In addition, under Article 954 of the Civil Code, a principal is allowed to terminate an agency agreement under a number of circumstances including cases where the agency arrangement has expired in fixed term agency contracts. There is no procedure required for an unregistered commercial agency other than the parties negotiating their commercial contractual provisions. It is increasingly becoming common to enter into unregistered commercial agencies which fall outside the Agency Law. The procedure for establishing a registered commercial agency is as follows:

→ Procedure for Establishing Registered Commercial Agencies

1 • Draw up a commercial agency agreement. This should include the provisions outlined above. The agreement should (as a matter of procedure) be produced in, or subsequently translated into Arabic.

2 • The commercial agency agreement should then be executed before the Notary Public in Dubai. If the agreement is to be signed outside the UAE, the following procedure should be adopted for executing and authenticating the agreement.

3 • The agreement should be signed before a notary public who should also notarise any documents authorising the signatory to sign on behalf of the company.

4 • The foreign ministry of the government of the country in which the agreement is executed should then authenticate the documents.

5 • The documents should then be certified by the UAE Embassy in the country in which they are executed (if there is no UAE Embassy in the country in question, any other GCC Embassy will suffice).

6 • Upon their arrival in the UAE, the documents should be authenticated by the Ministry of Foreign Affairs.

7 • The documents should then be translated into Arabic by a translator licensed with the Ministry of Justice.

8 • The commercial agency agreement should then be registered at the Ministry of Economy & Commerce's Commercial Agents Register either by the commercial agent or his legal representative.

Application to register a commercial agency agreement with the Ministry of Economy & Commerce is made by submitting the prescribed form together with the following:

1 • The commercial agent's trade licence and commercial register entry certificate together with copies thereof

2 • The duly executed and authenticated commercial agency agreement together with a copy thereof

3 • If the trade agent is a company, a certified copy of the memorandum of association together with a copy thereof and copies of the passport and family book of each partner or a certificate proving that the company is wholly owned by UAE nationals

4 • If the commercial agent is an individual, the passport and family book of the trade agent.

5 • The appropriate fee (currently Dhs 4,450)

The Ministry of Economy & Commerce is, under Article 11 of the Agency Law, required to issue its decision (an approval or a rejection) within 15 days of the date the application for registration is submitted. If the registration is accepted, the agent will be issued with an authenticated certificate, which testifies the registration, and details of the agency will be published in the Official Gazette. If the application is, on the other hand, unsuccessful, the Ministry must provide reasons for its refusal. It is possible to appeal against the Ministry's refusal to register the commercial agency agreement to the civil courts.

It is particularly important to ensure that the agency agreement contains accurate information, as the deliberate submission of incorrect information is punishable both under the UAE Penal Code and the Agency Law.

Once a commercial agency agreement is registered, the trade agent will be entitled to the exclusive rights to distribute and market the specified products and services in the specified territories. If the principal or any other person distributes or markets the specified products or services within the territory, they will be liable to compensate the trade agent.

Would be principals should also bear in mind that it can be very difficult to terminate a trade agency agreement without the trade agent's consent. In the absence of such a consent, a trade agency agreement can only be terminated if there is a justifiable reason. It is at the Ministry of Economy and Commerce's discretion to decide whether or not a justifiable reason exists. However, the Ministry's decision is subject to review by the Judicial Authority. In Dubai the party need not go to the Ministry and may proceed directly to court. A principal will also need to show a justifiable reason to refrain from renewing a trade agency agreement upon the expiry of its term. Wrongful termination or failure to renew a trade agency agreement may lead to the principal being obliged to compensate the former trade agent for any losses he may have suffered which can be substantial.

It should also be noted that under Article 21 of the Agency Law, registered commercial agents are required to take the necessary steps, where applicable, regarding the supply of spare parts for the maintenance of vehicles, engines, machinery, equipment and permanent consumable commodities.

Commercial Companies

Incorporated pursuant to Federal Law No. 8 of 1984 Concerning Commercial Companies as amended by Federal Law No. 1 of 1984 and Federal Law No. 13 of 1988 (the CCL).

The golden rule regarding companies established under the CCL is that they must have one or more national partners 'whose share in the company capital must not be less than 51% of the company capital'. (Article 22)

Under Article 23(1) of the UAE Commercial Code, a non-UAE national may not engage in commercial business in the UAE unless he has a partner or partners who are UAE nationals, and on the terms and within the limits provided for in the CCL.

Although the CCL fails to define what constitutes 'commercial business' this is defined under Article 5 of the Commercial Code which deems the following activities as commercial business:

a• The purchase of commodities and other tangible and intangible chattels for the purpose of sale at a profit, whether sold in their original condition or after processing or manufacture.
b• The purchase or hire of commodities and other tangible and intangible chattels for the purpose of lease.

c• The sale or lease of commodities and chattels purchased or hired as aforesaid

d• Banking, money changing and stock exchange transactions, investment company, trust fund and finance house transactions, and all other intermediary transactions of financial intermediaries

e• All transactions relating to commercial paper whatever the capacities of the persons involved and whatever the nature of the transactions for which it is established

f• All business relating to marine and air navigation, including:
- the building, sale, purchase, leasing, chartering, repair or maintenance of ships and aircraft, and sea and air consignments, including sea and air transport
- the sale or purchase of ship or aircraft stores, equipment or materials or their provisioning;
- forwarding and discharging business
- maritime and aviation loans
- employment contracts for captains and navigators of commercial ships and aircraft.

g• The incorporation of companies

h• Current accounts.

i• Insurance in its various forms, other than co-operative insurance.

j• Public auction premises.

k• The business of hotels, restaurants, cinemas, theatres, sports arenas and places of entertainment.

l• Water, electricity and gas distribution premises.

m• The publication of newspapers and magazines with the purpose of realisation of profit through the publishing of advertisements, news and articles.

n• Post, telegraph and telephone business.

o• The business of radio and television broadcasting, and recording and photographic studios.

p• General stores business, and pledges on property deposited therein.

Article 6 of the Commercial Code provides that the following businesses shall be deemed to be commercial business if practised as a profession:
- Brokerage
- Commercial agency
- Commission agency
- Commercial representation
- Supply contracts
- Purchase or sale of land or real estate in order to realise a profit on sale, whether in its original state or after conversion or division
- Land transport
- Real estate construction contracts, when the contractor undertakes to provide the materials and labour
- Industries for the extraction of natural resources
- Tourism and travel bureau business, import, export and customs clearance and services and employment bureau
- The business of printing, publishing, photography, recording and advertising
- Manufacturing
- Animal and fish resources
- The lease and hire of other people's labour for the purpose of hire
- The lease and rental of furnished or unfurnished houses, flats and rooms for sub-letting.

The DED has issued a standard classification of economic activities which fall under the following categories:

- Agriculture
- Fishing
- Mining and Quarrying
- Manufacturing
- Electricity, Gas and Water
- Construction
- Trading and Repairing Services
- Hotels and Restaurants
- Transport, Storage and Communications
- Financial Intermediation
- Real Estate, Renting and Business Services
- Education
- Health and Social Work
- Other Social and Personal Services
- Extra Territorial Organizations and Bodies

Therefore, foreign investors wishing to establish business operations in Dubai engaged in any of the commercial business activities defined above must do so with a partner who is a UAE national.

Those intending to establish service companies and/or branch offices, as discussed below, where 100% foreign ownership is permitted, will be restricted to non-commercial activities.

Under Article 5 of the CCL, there are seven different types of companies which may be established, namely:

- General Partnerships
- Simple Limited Partnerships
- Joint Participation (ventures)
- Public Joint Stock Companies
- Private Joint Stock Companies
- Limited Liability Companies
- Partnerships Limited with Shares

Each company is suitable for a particular purpose. However, before discussing these it should be noted that, according to Article 6 of the CCL, a company, which does not adopt one of the above forms, is considered void and individuals who conclude contracts on behalf of the business are personally and jointly liable for the liabilities arising from such contracts.

However, this is not to say that businesses, which adopt other formats than those permitted, are void in practice. This simply means that the parties are not subject to the CCL and may be personally liable and be subject to criminal sanctions under the law.

General Partnership

Articles 23 to 46 (inclusive) of the CCL govern general partnerships.

A general partnership is an arrangement between two or more partners whereby each of the partners are jointly and severally liable to the extent of all their assets for the company's liabilities. The CCL provides that only UAE nationals are allowed to be partners in a general partnership. This form of business organisation is therefore not appropriate for foreign investors wishing to set up in Dubai.

Nevertheless, the procedure for forming a general partnership is relatively straightforward and includes the preparation of a partnership memorandum, approval of the partnership name by the DED, inscription of the partnership into the Commercial Register at the DED, authentication of the partnership deed, publication of the firm's data in the Companies Bulletin issued by the Ministry of Economy and Commerce in accordance with provisions of Ministerial Regulation No. 65 of 1989 as amended, obtaining a trade licence and registering the partnership with the Dubai Chamber of Commerce and Industry.

Further, Article 26 of the CCL provides for the requirement of a general partnership memorandum. There is, incidentally, no prescribed minimum capital requirement for the establishment of general partnerships.

Simple Limited Partnership

Article 47 of the CCL defines a simple limited partnership or a partnership in-commendam as a "company formed by one or more general partners liable for the company liabilities to the extent of all their assets, and one or more limited partners liable for the company liabilities to the extent of their respective shares in the capital only."

Thus, a simple limited partnership is essentially a modified general partnership. As in a general partnership, only UAE nationals may be general partners in a simple limited partnership, although foreigners may be sleeping partners, who essentially do not have a role in the management as opposed to the administration of the company regarding third parties (Article 48). In addition, their liability is limited to the extent of their share capital in the partnership.

Sleeping partners should of course ensure that they do not lead third parties to believe that they are anything other than sleeping partners. Otherwise their limited liability will cease. The management of a simple limited partnership is vested in the general partners. As non-UAE nationals are excluded from assuming any form of management role, this form of business organisation is probably inappropriate for foreign investors.

Again there is a particular procedure which needs to be followed for establishing a simple limited partnership. This includes approval of the firm's name (which should include the name of one or more of the general partners) by the DED, drawing up of the firm's partnership memorandum which needs to be authenticated before the Notary Public of the Dubai Courts Department, inscription of the partnership at the DED Commercial Register, registering the firm as a member of the Dubai Chamber of Commerce and Industry and obtaining a trade licence from the DED.

Joint Participation Venture

Articles 56 to 63 (inclusive) of the CCL govern the establishment of joint participation ventures or consortium companies, and is defined as a "company concluded between two or more parties to share the profits or losses of one or more commercial businesses being performed by one of the partners in his personal name. The company shall be confined to the relationship between the partners and will not be effective towards third parties."

From the above, it is clear that the existence of such a company is restricted to the arrangement between the partners therein and must not be made known to third parties. Between the partners themselves the arrangement is essentially a partnership. Each partner conducting business will generally do so in his own name and will not declare the interest of the other partners to others. The liability of the partners who are conducting business is unlimited regarding the liabilities of the company. If the liability of the other partners is disclosed, the venture will be treated for every purpose as a general partnership.

Joint participation ventures are popular with foreign companies who wish to set up in Dubai on a short-term basis, perhaps to carry out a specific project. They are often formed where there is some participation by government bodies.

There are no registration formalities for this type of company as it is not a distinct legal entity. The business name and licence of the partner conducting the business are used by the company. A memorandum should, however, be prepared to indicate the rights and liabilities of the partners and the method of distribution of the profits and losses. The local partner should contribute at least 51% of the capital, but profits can be shared in different ratios to capital contributions. The decisions made in a joint venture have to be made by the unanimous consent of the partners, unless the memorandum provides that majority consent will be sufficient. However, decisions regarding the amendment of the memorandum must be unanimous.

Public Joint Stock Company (PJSC)

Public Joint Stock Companies are governed by Articles 64 to 214 (inclusive) of the CCL. Article 64 of the said law defines a public joint stock company as "any company whose capital is divided into equal value negotiable shares."

PJSCs are very similar to the public limited company in the UK. According to Article 64 of the CCL the shareholders of a PJSC are liable only to the value of their shares in the capital of the company. The nominal value of each share of a PJSC should not be less than Dhs 1 and not more than Dhs 100, and the minimum share capital requirements are Dhs 10 million for a general company, a banking entity Dhs 40 million and insurance and investment companies Dhs 25 million (Article 67 of the CCL).

Among the requirements for the establishment of a public joint stock company is the preparation of a founders' agreement, a prospectus or invitation for public subscription supported by an overall business plan/feasibility study and an auditor's certificate, a due diligence survey, a memorandum and articles of association which must be in accord with the specimen issued by the Ministry of Economy & Commerce. Any deviation from the specimen form must be approved in advance by the Ministry of Economy & Commerce. Further, the name of the intended company must end with the words 'Public Joint Stock Company'.

A PJSC must have at least ten founder members and its management should be vested in a board of directors consisting of a minimum of three and a maximum of twelve persons whose term of office may not exceed three years. Directors can be re-elected when their term of office has expired. A public joint stock company is required to have a chairman of the board of directors who must be a UAE national. In addition, the majority of the board of directors are required to be UAE nationals.

At least 10% of the net profit should be allocated to a reserve account until such reserve account amounts to half of the total paid-up capital of the company.

In addition, UAE nationals should hold at least 51% of the shares of the PJSC. The founder members must subscribe to a minimum of 20% and a maximum of 45% of the share capital of the company. If new shares are issued, the existing shareholders should be offered the opportunity to subscribe to such shares in accordance with their existing shareholdings.

There are additional requirements for the incorporation and operation of a PJSC stipulated under the CCL which should be considered by interested investors. However, given the fairly restrictive rules and controls governing the establishment and management of a public joint stock company and the substantial capital requirement needed, it is regarded as an inappropriate business vehicle for most foreign investors.

Notwithstanding that, the PJSC has become increasingly popular in recent years vis-à-vis the privatisation sector and there are currently about 100 PJSCs in the UAE. In addition, as it is the only business vehicle which allows shares to be offered to the public, it enables business to raise substantial amounts of capital, which is particularly the case when large-scale projects are concerned. This allows small foreign and local investors to participate in such projects.

It should also be noted that, where one is contemplating a business venture which involves insurance, banking or investment of funds on behalf of third parties, the establishment of a PJSC is a legal necessity and no other type of company may be established for such activities.

→ Procedure to establish a PJSC

Outlined below are the basic procedures necessary to establish a PJSC in the UAE.

1 • Draw up a founders' agreement which should be supported by a business plan/feasibility study.
2 • Draw up the company's constituent documents such as the memorandum and articles of association as per the Ministry of Economy & Commerce's approved formats, subject to approved changes.
3 • Present the company's constituent documents for approval to a committee jointly formed between the Ministry of Economy & Commerce and the concerned government authority.

4• Once the above approval has been obtained, send out the prospectus/invitation for public subscription and publish a summary of it in two local Arabic language newspapers. Before this, the founders must pay up their capital contributions to a specified UAE bank the receiving bank")chosen by the founders.

5• A minimum of 10 days and a maximum of 90 days is kept open for subscriptions with a provision for an extension of this period.

6• Convene the company's first general assembly of shareholders in order to ratify the issuance of any shares for assets in kind, elect the first board of directors and declare the establishment of the company.

7• A decision announcing the establishment of the company issued by the Minister of Economy & Commerce.

8• Register the company on the DED Commercial Register, obtain a trade licence from the DED and obtain membership of the company at the Dubai Chamber of Commerce & Industry

9• Upon issuance of registration, a receipt is presented to the bank and it releases the subscribed funds to the company and reimburses the founders for any expenses of incorporation.

Private Joint Stock Company

A private joint stock company is essentially the same as a public joint stock company, with the following differences:

• The minimum capital requirement is Dhs 2 million.
• The shares of a private joint stock company cannot be offered to the public.
• Only three founder members are required.

A private joint stock company may nevertheless be converted into a PJSC in accordance with Article 217 of CCL. In order to do so the following conditions must be satisfied:

a• The nominal value of the issued shares is fully paid up.
b• A period of not less than two financial years has expired.
c• During the two years preceding the application for conversion, the company had achieved net profits, distributable to the shareholders whose average is not less than 10% of the capital.
d• A resolution of the extraordinary general assembly for the conversion of the company is adopted by a majority of three quarters of the company capital.
e• The Ministry of Economy & Commerce's decision to convert the company from a private joint stock company to a public joint stock company is published in the Official Gazette.

Considering the lower capital requirement of Dhs 2 million, private joint stock companies are popular with foreign investors.

It is worth noting that the procedures for setting up a private joint stock company are the same as for a PJSC as covered earlier.

Limited Liability Company (LLC)

A popular, and frequently the most appropriate, method of establishing a business in Dubai by foreign investors is to form a limited liability company which is similar to private limited liability companies in the UK. However, as mentioned earlier, where the intended business involves banking, insurance and/or investment activities conducted on behalf of third parties, a LLC is not legally permitted to practice such activities and a PJSC will have to be established instead. In addition, the governing Articles of the CCL regarding LLCs are Articles 218 to 255 (inclusive). Article 218 of the CCL defines an LLC as one "with limited liability...where the number of partners may not exceed fifty and should not be less than two. Each of the partners shall only be liable to the extent of his share in the capital. The partners' participation should not be represented by negotiable certificates."

In addition, a LLC has the following legal and commercial characteristics:

Capital
- The minimum share capital must be Dhs 300,000 divided into equal shares with a minimum face value of Dhs 1,000 per share.
- UAE nationals must hold at least 51% of the shares.
- Public subscription for raising capital is not permitted.

Management
- Although a foreign partner is only legally permitted to own a maximum of 49% of the capital of the company, the day-to-day management of the company may be vested in a foreign manager.
- The manager or managers are appointed by the memorandum of association (Memorandum), by a separate management contract or the general assembly of the partners.
- Managers may be one or more of the partners or any other parties (including foreigners) provided that they do not exceed a total of five persons.
- In practice, national partners play no part in the operations of the company and may well give the foreign partner a power of attorney authorising him to vote in the general assembly on his behalf.

Profits and Losses
- It is possible to provide in the Memorandum that profit and losses will be shared in a ratio different to that of the share capital ratios.

Accounting Requirements
- It is necessary to appoint an auditor who must be accredited in the UAE.
- The auditor should be appointed by the general assembly (which is essentially a meeting of all the shareholders of the company).

Commercial Companies

→ Procedure to Establish an LLC

The following procedure should be satisfied for the establishment of a LLC:

1. Approve Company Name

The first step to be taken in establishing a LLC is to obtain the approval of the company name and activity by the DED. This is done by completing the prescribed form which is issued by the DED for this purpose. The name of the LLC should, among other things, end with the words "limited liability company" and either be derived from its objects or from the name of one or more of the partners. When the name and activities have been approved, a Memorandum should be prepared.

2. Prepare, Authenticate and Approve Memorandum of Association

The Memorandum should be prepared in accordance with Article 224 of the CCL which stipulates the information that should be included. It should be noted that the name of the company in the Memorandum should be the same as approved by the DED. The DED provides a standard memorandum of association which may be sufficient for some business ventures.

When the Memorandum has been completed and agreed, it must be authenticated before the Notary Public at the Dubai Court or the Notary Public at the DED. The Notary Public will not notarise the Memorandum if it does not comply with the CCL.

If one of the partners is a LLC (a juridical person), additional documents must be submitted with the Memorandum before it can be notarised. Furthermore, where the foreign partner is a company, additional notarised, legalised and authenticated documents, officially translated and further authenticated in Dubai, are required to be submitted. These are:

1• Certificate of incorporation or certificate of good standing of the company
2• Memorandum and articles of association of the company
3• Board resolution from the company calling for the taking up of the shares in the LLC and appointing an individual as its authorised attorney
4• Power of attorney from the company authorising the appointed individual to act on its behalf for the establishment of the LLC and the taking up of shares of the LLC

The documents listed above must be:
1• Notarised by a notary public in their country of origin
2• Legalised by the foreign ministry of the country from which they originate
3• Authenticated by the UAE Embassy in that country and
4• Authenticated by the UAE Ministry of Foreign Affairs upon their arrival in Dubai.
5• Translated into Arabic by a translator registered with the Ministry of Justice and thereafter the translation sealed by the Ministry of Justice.

If the documents of the foreign company are in any language other than English, it is highly recommended that they be officially translated into English in their country of origin prior to being notarised, legalised and authenticated.

Once JAFZA has reviewed and approved these documents, it will issue the necessary building permit. After receipt of the building permit, building works may commence which must be carried out by a locally registered contractor under the supervision of a registered consultant and will be subject to inspections by JAFZA.

Upon completion of the building, the consultant must obtain a Building Completion Certificate (BCC) which is issued by JAFZA, if upon satisfactory inspection of the completed premises. The DEWA only activates power supply to the premises upon presentation of the BCC.

Where the installation of machinery is involved, JAFZA will issue an Operation Fitness Certificate (OFC) when the machinery is installed in accordance with the detailed plans.

Equipment may be imported into the JAFZ while construction is taking place. However, procedures for the recruitment of JAFZ sponsored staff can start only after the BCC and the OFC are issued.

Mortgage of Buildings in the Jebel Ali Free Zone

In order to facilitate the raising of finance by investors who have constructed their own buildings on land leased from JAFZ, Local Law No. 1 of 2002 on the Mortgage of Immovable Property Erected at Jebel Ali Free Zone was enacted. Pursuant to this Law, an investor and lender may execute a Mortgage Deed in prescribed form and register the Mortgage Deed in the Register maintained for the purpose by JAFZA. Once registered, JAFZA recognises the lender's security over the building. If the lender needs to enforce its security at any time in the future, JAFZA is required to recognise the lender, or a third party to whom the lender sells/assigns the mortgaged building, in substitution for the original investor under the land lease.

JAFZA Manpower Service

Investors are free to employ their own staff or have the option to employ staff provided by JAFZ. In the case of the former, JAFZA handles the procedures required for the recruitment of employees under its sponsorship such as immigration requirements. In exchange, investors pay recruitment costs to the JAFZ, which involve entry permit fees, medical cover fees for each employee payable on the submission of the entry permit application, insurance cover fees (third party liability and workmen's compensation insurance) for each employee and bank guarantee fees. The bank guarantee is required for each employee sponsored by JAFZA. The amount of the guarantee is one and a half times the employee's salary plus the cost of a one-way air ticket to the employee's country of origin.

Under normal circumstances, investors are required to make the necessary payments prior to making entry permit applications, otherwise JAFZA may refuse to accept such applications.

Business in the JAFZ Zone

Costs of Setting up Business in the Jebel Ali Free Zone

Any Party interested in setting up an entity in the Jebel Ali Free Zone should be aware of the following associated costs:

		US$	Dhs
a)	Initial registration fees:		
	Branch of an established company	Nil	Nil
	Free Zone Establishment	2,725	10,000
	Free Zone Company	4,087	15,000
b)	Licence fees (annual):	1,500	5,500
c)	Name plates for offices:	136	500
d)	Issue of building permit (per square metre of developed floor space):	0.82	3
e)	Telecommunications installation charges:		
	Telephone	68	250
	Telefax	245	900
	Fax	41	150
	Internet	82	300
f)	Provision of PO Box:	57	210
g)	Dubai Chamber of Commerce & Industry Registration and Annual Membership Renewal fees:		
	Trading, Industrial and Service Licences	600	2,200
	National Industrial Licence	545	2,000
	National Industrial Licence (if foreign)	817	3,000
h)	Employee visa formalities: Provision of Employment Visa (including Entry Permit, Company Employment Card, Health Card, Medical & Residence Visa for 3 years)	370	1,360
i)	Provision of Entry Permit and Residence Permit for dependants of an employee	166	610
i)	Lease of Premises (per annum):		
	Standard Office Unit (26.88m^2)	9,537	35,000
	Multi-storey Office Unit	409/m^2	1,500/m^2
	Light Industrial Unit (510m^2)	29,973/36,060	110,000/125,000
k)	and Sites		
	2,500 m^2	5.45	20
	5,000 m^2	4.09	15
	7,500 m^2	3.27	12
	10,000 m^2	2.72	10

Business in the Dubai Airport Free Zone

The procedures for establishing a business in the Dubai Airport Free Zone (DAFZ) are quite similar to those of the Jebel Ali Free Zone. Parties wishing to set up in DAFZ, be they individuals or established companies, may do so by either setting up and registering a Free Zone Establishment (FZE), a Free Zone Company (FZCO) or a branch office.

Both the FZE and the FZCO are limited liability entities with a separate legal identity from that of its owners whose liability is thus limited to the extent of the company's paid up share capital which must be at least Dhs 1,000,000 for a FZE and Dhs 500,000 for a FZCO. At least one of the Directors and the Secretary are required to be resident in the Emirate of Dubai.

Licensing

In all cases, apart from registering a FZE, a FZCO or establishing a branch office, it is necessary for an applicant to obtain one of the three types of licences available at DAFZ. These licences are:

- Trade Licence:
  This allows for import, export, distribution and storage of all items specified in the licence
- Industrial Licence:
  The activities allowed are manufacturing, processing, assembling, packaging, importing of raw materials and exporting of finished products.
- Services Licence
  All services are permitted under this licence.

Under Article 5 of Law No. (2) of 1996, the activities of an entity at DAFZ must include one of the following activities:

a• The import and storage of goods for the purpose of re-exporting or importing them into the customs area in Dubai.
b• The assembling and packaging of some of the imported goods.
c• The establishment of light or advanced technology, industries and assembly plants for the purposes of export abroad or importing them into the customs area in Dubai.
d• The establishment of various business services such as banking, insurance, air shipment and other services.

Licences are issued depending upon the business activity of the applicant and more than one licence may be obtained.

→ Procedure for Registering a Free Zone Establishment (FZE), a Free Zone Company (FZCO) or a Branch Office in the DAFZ

 a• Submit the prescribed application form and application for licence form duly completed together with a one-page summary of the proposed project.
 b• The Licensing Department at DAFZ will notify the applicant within 30 days of receipt of the documents whether or not it has its permission for the formation of a FZE, FZCO or branch. If such permission is granted, the applicant will be required to submit the following documentation:

If the Applicant is an Individual

 a• Personal details and profile of the applicant
 b• Notarised specimen of the applicant's signature and notarised copy of the applicant's passport
 c• Original Banker's reference
 d• Attested specimen signatures of director, secretary and manager
 e• Original bank share certificate letter

If the Applicant is a Company

 1• The notarised and legalised copy of the parent company's Certificate of Incorporation or Certificate of Good Standing
 2• An attested and notarised copy of the parent company's Memorandum and Articles of Association
 3• An attested and notarised Board resolution of the parent company calling for the establishment of the FZE or FZCO in the DAFZ, and appointing the manager in charge
 4• Attested and notarised specimen signatures and passport copies of director, secretary and manager.
 5• Original share certificate letter from a local bank

If the Applicant is a Foreign Company wishing to establish a branch

 1• A notarised and legalised copy of the Certificate of Incorporation or Certificate of Good Standing of the parent company
 2• A notarised and legalised copy of the Memorandum and Articles of Association of the parent company
 3• A notarised and legalised board resolution calling for the establishment of a branch in the DAFZ, guaranteeing the full financial commitment for the intended operation and appointment of a manager
 4• Copy of the manager's passport and a notarised specimen signature

FZE's and FZCO's in the DAFZ are also subject to various requirements under DAFZ laws which include, but are not limited to, the following:

1• An FZE or FZCO must at all times have an office registered in the DAFZ.

2• The name of the FZE or FZCO must end with the initials FZE or FZCO respectively. The business's stationary must clearly state the FZE's or FZCO's name and registered office. This also applies to other documentation such as promissory notes and cheques.

3• A FZE or FZCO is required to keep accounting records which adequately explain the transactions entered into.

4• An auditor approved by DAFZ must be appointed to report on the FZE's or FZCO's annual accounts and ascertain whether the annual accounts have been prepared in accordance with Regulation No. 1/98 pursuant to Law No 2 of 1996.

Customs Duties

The goods imported into DAFZ or manufactured there are exempt from customs duties. If they are exported abroad they also benefit from export customs duties exemption. However, if an investor wishes to sell or distribute the products in Dubai area (outside the DAFZ) the goods are regarded as having been imported from abroad and as such are liable to customs duties in accordance with the customs tariffs applicable.

Companies in the DAFZ are regarded as offshore companies, hence the laws relating to the imposition of customs duties.

FZEs and FZCOs in DAFZ which are fully or 51% owned by UAE nationals or nationals of other Gulf Cooperation Council countries are entitled to customs duty exemptions on their products provided that they are licensed by the Ministry of Finance & Industry in the UAE or the applicable states. In such cases, the products are deemed to be national products, and are subject to the laws of the Emirate of Dubai as distinct from Law No. 2 of 1996 regarding the Establishment of a Free Zone in Dubai International Airport.

Costs of Setting up Business in the Dubai Airport Free Zone
Any Party interested in setting up an entity in the DAFZ should be aware of the following associated costs:

	US$	Dhs
a) Initial registration fees:		
Branch of an established company	Nil	Nil
Free Zone Establishment	2,722	10,000
Free Zone Company	4,083	15,000
b) Licence fees (annual):	1,370	5,000
c) Telecommunications installation charges: Telephone	96	350
Telefax	69	250
Internet	82	300
d) Dubai Chamber of Commerce & Industry Registration and Annual Membership Renewal fees:	690	2,500
e) Employee visa formalities: Provision of Employment Visa (including Entry Permit, Company Employment Card, Health Card, Medical & Residence Visa for 3 years)	399	1,460
f) Provision of Entry Permit and Residence Permit for dependents of an employee	191	700
g) Lease of Premises (per annum): Land Minimum size 2,500 m² (per metre square)	29-35/m²	108-130/m²
h) Light Industrial Units (Pre- built) 317 m² Plus service charge @3.5%	147/m²	540/m²
i) Free Space Offices Minimum 50 m² Plus service charge @3.5%	381/m²	1,400/m²

Business in the Dubai Technology, E-Commerce and Media Free Zone

The Dubai Technology E-Commerce and Media Free Zone (TECOM) encompasses the Dubai Internet City (DIC), Dubai Media City (DMC) and the Knowledge Village (KV). Parties wishing to set up in DIC, DMC or KV be they individuals or established companies, may do so by either setting up and registering a Free Zone Limited Liability Company (FZ LLC) or a branch of a foreign company or a UAE established company.

To qualify for establishment in the either the DIC, DMC or KV, applicants must belong, as a general rule, to one of the following activity categories:

DIC: Information and communications sector
DMC: Media related service sector
KV: Institutions for the provision of education and learning

The FZ LLC is a limited liability entity with a separate legal identity from that of its owners and liability is thus limited to the extent of the company's paid up share capital. At least one of the Directors and the Secretary are required to be resident in the Emirate of Dubai.

Licensing

Applications for obtaining licences at the DIC/DMC/KV are made to each respective entity within TECOM. Generally the following steps are required to be taken to operate within TECOM:

1 • Submission of the relevant application form and business proposal by the applicant for assessment.
2 • If the application is approved the applicant will receive a provisional approval letter requesting the relevant legal documents and the time within which these should be submitted. In addition, the applicant will receive a personal sponsorship agreement (PSA), employment contract, general terms and conditions of the sponsorship agreement and a letter to the applicant's nominated bank to open an account to receive the share capital.
3 • If the applicant is establishing a branch of an existing company, the following notarised and attested documents from the parent company are required to be submitted:
   a • Certificate of Registration or a Certificate of Good Standing
   b • Memorandum and Articles of Association
   c • Board resolution calling for the establishment of a branch in either DIC/DMC/KV, guaranteeing its full financial commitment to the branch, appointing the company's negotiator or legal representative and the appointment of the branch office's manager
   d • Power of attorney in favour of the company's negotiator or legal representative,
   e • Specimen signature of the company's negotiator or legal representative and his passport copy
   f • Power of attorney in favour of the company's manager or representative for the branch
   g • Specimen signature of the company's manager or representative and a copy of his passport.

The documents listed above must be:
1 • Notarised by a notary public in their country of origin
2 • Legalised by the foreign ministry of the country from which they originate
3 • Authenticated by the UAE Embassy in that country

If the documents of the foreign company are in any language other than English, it is highly recommended that they be officially translated into English in their country of origin prior to being notarised, legalised and authenticated. TECOM may require additional documents if it deems necessary.

If the applicant is establishing a FZ LLC, the documentation required is as follows:
If the applicant is an individual/s:
1 • Personal profile/s of the applicant/s, such as business background
2 • Notarised specimen of the applicant/s signature/s
3 • Copy of the applicant/s passport/s
4 • Original bank reference letter/s, on the bank's letter head and stamped
5 • Notarised declaration calling for the establishment of the FZ LLC, appointing the negotiator or legal representative, stating the shareholder/s, director/s, secretary and manager as well as notarised specimens of their signatures and copies of their passports
6 • Power of attorney for the negotiator or legal representative, the notarised specimen signature and a copy of his passport
7 • Bank Certificate of deposit of the share capital of the FZ LLC
For individual applicants, the notarised documents required for submission to TECOM may be signed before the Registrar at the TECOM.

If the applicant is a company:
The following notarised and legalised documents are required:
1 • Certificate of Registration or Certificate of Good Standing of the parent company
2 • Memorandum and Articles of Association
3 • Board resolution of the parent company calling for the establishment of a FZ LLC, appointing the negotiator or legal representative, and the Manager, Directors and Secretary of the company
4 • Power of attorney for the negotiator or legal representative
5 • Specimen signature of the negotiator or legal representative and a copy of his passport
6 • Specimen signatures of the Manager, Directors and Secretary and copies of their passports
7 • Bank Certificate of deposit of the share capital of the FZ LLC

Upon submission and approval of the relevant legal documents, the applicant are issued with a final approval letter together with details of office space available, an invoice for the licence fee and a 20% deposit on the lease office, and a copy of the specimen lease agreement.

Once the applicant has paid the invoice amount, the lease agreement is issued, which the applicant signs together with the PSA and pays the balance of the 80% of the rental amount for the lease office.

Business in the Dubai Cars and Automotive Zone

The Dubai Cars and Automotive Zone (DUCAMZ) has been established with the objective of facilitating the re-export of automotive vehicles to the African, Asian and Middle Eastern markets, and comes under the administration of JAFZA, and is therefore governed by JAFZ rules and regulations.

Investors can establish a Free Zone Company (FZCO) and these are separate legal entities with limited liability limited to the extent of the company's paid-up share capital which must be at least Dhs 100,000. Minimum shareholders are two, with a maximum of five.

Business in the the Dubai Gold and Diamond Park

Also operating under the auspices of the JAFZ and located on an adjacent site, is the Dubai Gold and Diamond Park (DGDP). The DGDP is similar in concept to the DUCAMZ, its inspiration being the recognized advantages in terms of convention and economy of service provisions of grouping similar commercial activities in one place. As its name indicates, the DGDP accommodates dealers in precious metals and valuable stones and the associated craft industry.

Specific Industries & Professions

Industrial Projects

The law regulating industrial projects is contained in, among other things, Federal Law No. 1 of 1980 on the Regulations of Industrial Affairs. An industrial project is one, which involves a manufacturing process including processes such as packaging, and is subject to specific procedures. Those who may practise industrial activities are limited to entities which are either wholly owned by UAE nationals or other GCC nationals, or entities which are at least 51% owned by such nationals. This rule, however, does not apply to companies established in any of the free zones in Dubai.

Before one contemplates setting up an industrial project, it is advisable to first refer to the activities which are encouraged by the government policies in the area of industrial development. One body which contains extensive data with regard to industrial projects, including statistical information, is the Dubai Chamber of Commerce and Industry.

There are several designated industrial areas in Dubai such as Al Quoz which was established in 1974 and extends over 1,838 hectares, and Al Khabisi which was established in 1965 on a 102-hectare area. Various incentives are available to businesses practising or involved in industrial projects. These include exemption from customs duties on imports for the use of industrial projects such as raw materials and machinery in addition to a 10% price preference in government purchases over imported goods.

The operations industrial projects may be engaged in are legally defined as including the undertaking of one of the following operations:

- The extraction of raw materials from natural mineral ores and their transformation, purification and preparation into marketable products.
- The transformation of raw materials in accordance with the substance, components or shape into a final product or semi-manufactured product including mixing, purifying, assembling, forming and/or packing the product.
- The addition of production capacity to an existing industrial project or the formation of new production assets in order to replace the old and fully depreciated ones.

The minimum capital requirement for an industrial project is AED 250,000 if the owner is a UAE national, and AED 300,000 if the owner of the project is a limited liability company. Further, an industrial project must have a work force of at least 10 individuals.

In addition to the operations outlined above, the activities the industrial projects may be involved in are set out or classified and become relevant when the application for a licence is being made.

→ Procedure to obtain a licence for an Industrial Project

After fulfilling conditions such as the capital requirement, the nationality of the entity launching the industrial project and its activity, a prospective investor must fulfil five main requirements to establish an industrial project. These are:

1. Obtain No Objection Letter ('NOL') from Municipality

In order to start an industrial project, it is first necessary to approach the Industrial Unit of the Planning Department at the Dubai Municipality (the Municipality). The Municipality, among other things, is responsible for the safety and health aspects of the project. The unit advises and guides investors on its regulations on the basis of the technical and feasibility studies of the proposed project. It also evaluates various factors such as suitability of the designated site and the need to maintain high quality in the products produced. The unit has rejected projects which consume large quantities of water, adversely affect the environment and/or are dangerous to human health.

If the project is likely to have adverse effect on the environment it is referred to the Public Health Department of the Municipality in order to ensure that the necessary legal conditions have been complied with. Various conditions have to be met in addition to those discussed above and these will depend on the characteristics of the particular project. Once these conditions have been fulfilled, the Municipality will issue a letter addressed to the Ministry of Finance & Industry (the Ministry) confirming that it has no objection to the Ministry approving the establishment of the project.

2. Obtain Initial Approval from the Ministry of Finance & Industry

Initial approval of the project needs to be obtained from the Ministry. In order to do so, either the owner of the project or his authorised manager should submit the prescribed application form and the following documents to the Industrial Department at the Ministry:

1 • A detailed report of the project including technical and economic feasibility studies, the annual production cost, the required capital and the labour requirements

2 • The NOL obtained from the Municipality, a site plan of the allocated plot of the project

3 • A document issued by a bank operating in the UAE confirming the financial capability of the owner of the planned project

4 • Three passport copies of the owner of the project or his identity card

When these documents have been submitted, the Industrial Department will study the project from a technical and economical standpoint in order to ensure that they comply with the relevant regulations and laws. The application is then referred to the Consultative Industrial Committee (the Committee) at the Ministry which will study the application in the light of the recommendation made by the Industrial Department.

On an average the Ministry takes 15 days to study the application. It then refers the matter to the Minister of Finance & Industry who normally issues his decision within 30 days of the date of receipt of the application.

The project owner is then notified of the Minister's decision. If the Minister grants approval, construction on the project should commence within six months of the approval. The project owner also receives the following documentation with the approval:

• A letter of approval from the Municipality for the establishment of the project which will enable him to obtain a plot for the construction of the factory

• A letter addressed to the DED for completing the necessary procedures to obtain an industrial licence

• A letter addressed to the Ports & Customs Department enabling the owner to benefit from exemption of custom duties on the import of machinery and raw materials for the project

• A letter addressed to the Ministry of Labour & Social Affairs enabling the owner to recruit the necessary manpower for the project.

3. Obtain Industrial Licence from DED

After the Ministry has granted its approval, an application for an industrial licence should be made at the DED on its prescribed form. The following documents should also be submitted:

1 • A document stating the proposed trade name of the industrial firm

2 • The letter issued by the Ministry of Finance & Industry approving the project

3 • If the owner of the project is a partnership company, the partnership agreement, notarised by the Notary Public at the Dubai Court. If the owner is a share holding company incorporated by an Emiri Decree, a copy of the decree, the company's memorandum and articles of association. If the owner is a joint stock company or a limited liability company, the company's memorandum and articles of association.

4 • A copy of the passport of the owner of the project and copies of the non-national partners' passports if the project is owned by individuals

5 • The site plan of the project (attested by the concerned authority) or photocopy of the lease agreement of the place of business

6 • A copy of the tenancy contract for the employee's quarters

4. Prepare Factory Site

When the DED approves the licence application, the owner(s) must commence the preparation of the factory site, i.e. the installation of machinery, the importation of the raw materials needed and the recruitment of labour. The DED issues a provisional licence to the owner for these purposes.

After the preparation work of the factory is completed, the owner should inform the DED so that an inspection can be conducted by the technical departments of the Municipality, namely, the Planning & Public Health Sections and the Fire & Civil Defence Department.

These two departments will prepare technical reports on the extent of compliance with the regulations regarding professional safety, health and environment. If the inspections are completed without major problems, the fees for the industrial licence are assessed. When the DED is satisfied with the documentation, the fees are paid and the provisional industrial licence issued. The installation of machinery in the factory may commence at this stage.

The Ministry and the Municipality will conduct further safety and environment inspections. If these are satisfactory, a Certificate of Conformity is issued. The Ministry will then issue a letter addressed to the DED to release the original industrial licence.

5. Register industrial firm with the Dubai Chamber of Commerce and Industry (DCCI)

6. Register project in the Industrial Register at the Ministry (Industrial Department)

The project must be registered in the Industrial Register at the Ministry of Finance & Industry by submitting the prescribed application form to the Industrial Department with the following documents:

1 • A copy of the industrial licence issued by the DED
2 • A copy of the partnership agreement or the memorandum and articles of association duly attested by the Notary Public
3 • A copy of the registration certificate of the industrial project with the DCCI

After the Industrial Department has carried out inspections to ensure that the activity specified in the licence is being practised, the project is entered in the Industrial Register.

This entitles the company to obtain a certificate from the Ministry stating the value added to the product(s) produced. This certificate clears such product(s) to be exported to other GCC states duty-free and without restriction.

In addition, when the project is entered in the Industrial Register, a licence for industrial production is granted to the owner which entitles him to benefit from the incentives and exemptions provided by the Dubai government.

It should be noted that it is necessary for the owner of the project to fulfil certain obligations stipulated by law which include submission of annual reports, amendment of the project's data to the

Industrial Department and notification to the Ministry of any changes made to the data entered into the application for registration form. The Industrial Department should also be informed of any sales, assignments, or leases made regarding the project. Incidentally, all data submitted by the owner regarding the project is subject to confidentiality.

Insurance Companies, Agents & Brokers

Insurance is regulated under Federal Law No. 9 of 1984 pertaining to Insurance Companies and Insurance Brokers (the Insurance Law). Additionally, Ministerial Decision No. 32 of 1984 was issued to include the executory rules pertaining to the Insurance Law (Executory Rules). Further, Ministerial Decision No. 22 of 1985 pertaining to conditions and procedures for registering in the actuarial expert's register and Ministerial Decision No. 23 of 1985 pertaining to the regulation of Insurance Consultancy Professions, were issued.

Setting up Insurance Companies

The rules and procedures for setting up insurance companies in the UAE are stated in the Insurance Law and the Executory Rules.

Article 11 of the Insurance Law states that "All insurance companies that are established or will be established in the State shall be public joint stock companies, all the stocks of the same shall be nominal and the share capital of the same shall be owned by UAE natural or juridical persons that are fully owned by UAE nationals".

Therefore, an insurance company established in the UAE should be a public joint stock company.

Further, the Insurance Law states in Article 12 that the paid up share capital of an insurance company established in the UAE shall not be less than Dhs 50,000,000 in all cases.

An insurance company may not be established unless it obtains a licence from the Ministry of Economy & Commerce. The Insurance Law and the Executory Rules have determined the rules and procedures for obtaining an insurance licence in the UAE. The said rules also regulate the insurance operations of the company to be established, its founders, structure and activities.

In addition to obtaining a licence and prior to undertaking its business in the UAE, any insurance company should be registered in the Insurance Companies' Register at the Ministry of Economy & Commerce. Registration has been enacted to include all the companies that have fulfilled the requirements of the law including the share capital thereof and licensing requirements, and that are commencing business in the UAE. Prior to being registered, an insurance company is required to deposit with a bank operating in the UAE, a reserve amount to cover its activities under each of the insurance branches.

Licensing and Registering an Operating Branch of a Foreign Insurance Company

The Insurance Law has allowed for foreign insurance companies, duly organized and registered in foreign jurisdictions, to license and register an operating branch of the same in the UAE.

The requirements for licensing and registration of a branch are set out in the Insurance Law and the Executory Rules. Most of the licensing and registration requirements of insurance companies established in the UAE apply to the licensing and registration of operating branches of foreign insurance companies save for some requirements that do not apply to branches of insurance companies and some additional requirements that are not required by the law to establish a local insurance company. The most significant requirement pertaining to the licensing and registration of a branch of a foreign insurance company is the requirement to have a local service agent and to provide notarised, legalised and attested incorporation, registration and good-standing documents from the country of origin.

Insurance Individuals

The Insurance Law has determined two groups of individuals working in specific areas of insurance business who need to be qualified and registered in order for them to undertake the work in that specific field. The two types of insurance individuals set out in the Insurance Law are:

1• Insurance Brokers: Article 30 of the Insurance law defines an insurance broker as being anyone who "mediates or offers or concludes an insurance contract on behalf of an insurance company that is registered in the Insurance Register with the Ministry of Economy & Commerce in return for an allowance, bonus or commission."

An Insurance broker may not undertake activities if he is not registered in the Insurance Brokers' Register with the Ministry of Economy & Commerce. Registration with the Ministry must be renewed on an annual basis.

The registration of a broker in the Insurance Brokers' Register is conditional upon:
- Being a UAE national
- Being of good conduct and demeanour, and not having been convicted of a crime of dishonour or dishonesty unless discharged or pardoned by the competent authorities
- Being at least 21 years of age and fully competent under the law
- Not having been declared bankrupt unless discharged
- Conducting the business at a permanent location.

If an insurance broker is a company, it should be established in the UAE and should be wholly owned by UAE nationals.

2• Surveyors and Loss Adjusters: Surveyors and Loss Adjusters under the Insurance Law are persons who carry out a survey and assessment of the damage of an accident, which is the subject of insurance. The Insurance Law forbids any person to engage in the profession of Surveyors or Loss Adjusters unless his name is entered into the Register of Surveyors and Loss Adjusters held with the Ministry of Economy & Commerce.

Insurance Individuals

Further, Ministerial Decision No. 22 of 1985 listed the procedures and requirements for registering actuary experts. No person may practise the profession of actuary unless he is registered in the Actuary Register with the Ministry of Economy and Trade. An insurance actuary will not be registered unless the individual:

- Holds an associate or fellow degree from the Actuary Experts Institute in the United Kingdom or from the Actuary Experts Association in the United States of America or one of the institutes or associations for actuary experts which are approved by the Ministry of Economy & Commerce
- Has practical experience in the field of actuary mathematics that is not less than three years
- Is at least 25 years of age
- Enjoys full legal capacity
- Is of good conduct and demeanour and has not been convicted of a crime of dishonour or dishonesty unless discharged or pardoned by the competent authorities and
- Has never been declared bankrupt unless discharged.

Engineering Consultancies

The field of engineering consultancy in Dubai is mainly regulated by Local Order No. 89 of 1994 on Regulating the Practice of the Engineering Consultancy Profession in the Emirate of Dubai (the Order).

Under the Order, all persons who intend to practise engineering consultancy in Dubai must have their names entered in a register at the Dubai Municipality.

In order to be registered in the register, an individual must:
1• Be a UAE national
2• Be fully competent
3• Be of good conduct and reputation
4• Have not been previously convicted of a crime or misdemeanour relating to honour or honesty, unless he has been granted a pardon for such crimes or been rehabilitated
5• Hold a Bachelor of Science (B.Sc.) Degree in engineering from a recognised university in an engineering field for which he is applying for a licence
6• Have at least three years experience in his specialist field after obtaining his university degree
7• Be a member of the Engineers' Association in the UAE
8• Not be an owner or a partner in a contracting company or a building material trading company in the UAE.

As an exception to points 1 and 6 above, foreigners who wish to practice engineering consultancy in Dubai may do so provided they satisfy the following conditions:
a• Their only work is in engineering consultancy.
b• They have at least three years experience in the concerned engineering field after obtaining a university degree.

    c• Where a licence is being issued for the establishment of an engineering firm, their actual period of residence in the UAE is at least nine months in a calendar year.

Engineering consultancies in Dubai must adopt one of the following forms:

• Local Engineering Firm

This type of firm is owned by one or more UAE nationals. Foreigners may have a share in it providing their names are entered in the Register and this share does not exceed 49%.

• Associate Engineering Firm

This firm is the association of a local engineering firm (as above) with a foreign engineering firm that has at least 10 years practice in the field.

• Expert Engineering Firm

An expert engineering firm is one which is owned by one or more UAE nationals and is engaged in the provision of opinion or advice to local engineering firms, associate engineering firms or official bodies. The appointment of a local service agent is required where none of the licence applicants is a UAE national. Various conditions need to be satisfied in order to establish such a firm. One of these is that the owners must have a minimum of 15 years specialist experience.

• Branch of a Foreign Engineering Firm

This firm, as the name suggests, is a branch of a foreign engineering company. In order to set up such a firm a number of conditions have to be fulfilled which include (but are not limited to) the following:

    a• The foreign office is technically highly qualified and has been established for at least fifteen years

    b• The manager of the firm has at least fifteen years experience in the engineering profession and his name has been entered in the Engineering Consultancy Register

    c• The parent company has taken on large scale projects of high technical and financial value (a list of these has to be provided when the firm's application is being made)

From the above, it is clear that to set up an engineering consultancy firm, it is necessary to obtain a licence which is issued by the Committee for Registration & Licensing at the Municipality for a two year term. There are other conditions and procedures too, which should be carefully studied.

Auditing Firms

The Audit profession is regulated under Federal Law No. 22 of 1995 with regard to the organisation of auditing profession ('Auditing Law'). Under the Auditing Law, no natural or juridical person may practice auditing without being registered at the Auditors Register with the Ministry of Economy & Commerce.

Requirements to enlist UAE nationals in the Auditors' Register

    1• A copy of the family book

    2• A copy of university degree in the field of accounting from one of the accredited universities or the equivalent thereof

    3• A copy of certificate of membership in any of the institutes or auditor's associations that are determined by a decision from the Minister of Economy & Commerce

4• A certificate of good standing from the Dubai police
5• A statement signed by the applicant stating that he has not been convicted of any professional crime relating to honour or ethics of the profession
6• Experience certificate
7• Undertaking to be dedicated to the profession of auditing unless he/she is a university professor
8• Three personal photographs

Requirements to enlist non-UAE nationals in the Auditors Register:
1• A copy of the applicant's passport and residency visa
2• Birth certificate
3• A certificate proving that he/she is a partner with one of the UAE nationals listed in the Auditors Register or is working for the same
4• A copy of a certificate of membership in one of the institutes or auditors association which are determined by a decision issued by the Minister of Economy & Commerce
5• A copy of the university degree in the field of accounting, or the equivalent thereof, from one of the   accredited universities or institutes
6• Certificate of good standing from the competent authority
7• Statement signed by the applicant stating that he/she has never been convicted of a professional crime relating to honour or ethics of the profession
8• Undertaking to be dedicated to the profession
9• Three personal photographs

Requirements for registration of a foreign audit firm in the Auditors Register:
1• A certificate proving the registration and licensing to undertake the auditing profession in the UAE prior to the enforcement of Law No 22 of 1995
2• A certificate of the company's licence to undertake auditing in its country of origin
3• A certificate stating that the representative of the company is a partner and a member in one of the auditors associations that has international recognition which shall be stated in a decision of the Minister of Economy & Commerce
4• A certificate stating that the representative of the company has a residency visa in the UAE
5• A list of all employees of the company who undertake auditing accounts along with their nationalities, in addition to an undertaking to provide the Ministry and the competent authority with   any amendments occurring to that list within two months from the date such amendments take place
6• Insurance certificate to cover the business of the company to include all the risk of the profession in the UAE
7• A statement affirming full dedication to the profession with regard to partners and managers

Activities under the ambit of the Government of the Dubai Department of Tourism & Commerce Marketing:
Hotels, Guesthouses and Furnished Apartments

The procedures involved in obtaining a business licence are normally conducted at the DED. Certain areas, however, fall within the ambit of the Dubai Department of Tourism & Commerce Marketing (DTCM). These include the following:

- Hotels
- Hotel administration
- Rentals of furnished apartments and guesthouses
- Organisation of tourist expeditions
- Travel agencies
- Sale of airline tickets
- Ship rentals and rentals of leisure boats
- Organisation of boat trips for tourists
- Floating restaurants
- Amusement parks

The establishment of hotels, guesthouses and furnished apartments in Dubai are subject to special requirements, which are outlined in the local by-law No. 1 of 1998, Concerning Licensing and Classification of Hotels, Guesthouses and Furnished Apartments (the By-law).

According to Article 2 of the By-law, a hotel is defined as "a building or independent part of a building which incorporates not less than 10 bedrooms available for board and lodging services against a financial consideration."

A guesthouse is defined as "a building or part of a building which incorporates not less than 10 bedrooms and provides lodging services only against a financial consideration."

Furnished apartments are defined as "a group of furnished villas or apartments providing not less than eight accommodation units which are rented to guests on a daily, weekly, monthly or yearly basis."

It should be noted that a business involving hotels, furnished apartments or guesthouses must be 100% owned by UAE nationals in the form of establishments.

→ Procedure to set up a Hotel, Guesthouse or Furnished Apartment
  1• Obtain the preliminary approval of the DTCM
  2• Obtain classification where a hotel or furnished apartments are concerned
  3• Obtain a licence from the DTCM.
     The classification of hotels is based on a five-grade system and for furnished apartments on a two-grade system, i.e. standard and deluxe. The DTCM is the body which decides on the classification after inspections to determine whether the criteria and conditions outlined in its Licensing & Classification Manual for Hotels, Guest Houses & Furnished

Apartments in the Emirate of Dubai are met. Applications for preliminary approval, licensing and classification are made to the Department on the prescribed forms supported by the necessary documents. The licence fees are determined by the DED in accordance with factors such as the number of rooms available.

The Administrative Section of the DTCM will review the applications and the results of the inspections. It will then submit its recommendations to the Director General of the Department who will subsequently issue a decision.

If the applicant is not satisfied with the classification granted, he can appeal against it to the Director General of the DTCM within 15 days of being notified of the decision. The Director General's decision on the appeal will be issued one month from the date the appeal is submitted and is final. If such a decision is not issued within this time, the appeal is regarded as rejected.

After satisfying that the necessary conditions have been met, the DTCM will issue a license and a classification certificate, which are renewable every year. Applications for renewals are made to the DTCM at least 30 days before the expiry date of the licence or classification certificate. It is possible to apply for the amendment of the classification issued in accordance with the procedures outlined above. The Director-General's decision in this regard can also be appealed.

In addition, businesses in the tourism industry, such as hotels must be registered in the Commercial Register at the DED and become members of the DCCI after obtaining the licence. Should the business wish to sell alcohol, it must apply for a liquor licence to the police authorities.

Once a new hotel, guesthouse or a building containing furnished apartments has been established, various obligations must be fulfilled. These include providing the DTCM with records of guests, maintaining accounts books and records, displaying a list of the tariffs and the timings of the services provided in a prominent place in the building in at least the Arabic language and one other foreign language.

There are penalties under the By-law against those who violate its provisions. These vary from the imposition of fines (minimum Dhs 100, maximum Dhs 100,000), lowering of the grade of the hotel or furnished apartment, temporary or permanent closure of the hotel, guesthouse or furnished apartment and/or the cancellation or withdrawal of the licence.

Medical Establishments

The establishment of private medical institutions in Dubai is primarily governed by Federal Law No. 2 of 1996 (the Law) regarding private health care institutions. The concerned authorities in this regard are mainly the Ministry of Health (MOH) and the Dubai Department of Health and Medical Services (DOHMS). Under the Law all medical institutions must be wholly owned by UAE nationals as civil companies. This implies that the entity must be an establishment. Establishments, as discussed earlier, are the equivalent of sole proprietorships where the sole proprietor's liabilities are unlimited. Civil companies, as opposed to commercial companies, as mentioned earlier, involve activities that are performed through the exploitation of the expertise of the partners whereas commercial company activity generally involves activities of a commercial nature.

Although various hospitals in the UAE have been established as limited liability companies (LLCs), these are exceptions and are to be found among large-scale projects like hospitals rather than clinics. Also, although LLCs allow 49% foreign ownership, in order to comply with the law, if a LLC is to be established as a medical practice, it needs to be wholly owned by UAE nationals.

It is necessary for the establishment of all medical practices in the UAE to obtain a professional licence from the MOH as stated under Article 3 of the Law. This licence is issued to UAE nationals. However, under Article 6 of the Law, non-UAE doctors who have practised in the UAE for 2 years (in the case of specialists) and for 5 years (in the case of consultants) may, in collaboration with a UAE national, obtain a licence to establish a specialised medical practice.

Under Article 1 of the Law, the various medical establishments permissible in the UAE are defined as follows:

- A private clinic or medical practice is defined as "a facility equipped and licensed by the competent authority in order to receive patients and provide them with health care services, in which a licensed human physician or a dentist practises his profession."
- A general clinic is defined as "the clinic in which patients are provided with health care services by one or more general physicians."
- A specialised clinic is defined as "a clinic in which one or more specialist physicians operate on a permanent ongoing basis. Such a specialist shall practise in one medical discipline."
- A multi-disciplinary medical clinic is defined as "a clinic in which more than one physician operate in various medical disciplines."
- A hospital is defined as "a health care institution licensed by the competent authority for examining patients, providing them with health care services and providing facilities for in-patient stay during clinical treatment."
- A convalescent home is defined as "a health care institution licensed by the competent authority for providing post-clinical services for people to convalesce."
- A medical test centre is defined as "pathological laboratories, x-ray and radio imaging centres and the like."
- A rehabilitation centre is defined as "dental manufacturing labs, optical, acoustical and communication centres, physiotherapy centres, manufacturing facilities for prosthesis, orthodontics and the like."

The UAE law distinguishes between the establishment of hospitals and other medical institutions. The main difference between the two relates to the activities they may practice and hospitals require the approval of His Highness Sheikh Hamdan Bin Rashid Al Maktoum's approval. Hospitals, for instance, may have in-patient facilities and administer both local and general anaesthetic to their patients. Clinics however may not have in-patient facilities and may not administer general anaesthetic but may operate consultancy services and have outpatient facilities. A clinic desirous of engaging in activities restricted to hospitals, such as conducting operations involving general anaesthetic, may enter into an arrangement with a hospital to rent rooms for this purpose, subject to obtaining the approval of both the MOH and DOHMS.

As the Law permits foreign participation in the establishment of clinics rather than hospitals, only the procedure for the former has been outlined below.

→ Procedure to Establish a Clinic in Dubai

a• Obtain a No-Objection letter from DOHMS

To establish a medical practice in Dubai, it is first necessary to obtain a no objection letter from the DOHMS The application is made in a letter addressed to the DOHMS outlining the intended venture. The purpose of this letter is two-fold: (i) to obtain the DOHMS' preliminary approval for the venture; and (ii) to ascertain whether both the intended local owner and the first practising doctor meet the eligibility criteria set by the DOHMS, as mentioned below. The national owner will, according to the DOHMS, be eligible if he fulfils one of the following criteria:
- He is a college graduate and holds a medical degree. If so, he will be limited to employing three doctors.
- He has a Medical Doctorate degree (PhD.). In this case, the number of doctors he may employ is unlimited, subject to other factors, such as the amount of space available for the practice.
- He is a businessman (presumably without a medical degree or doctorate). Here the medical committee's approval at the DOHMS is required and the number of doctors that he may employ is limited to three.

The first doctor will be eligible if he satisfies the following:
- He holds a Bachelor of Medicine and Surgery degree or the equivalent; or
- He is a specialist; he must have a master's degree in medicine and at least three years experience. In addition, foreign doctors who wish to practice in the UAE must have relevant experience of at least three years (in the case of specialists) and submit to the DOHMS a testimonial indicating the length of time they have practised.

Those who wish to establish private medical institutions in Dubai will therefore, need to consult with the MOH and DOHMS in order to obtain information on the necessary procedures as there is no written document in the UAE or in Dubai outlining them.

Future Business Options

Dubai International Financial Centre   www.difc.ae

As discussed in Chapter 3, The Dubai International Financial Centre (DIFC) has been created to attract global financial institutions and professional financial service firms for the provision of institutional finance, capital and investment. The DIFC will initially focus on five main areas activity:

- Asset Management
- Islamic Finance
- Regional Financial Exchange
- Re-insurance
- Back-office Operations

The DIFC is expected to begin licensing entities in end 2003.

Dubai Healthcare City   www.dhcc.ae

The Dubai Healthcare City (DHCC) has been established to create a concentration of health care and medical professionals and service providers in Dubai for the provision of world class specialist medical services, medical education, life science research and technology leveraged healthcare services by providing access to a unique healthcare community.

Final completion of the DHCC is expected by 2010, and companies and investors have begun reserving land and commenced related activities.

Dubai Maritime City

The Dubai Maritime City is expected to attract six main sectors from the maritime industry:

- Ship repair and maintenance services
- Ship design and manufacturing
- Marine management services
- Marine related marketing
- Marine research and education
- Marine recreational services

The first phase of the Dubai Maritime City is due for completion in mid-2004.

Offshore Companies

In May 2003, the Jebel Ali Free Zone Authority issued new regulations allowing for the formation of offshore companies. The new JAFZ Offshore Companies Regulations 2003 have been designed in line with the latest international practices, and are aimed to enhance JAFZ as a centre for registration of offshore companies. Any one or more persons may, by signing and delivering to the registrar an application for certificate of incorporation, apply for the formation of an incorporated offshore company with limited liability.

The offshore company must have a minimum of two directors and one secretary, and should issue a single class of shares. It must also maintain a registered office at the JAFZ or through a registered agent approved by the JAFZA. In addition, it must hold at least one shareholders meeting every year and produce financial statements to be audited by an approved auditor.

Activity of an offshore company will cover trade and allied services, but activities of banking and/or insurance will not be permitted. However, offshore companies can open bank accounts in the UAE.

Other Investment Considerations

Exchange Controls and Customs Union

One of the strong incentives for foreign investors in the UAE is the fact that there are no restrictions regarding currency accounts, the repatriation of capital, profits and fees. The UAE Dirham (Dhs) or the Arab Emirates Dirham (AED) has, since 1980, been fixed against the US dollar at the rate of US$1 to Dhs 3.671.

Pursuant to the Doha Declaration issued on 23rd December 2002 by the 23rd GCC summit held in Qatar, the GCC states established a Customs Union effective from 1 January 2003 and a transitional period of three years, ending in 2005.

Under the Customs Union, all fees, taxes, customs and other obstacles to trade within the GCC will be replaced with unified customs measures that will see all GCC states implementing a 5% duty on foreign imports (subject to certain exempted categories). Commodities and goods manufactured in the GCC will not be subject to customs tariffs if the commodities and goods are moved between member states.

Taxation

Strictly speaking, all companies in Dubai are required by law to pay tax on their earnings. The rates of tax are on a sliding scale up to a maximum of 50%. In practice, however, only oil, gas and petrochemical companies, hotels and the branch offices of foreign banks are required to pay tax, although there is no provision for this in the Law. Such taxes are normally determined by agreement with the relevant bodies. There is no federal tax legislation on the taxation of corporations in the UAE, instead each emirate has its own tax laws.

Income tax is non-existent in the UAE and the only tax which is charged on individuals, albeit indirectly, is the municipal tax which is imposed on hotel services, business and residential property rentals.

There are currently double taxation agreements with Algeria, China, Egypt, Finland, France, Germany, India, Indonesia, Italy, Jordan, Kuwait, Malaysia, Pakistan, Poland, Romania, Singapore Sudan, Syria, Turkey and Yemen, and there are plans to sign further such treaties with other nations.

Securities

The Dubai Financial Market (DFM), the UAE's first stock exchange, was established on 26 March 2000. Regulated by the Emirates Securities and Commodities Market Authority and equipped with state of the art technology, the DFM provides investors with an efficient and accurate system by which to trade in securities. Foreign investors in the DFM have been limited up to now, although this is expected to grow in the near future.

Ownership of Real Estate

There is no specific Federal Land Law in the UAE. Instead each Emirate has established its own specific land ownership policies through local orders and decrees and in accordance with its own economic and political circumstances. Residential, commercial, agricultural and industrial land is all held in the Dubai Emirate by UAE nationals, and in exceptional cases by other GCC nationals. Recently, however, various developers have announced that they are offering land in their residential developments for sale to UAE and foreign nationals on a freehold basis (see page 210). As at the date of publication hereof the empowering Decree allowing foreign nationals ownership of freehold land had not become law.

The Protection of Intellectual Property Rights

Although Dubai has for some time been regarded as a major centre for international trade, it originally had an unfortunate reputation for being a centre for the trade of counterfeit goods. Things have, however, witnessed a rapid change as over the past years, the UAE has managed to earn a reputation for being the leading country in the Middle East for the protection of intellectual property rights.

This has been possible as a result of the firm and efficient enforcement campaigns led by government bodies such as the Ministry of Information & Culture, the DED, the Municipality and Economic Department in Sharjah, the Police, private organisations and right holders.

Even prior to its entry into the World Trade Organisation (WTO), the UAE put into place laws to protect intellectual property rights in 1992 as outlined below.

Trademark protection is afforded by Federal Law No. 37 of 1992 as amended by Federal Law No. 8 of 2002 (the Trademark Law) which came into force on 12 January 1993 and 31 July 2002, respectively. The Trademark Law provides for a comprehensive trademark registration scheme for marks relating to both goods and services. The categories of goods and services which can be registered correspond with the International Classification of Goods and Services under the Nice Agreement. However, alcoholic beverages are excluded.

The Trademark Law provides protection of trademarks for a period of ten years, which may be renewed indefinitely for recurring periods of ten years. Owners of trademarks can file civil proceedings against infringements which can lead to the confiscation of offending goods and to the imposition of other civil remedies. Criminal sanctions also exist in the Trademark Law. An infringer of a registered trademark can be fined and/or have his business premises closed down and the offending goods destroyed. Administrative action by the local government authority such as the DED and Economic Department or Municipality in Sharjah is also possible and is efficient due to the fact that it is fast and effective. The authority can fine the offender, confiscate and destroy the goods and seek an undertaking.

Patent protection was introduced by Federal Law No. 44 of 1992 (the Patent Law) which came into force on 12 January 1993. The Patent Law affords protection for inventions, industrial designs and models. There are some exemptions in the Patent Law such as the absence of protection for pharmaceutical products. However, measures are being taken to amend the Patent Law. Registration of patents commenced as of July 2002 when the first 9 patents were issued.

Copyright protection was introduced by Federal Law No. 40 of 1992 which came into force on 12 April 1993. However, this was repealed by Federal Law No. 7 of 2002 on Copyright and Related Rights (the Copyright Law) which came into force on 14th July 2002. The Copyright Law affords protection to the original author (foreign or national) of a variety of works automatically upon creation, including, but not limited to, literary work and written matter, computer software, choreographic works, theatrical plays, musicals and cinematographic works. Although it is possible to register one's copyright with the Ministry of Information & Culture, failure to do so does not prejudice the rights of the copyright holder. The period of protection granted depends on the nature of the work. Generally, however, the protection granted is the period of the author's life plus 50 years.

There are some works which cannot be copyright protected. These include matters such as court decisions and official documents.

In terms of sanctions, the Copyright Law imposes civil, as well as, criminal liability on copyright infringers. The Ministry of Information & Culture has also been very active in the administrative enforcement of the law by conducting raids, confiscating goods and even closing down shops selling pirated material such as cassettes, software and videos.

Pollution Control

It has long been a strong policy of the UAE government to protect the environment and several laws and regulations have been passed in this regard. These need close scrutiny by any investor contemplating projects in the UAE, particularly in the industrial sector.

Any investor seeking to practise such activities has to prepare what is known as an environmental impact statement for the premises where the industrial project is to be set up. This is one of the procedural requirements of the Dubai Municipality when seeking approval for such a project. This statement must, depending on the size and nature of the project include details regarding, among other things, air emissions, water discharges, solid waste discharges, safety and health aspects, construction issues and chemicals and dangerous goods which may be used at the project's premises.

The Dubai Municipality has a specialised Environmental Department (Page 99), which is responsible for providing effective environmental protection and safety as well as waste management services throughout the emirate.

Environmental protection and safety section under the Environmental Department monitors the level of pollution; in water, air and soil. Additionally, it carries out routine monitoring of creek and marine waters to protect them from pollution, operates an effective hazardous waste disposal permit system, monitors industrial safety, assesses environmental risks, applies relevant environmental protection regulations, promotes public awareness issues relating to the preservation of the environment and executes regulations concerning the protection of natural life and preservation of marine and land sanctuaries.

The waste services section at the Environmental Department undertakes daily waste collection and street cleaning, and promotes waste minimisation and recycling throughout the Emirate.

The waste treatment section of the Environmental Department provides effective facilities for the disposal of all domestic and industrial waste and supervises disposal of hazardous materials.

There are also environmental guidelines investors must take on board when establishing businesses or projects in the JAFZ and DAFZ. Environmental impact assessment studies are also a requirement laid down by JAFZA. Investors are provided with guidelines on this.

UAE Federal Law No. 7 of 1993 established the Federal Environmental Agency, which issued UAE Federal Law No. 24 of 1999 on the Protection and Development of the Environment and came into effect in February 2000.

The intention of this law was to unify and embody the approach to environmental issues across the Emirates. The law deals with the general protection of the environment and has specific chapters on water, soil, noise and air pollution, handling hazardous substances and hazardous waste, protected 'natural reserves', environmental disasters and the respective penalties for violation of any of these provisions.

Obtaining Office/ Warehouse Premises in Dubai

Office space in Dubai is easy to obtain. Dubai is currently in the midst of a construction boom and many office developments are being completed. The most popular locations in which commercial organisations locate their offices are the Dubai World Trade Centre, Sheikh Zayed Road, Bur Dubai, Al Riqqa Street, Creek Area, City Centre Area and Al Maktoum Street. Many other commercial centres are, however, developing in and around Dubai. If location is not important, an office can be established at relatively low cost by renting an apartment and obtaining a commercial licence for the premises. Office space is available through most of the real estate agents operating in Dubai.

The premises for a new business should be rented before the business licence is obtained from the DED and after initial approval of the business's name and activity has been issued by the DED. In addition, the premises should be rented or leased in the business's name rather than the name of its partner(s) or owner(s). Businesses which are building their own premises should also do so before a licence is issued by the DED. The reason for this is that before issuing the licence, the DED needs to inspect the premises.

Foreign companies can lease premises in Dubai for their offices, warehouses or other premises whether flats or villas at any location in Dubai. However, they may not be able to lease land for commercial industrial projects from the government unless the project is at least 51% owned by UAE nationals.

Lease agreements are usually private transactions between the landlord and tenant. Rent is paid on annual basis though it is not uncommon for the landlord and tenants to agree to split the payment through the provision of 3-4 post-dated cheques to run through the year. It is not uncommon nowadays, especially for prestigious commercial buildings for the landlord and tenant to enter into long leases especially if the fit out on those premises is expensive.

There is no tax or customs duty payable for lease or rental other than the fee, which is paid to the DED upon issuance and subsequent renewal of the company licence. The DED base some of their fee on the rent agreed for the office premises and the residential premises rented by senior employees of the entity. This fee is collected by the DED on behalf of the Dubai Municipality.

Water and electricity charges are normally the responsibility of the tenants and are paid on a monthly basis, unless otherwise provided in the lease agreement. Tenants will also have to make their own arrangement for insurance.

Rent dispute is normally a matter of commercial contract and any dispute must be put before the Rent Committee, which is situated at the Dubai Municipality. The Committee has judicial powers and their decision is final and not subject to appeal. They normally deal with the dispute in a rather relaxed fashion aiming to mediate between parties to reach an amicable settlement of their rental dispute in a way that balances the rights and obligations between both parties. There is no formal procedure for the Committee, though both parties will be given the right to put forward their case and arguments before the Committee, who will decide on the subject matter.

The checklist below indicates points that investors and their advisors should consider when contemplating setting up a business in the UAE.

Market - Existing and Potential
- Existing market for products/services
- Potential market for products/services
- Competition
- Market surveys
- Patents, trademarks and copyrights
- Licences to trade
- Franchising

Preparation of Business Plan
- Determination of overall strategy
- Assistance from professional advisors
- Discussion of plans with regulatory authorities

Form of Entity to Adopt
- Corporation
- Commercial Company
- Civil Company (services)
- Commercial Agency
- Foreign branch or representative office
- Free Zone Entity

Initial Capital Requirements
- Outside capital
- Raise capital from local sources
- Repatriation of capital and earnings

Capital Requirements
- Availability of financing - local source/ foreign source
- Repatriation of interest and principal of foreign-sourced loans
- Bank borrowings
- Injection of cash from holding company/parent
- Other forms of finance
- Government assistance
- Lease and/or purchase of assets
- Obtain professional advice from bankers, lawyers and accountants

Premises
- Type required
- Own or lease? (Ownership of land currently subject to local laws)
- Current requirements
- Expansion possibilities
- Storage
- Insurance requirements

- Health and safety requirements
- Approvals required

Location
- Where to set up operations
- Accessibility to ports of entry

Management: Availability and Compensation
- Requirements
- Compensation levels
- Availability locally; recruitment
- Possibility of bringing in own staff from outside
- Permits needed
- Cost of expatriate staff
- Company housing and accommodation

Labour: Availability and Compensation
- Numbers and types needed
- Protected costs
- Terms of employment
- Work permits for expatriates
- Recruitment
- Wages, salaries and fringe benefits
- Accommodation
- Training courses
- Severance pay

Production Capabilities
- Capital commitments-current and projected
- Capacity-current and projected
- Raw materials-sources and availability
- Projected costs

Selling the product
- Projected costs
- Sponsorship
- Commercial agent
- Exhibitions and trade shows
- Exporting process
- Customs duty exemptions

Formation Procedures
- Appointment of professional advisors, such as lawyers, bankers, auditors, tax advisors
- Conduct of the entity
- Registration of name
- Ordering stationery
- Company secretarial and admin. services

Checklist

The Dubai Chamber of Commerce & Industry Administrative Fees & Arbitrator's Remuneration				
	Conciliation	Arbitration	Minimum	Maximum
Disputed amount Chamber's Administrative fee (in Dirhams) Arbitrator's Remuneration in Dirhams as percentage				
Up to 200,000	500	1,000	3,000	7.5% of the disputed amount (up to a maximum of 15,000)
From 200,000 to 500,000	1,000	2,000	3,000+1.5% of the amount over 200,000	15,000+6% of the amount over 200,000
From 500,000 to 1,000,000	1,500	3,500	7,500+1% of the amount over 500,000	33,000+4% of the amount over 500,000
From 1,000,001 to 2,500,000	2,000	5,000	12,500+0.5% of the amount exceeding 1,000,000	53,000+2% of the amount exceeding 1,000,000
From 2,500,001 to 5,000,000	3,000	10,000	20,000+0.3% of the amount exceeding 2,500,000	83,000+1.5% of the amount exceeding 2,500,000
From 5,000,001 to 10,000,000	4,000	15,000	27,500+0.2% of the amount over 5,000,000	120,500+0.8% of the amount over 5,000,000
From 10,000,001 to 20,000,000	5,000	20,000	37,500+0.1% of the amount over 10,000,000	160,000+0.4% of the amount over 10,000,000
From 20,000,001 to 50,000,000	7,500	25,000	47,500+0.05% of the amount over 20,000,000	200,000+0.2% of the amount over 20,000,000
More than 50,000,000	10,000	30,000	62,500+0.02% of the amount over 50,000,000 of 7.5% of the disputed amount (up to a maximum of 15,000)	260,000+0.1% of the amount over 50,000,000
Registration fees for conciliation & arbitration cases		Dhs 200 (non-refundable)		
Complaints dealt with by the Chamber's Administrative Apparatus		Dhs 200		

Charges at the Chamber of Commerce

Rates for the use of the Dubai Chamber of Commerce & Industry's Facilities				
Name of the Hall	Area	No. of Seats	Location	Daily Rent
Exhibition Hall	1,000 sq.m		Ground Floor	Dhs 10,000
Conference Hall	-	200	Floor/ 13	Dhs 5,000
Auditorium	-	700	First Floor	Dhs 20,000

* A discount of 10% is given on the above rates if the premises are hired for three consecutive days, a 15% discount for a week and 20% for over a week.

DCCI Membership Fees - in Dirhams	
National Establishments and Companies:	**Annual Fee**
Agriculture and fishing activities	500
Mining and exploitation of natural resources and all activities related to oil and natural gas	2,500
Conversion industries	1,000
Energy production and distribution	2,000
General contracting for civil installations and the construction of buildings seven or more storeys high	2,500
Contracting for buildings of four floors or less	1,500
Contracts for preparing building sites and finishing work, general trading, commercial agents	1,000
Middlemen and agents on commission	2,000
Consumer complexes, co-operative societies and department stores	2,000
Special offices for commercial representation and liaison	3,000
Simple trade activities	500
(grocery stores, greengrocers and shops selling livestock, consumer and other goods)	
Repairing vehicles, gadgets, machines and equipment	1,000
Two-star hotels and above	3,000
One-star hotels and lower, and short stay houses	2,000
Restaurants, food and beverage shops	1,000
Transport, land freight and storage	1,500
Sea and air freight and travel agents	2,000
Transport-related services	1,500
Communications and postal services	1,500
Banking, financing, financial and monetary establishments	3,000
Buying and selling foreign currency and travellers' cheques	2,000
Insurance services and agents	3,000
Insurance support services	2,000
Real estate services and renting machines and equipment	1,500
Renting machinery and household and personal goods	1,000
Computer activities, studies, development, business services (legal, accounting, engineering, consultancy, managerial, economic and other business services)	1,000
Educational, medical, health and social services	1,000
General cleaning services and the cleaning of buildings	1,000
Producing films and programmes for radio and cinema, advertising and news services	1,500
Culture, sports and entertainment	1,000
Personal and household services (washing and cleaning, barbers, beauty saloons, tailors)	1,000
Offices of government representatives and branches of international and regional organisations and associations	1,000

JAFZA Fees

JAFZA Administration Charges

Charges for processing Licences and Permits	US$	Dhs
All types of Licences	954	3,500
Revision of Licences (activity)	954	3,500
Revision of Licences (other than activity)	136	500
Registration of FZE	2,725	10,000
Sub-lease fees	2,725	10,000
Issue of Building Permit (per square metre of developed floor space	0.82	3
(Facilities other than buildings will be quoted separately)		

Installation charges for telecommunications		
(All costs billed by ETISALAT as the supplier)	US$	Dhs
Telephone	68	250
Telex /fax	245	900
Fax	41	150
Attendance of ETISALAT per application	27	100
Provision of PO Box by General Post Office (inc. service charge)	57	210

Dubai Chamber of Commerce Charges	US$	Dhs
Registration & Membership Renewal:		
A. Trading, Industrial & Service Licences	817	3,000
B. National Industrial Licences	545	2,000
C. National Industrial Licences if a partner is a foreign company	817	3,000

Certificates of Origin		Authentication Charges	
Value of the goods (in Dhs)	New Charges (in Dhs)	Categories	Charges (in Dhs)
Less than 1,000	20	Signature Verification	50
From 1,001 – 5,000	40	NCV & Samples	50
From 5,001 – 20,000	60	Used Personal Effects	50
Fom 20,001 – 40,000	80	True Copies	30
From 40,001 – 100,000	100	Exchange of C.O.	30
From 100,001 – 500,000	200	Amendments of all kinds	30
Over 500,000	300	Authentication of the Documents after the original copy	10

Special Approval Activities

Activity	Parties from which the Special Approvals are Required
Pharmacies	Ministry of Health
Cassette and video shops, bookshops, publishers and printers, newspapers, magazines, advertising and translation offices, news agencies, party contractors, calligraphic and painting shops, photographic studios, computer software importers, satellite receivers (dishes), and TV decoders	Ministry of Information & Culture
Explosives and arms	Ministry of Defence
Financial investment companies and banking, financial investment consultancies	UAE Central Bank
Private clinics	Department of Health & Medical Services (Medical Committee)
Contracting companies, engineering consultants and technical services related thereto and laboratories	Dubai Municipality (Technical Committee)
Travel agents and air cargo offices. Carriage by sea of passengers and cargo and freight forwarding & clearing offices	Department of Civil Aviation
Advocate and Legal consultants and gas stations	Ruler's Office
Nurseries, private schools and institutes	Ministry of Education (Private Education Department)
New industrial projects and expansions	Ministry of Finance & Industry (Industrial Department)
Chartered accountants and auditors	Ministry of Economy & Commerce

Activities that require Special Approval

Chapter Five

Employment Issues

Introduction

Dubai is a youthful and growing economy which has not been hindered by the recession witnessed recently by many of the world's leading economies. Employment opportunities are available in nearly every sector, particularly the oil, transport and communications sectors. Accountants and doctors are in demand and there are vacancies for high class managers. The emergence of Dubai as a major tourist centre has also created a number of opportunities in the hotel and leisure industries.

However, despite the opportunities available to expatriates, there have been recent moves led by the government to increase the employment of UAE nationals and thus decrease the UAE's dependence on the expatriate work force. The scheme which is commonly known as the 'Emiratisation Plan' involves, among other things, the encouragement of companies and establishments in the country to employ nationals in all sectors, particularly in medium to high positions as well as provide them with quality training and education.

The sections below aim to give the reader an overview of the labour practices in Dubai, the formalities a new business will need to complete regarding labour aspects and a summary of the UAE Labour Law.

The Ministry of Labour & Social Affairs   www.mol.gov.ae

▲ The Ministry of Labour & Social Welfare is located in Deira.

The Ministry of Labour and Social Affairs (the Ministry) is the main body responsible for the regulation of manpower recruitment. Many of the procedures a business will need to complete regarding labour matters will, therefore, involve a fair amount of dealings with the Ministry.

In order for a new business to recruit employees, it will need to register itself or open a file with the Ministry and obtain a card which is known as the firm or establishment card. Following the submission of the application, the Ministry is responsible for inspecting the business premises to ensure that the workplace is large enough for the size of the manpower required by the employer. Once the Ministry is satisfied with the inspection and the necessary documents have been submitted, a firm card is issued to the company or establishment.

The purpose of such registration is to enable the Ministry to maintain a record of the staff employed by businesses. By obtaining a registration card, a business is able to apply for employment visas. The procedures for registering a business with the Ministry are discussed below.

Apart from registering businesses, the Ministry is also responsible for other aspects relating to the health and safety of the employees. These include conducting random inspections of business premises and equipment. In addition, where an establishment or a company involves steam boilers, pressure receptacles, cranes, towing machines, tools and other accessories, it may be inspected by the Ministry in the interests of safety.

Legally speaking, the Ministry plays an important role in settling labour disputes between employees and their employers. A majority of such disputes are settled by the Ministry rather than the court. It is worth noting that all disputes between employers and their employees must first be filed with the Ministry. If either of the parties is not satisfied with the Ministry's recommendations it may go to the court within two weeks of the date the recommendations are made. The Ministry does not act in a judicial capacity but aims to expedite labour related claims by reaching amicable settlements.

As was discussed in Chapter 2, in order to work in the UAE one must be sponsored. The transferring of one's sponsorship is subject to a number of conditions and requirements. However, the Ministry often handles sponsorship transfers without requiring the individual to leave the country.

Working Hours

The working hours for local businesses are usually split. That is they work from 8.00 am to 1.00 pm and then from 4.00 pm to 7.00 pm. However, many businesses now operate a single or straight shift system where employees work from 9.00 am to 1.00 pm and then again from 2.00 pm until 6.00 pm. The weekend generally starts on Thursday at 1.00 pm with Friday as the only complete day off. However, some firms, particularly international firms, have a two-day weekend on Fridays and Saturdays.

Salaries and Packages

Salaries and employee packages tend to vary from industry to industry although there is no maximum or minimum salary requirement in Dubai. Unlike some countries, pay packages in the UAE are divided into a basic salary and other allowances. The basic salary is a monthly lump sum paid to an employee and excludes any of the allowances the employee may be offered such as accommodation, car and travel allowance. The total salary on hand consists of both the basic salary and any or all allowances paid to an employee. The legal significance between the basic salary and the total salary is that the gratuity or end-of-service benefits an employee is entitled to (if any) on the termination of his employment will be calculated according to the basic salary, rather than the total salary.

In order to provide potential investors with an idea of the average salary packages currently being offered in the UAE, we have provided the 2002 Gulf Business Annual Salary Survey conducted by Gulf Business Magazine below, which illustrates the monthly average salary in US dollars for Gulf Arab national employees, western expatriate employees, Asian expatriate employees and Arab expatriate employees working in a range of positions. The figures are exclusive of housing benefits and include the statistics provided by the above survey for the UAE alone.

UAE AVERAGE MONTHLY SALARY (EXCLUDING HOUSING ALLOWANCE)				
Designation	Gulf Arab National US $	Western Expatriate US $	Asian Expatriate US$	Arab Expatriate US$
CEO/Managing Director/ General Manager of Company with sales of $50M+	16,345	15,294	10,676	14,694
CEO/Managing Director/ General Manager of Company with sales of $25-50M	13,638	12,025	8,919	11,775
Head of Finance	10,871	10,595	7,633	9,845
Head of Engineering	9,642	9,506	6,825	8,756
Head of Human Resources	9,926	9,860	7,361	9,860
Head of Information Technology	9,232	10,360	6,317	9,210
Head of Sales/Marketing	9,535	9,535	6,375	9,535
Executive Secretary/PA	2,630	2,995	2,051	2,759
Accountant	4,258	4,280	3,137	4,184
Sales Engineer	3,511	3,699	2,669	3,395
Systems Analyst	3,409	3,409	2,685	3,123
Computer Programmer	3,052	3,052	2,359	2,923
Banking - Branch Manager	6,989	5,978	5,519	6,038
Banking - Treasury Manager	8,662	9,511	6,497	7,247
Banking - Retail Personal Banking Manager	8,512	9,511	6,247	7,097
Advertising - Creative Director	7,737	7,837	5,424	7,157
Public Relations - Account Director	7,287	7,387	4,874	6,367
Publishing - Editor	6,539	6,639	4,195	5,824
Construction - Project Manager	4,925	6,846	4,267	5,684
Hotels - General Manager	6,219	6,319	4,570	5,710

Source: 2002 Gulf Business Annual Salary Survey, www.gulfbusiness.com

Recruitment Agencies

A list of recruitment agencies is provided in the directory on CD. There are a number of employment agencies in Dubai that offer recruitment consultancy. The agency takes its commission from the registered company once the position has been filled. No fees are levied on candidates for this service.

Personal Taxation

As discussed in Chapter 3, there is no personal income tax payable in Dubai and the only tax payable by persons living and working in Dubai is a 10% Municipality Tax which is payable on food purchased in hotels. Hotels also charge an additional 15% service charge on the services they provide including room rates.

Labour Requirements for New Businesses

Registration with the Ministry of Labour & Social Affairs

If a business organisation intends to employ staff and fulfill the necessary procedures for doing so, such as the immigration requirements, it must open a file at the Ministry of Labour and Social Affairs and obtain an establishment/labour card. It should be noted that for a manager to obtain residency it is a prerequisite that the business is registered with the Ministry:

→ Procedure to Register a Business with the Ministry

In order to register a business with the Ministry, the local partner, the national agent or the duly authorised representative of the business should submit the following to the Ministry

1 • Copies of the trade licence including the page showing the partner's names
2 • Copies of the local partners' passports
3 • Copies of non-local partners' passports and visas
4 • Copies of the civil registration for local partners
5 • Immigration card forms. Note that the Ministry computer generates this form. The fees are Dhs1000
6 • Computer data form.
7 • Power of attorney for any non-partner authorised signatory, who must be under the same company's sponsorship
8 • Letter of undertaking (in case the sponsor is a services sponsor)
9 • Copy of the memorandum of association
10• Copy of the trade license
11• Copy of the Immigration card from Immigration Department

Provided the correct documents have been submitted and the appropriate fee paid, the Inspection Section at the Ministry will inspect the applicant's business premises to ensure that the following conditions have been satisfied:

a • No employees are present at the premises and that only the national agent, the local partner or the duly authorized representative of the business are present.

b • The applicant's signboard is placed on the floor at the building entrance and on the applicant's office door.

The national agent's and/or local partner's representative should meet the inspector at the Ministry to conduct him to the business premises.

The above procedure should take an average of ten days to complete.

Representative Cards

As local partners and/or national agents are unlikely to have sufficient time to deal with the Ministry regarding labour matters, it is common for most businesses in Dubai to appoint a representative from their staff to deal with such matters. However, in order to conduct dealings on behalf of a business with the Ministry of Labour and Social Affairs, it is first necessary for one to obtain what is known as a representative card. A representative card allows the holder to deal with the Ministry regarding labour issues on the business's behalf, without which only the business's sponsor, local partner or manager may conduct such dealings.

→ Procedure to obtain a Representative Card

A representative card can be obtained by filing the following with the Ministry:

1 • Two copies of the prescribed application form, typed in English and Arabic. The application should be filled in and signed by the authorized signatory of the business who will take full responsibility for its contents. The application must confirm that the intended representative is a literate adult, able to speak and write Arabic working under the applicant's sponsorship, is employed by the applicantand is a legal resident of the UAE.

2 • Paid PRO card form. Note that the Ministry computer generates this form. The fees are Dhs 400 and the card is valid for 2 years.

3 • Copy of the trade licence

4 • Copy of the Immigration Card

5 • Letter from the company confirming that the representative is an employee

6 • Copy of representative's passport

7 • Copy of the representative's labour card

8 • Two passport size photographs

9 • The expired representative card (if any).

The representative card will automatically terminate in the event of the representative's dismissal or resignation from employment, the cancellation of his residency or his conviction of a crime relating to honour or honesty. It should be renewed every two years, through the same procedures and payment of the appropriate fee (currently Dhs 410).

It is necessary for the representative to present his representative card to officials at the Ministry of Labour and Social Affairs every time he makes an application or inquiry at the Ministry.

Employment Visas

A non-UAE national may only be employed after the approval of the Labour Department. An employment visa should be obtained in accordance with the procedures of the Ministry and the immigration authorities. The following conditions must be satisfied:

1 • The employee should have at least secondary school certificate (this condition does not apply to Arab nationals)
2 • The employee must be skilled or possess educational qualifications needed by the country.
3 • The employee must have entered the country legally and have satisfied the conditions prescribed in the country's residency rules.
4 • The Labour Department will not approve the recruitment of non-nationals until they are satisfied that there are no unemployed nationals who are able to perform the required jobs.

→ Procedure to Obtain an Employment Visa

As discussed in Chapter 2, an application for an employment visa is made to the relevant immigration authorities after the approval of the Ministry has been obtained to employ the individual (where applicable) by submitting the prescribed visa application form together with:

1 • A copy of the establishment card of the company
2 • A copy of the employer's trade licence
3 • A copy of the immigration card.
4 • The prospective employee's university certificates (notarized by the UAE Embassy abroad and the Ministry of Foreign Affairs in the UAE)
5 • The appropriate fee (currently Dhs 200).
6 • Paid employment visa application form. Ministry computer generates this form, which needs to be completed by typewriter. Fees are Dhs 200 per person at application stage, and Dhs 1000 per person at approval stage.
7 • A copy of the Business trade license.
8 • A copy of the authorized signatories card (Immigration Card) at the labour office
9 • A copy of the authorized signatories card (Immigration Card) at Immigration Department.
10 • An official envelope for fee Dhs. 15. The address and the Immigration Card No. should be typed .
11 • A copy of the employee's passport, including any page that contains renewal of the passport.
12 • One passport size photograph
13 • An attested copy of the secondary school certificate
14 • A map showing the location of the company
*In case of higher standard qualifications the following additional documents are needed:
15 • A copy of the college certificate attested by UAE Ministry of Foreign Affairs, for the following professions:

Doctors, Pharmacists, Nurses, Accountants, Advocates, Consultants, Directors, Vice-Directors

The Ministry of Labour & Social Affairs will receive the documents and issue a receipt. The approval or the rejection will be received by mail. Applications normally take between seven and fifteen days to be processed, as they must be considered by the Employment Visa Committee. This Committee carefully considers the employment needs of the applicant (the employer) and whether those needs can be satisfied by the employment of UAE nationals. If the Committee finds that a UAE national can be employed instead, the application is usually rejected. Nevertheless, if the visa application is accepted, the ministry issues a letter asking for a bank guarantee (for the companies included in the bank guarantee decision). If the company is required to submit a bank guarantee it should submit a bank guarantee of Dhs 3,000 for each approved employee, then the Ministry of Labour issues a letter addressed to the Immigration Department setting out the name, passport number, title etc of the employee (or employees) that has/have been approved to have an employment visa. A fee of Dhs 1000 per employee must be paid. This letter should then be taken and submitted to the Immigration Department together with a copy of the applicant's Immigration Department establishment card, a copy of applicant's trade licence and fees of Dhs 200 for each approved employee.

A photocopy of the employment visa (after being issued by the Immigration Department) should be sent to the proposed employee in his home country and the original handed to the immigration authorities at the airport at least one hour before the employee's arrival into the country.

An employment visa allows the holder to remain in the UAE for 60 days. The remaining immigration requirements should be completed within this period. These are the medical test, labour card and residence permit as outlined in Chapter 2.

The companies included in the bank guarantee decision are:

• Construction
• Transportation
• Readymade Garment Factories
• Oil Field Services
• Maintenance
• Private Schools
• Selling and Importing Vegetables and Fruits
• Garages
• Cleaning
• Tailoring of Clothes and Leather Products Activities
• Simple Handicraft
• Groceries
• Cafeterias
• Restaurants & Cafés and all companies which are not included in this list, but are sponsored by a local agent (service agent)

If an individual has entered Dubai on an employment visa, he must apply for a labour card within 30 days of his arrival. This requires:

1 • A labour card and the prescribed contract of employment forms signed by both employer and employee. A contract is not approved if it is for a relatively simple job and the salary is unduly high (this is to prevent attempts to circumvent the new family visa rules)
2 • A medical report. The employee must go to any government hospital in the emirate in which his employment visa has been issued. He must take a copy of his passport, a copy of his employment visa, four passport size photographs and the appropriate fee (currently Dhs. 500, which is Dhs 200 for the blood test and Dhs 600 for medical card valid for two years)
3 • Labor card and contract application form (no fees for this application, because it is already paid by virtue of approval of visa application). In case of renewal, the fees are Dhs 500
4 • A copy of the medical report. (blood test report)
5 • A copy of the authorized signatories card (Immigration card) at labour office.
6 • A copy of the employee visa, which should display the seal of entering the UAE
In case of renewing the employee's labour card, a copy of his residence visa (from his passport)
7 • An official envelope costing Dhs 15
8 • The original Labour Card (in case of renewal)
9 • A copy of the labour contract (in case of renewal)
10 •Two colour passport size photographs of the employee
11 •A copy of the business' trade licence
12 •A copy of the Ministry of Labour and Social Affairs Establishment Card
13 •A copy of the employee's Passport
14 •A copy of the employment entry permit that has been issued by the Immigration Department
A labour card is valid for three years.

Labour Card for ladies sponsored by relatives (father or husband)

If the proposed employee is a female and is already a resident in the UAE (that is, sponsored by her husband or father), the procedure is slightly different. An application for employment permit (for ladies sponsored by relatives) is made to the Ministry of Labour and Social Affairs by submitting the prescribed application form together with the following:

• A copy of passport and residence permit of the employee and her sponsor
• A copy of the employer's trade licence
• A copy of the employer's Ministry of Labour and Social Affairs establishment card
• A copy of the employer's Establishment Card at Immigration Department
• One passport size photograph of the employee
• The appropriate fee (currently Dhs 200)

The approval of this employment permit (if any) will be sent to the employer by mail, he should pay the fees of Dhs 1000, prepare and submit the application for the labour card for her together with the following:

1 • A copy of her passport and her sponsor's passport
2 • A copy of the employer's trade licence
3 • A copy of the employer's Ministry of Labour and Social Affairs Establishment Card
4 • Two passport size photographs
5 • The approved work permit

This type of labour card is only valid for one year and terminates automatically upon expiry.

The Visa Transference

The Cabinet of Ministers' Decision No. 30 of the year 2001 was issued to state the categories of employees allowed to transfer their residency visa, exceptions from the prohibition of transfer of residency visa and requirements for any allowed or exempted transfer. The general categories that were granted exemptions from the prohibition of the transfer of the residency visa and the requirements for such transfers are dealt with below. These exceptions and terms are from the explanatory note of Decision No. 30 of the year 2001 regarding the transfer of employees that came into force on 19 March 2002.

1 • Engineers holding bachelor's degree in Engineering or more
2 • Medical doctors, pharmacists and nurses with a minimum bachelor's degree in the relevant field
3 • University and higher institute professors with a minimum of master's degree or more
4 • Experts and legal, economic, financial and business consultants holding a minimum of master's degree or the equal to the same. However, for financial experts, a certified public accountant (CPA) certificate will be enough for the purposes of transfer of the visa
5 • Computer programmers and analysts holding a university degree in the relevant field
6 • Experts and technicians working in the field of exploitation and refining of oil and gas and all the related professions
7 • Physical instructors and sports coaches in all fields of sports with appropriate education
8 • Experts and specialist in the field of nautical and air sciences and piloting ships and airplanes with relevant education
9 • Specialisations that include:
    a • TV presenters, reporters, editors, journalists and technicians in the same field holding a minimum of bachelor's degree
    b • Legal translators
    c • Chefs working in first class hotels with specialised certificates and practical experience
    d • Artists, graphic designers and animators provided that their work will be in specialized establishments
    e • Drivers of heavy duty vehicles and light taxis provided that they are allowed to drive such vehicles by virtue of a valid driving licence
    f • Assistant pharmacist holding a diploma in pharmacy and previous experience in the UAE

g • Lawyers and legal researchers provided that they obtained a bachelor's degree from an accredited university

h • Medical and laboratory technicians and nutrition experts holding proper certificates provided that they work in specialised establishments

i • Education experts, including teachers, supervisors and social experts holding a proper degree in these fields provided that they work in specialized establishments

j • Managers with extensive or rare experience being transferred to fields of economic importance for the UAE

k • Agricultural supervisors and specialists with certified university degrees

l • Accountants holding masters degrees or the equivalent of the same such as CPA or Chartered Accountant certificates.

If an employee falls within one of the above categories, he/she is eligible for the transfer of his residence visa provided that he/she meets the following conditions:

1 • To Work with a new employer in the same field as the previous employer or is responsible for the same duties

2 • Holds a valid residence visa stipulated in his/her passport

3 • Has spent at least 2 years with the previous employer

4 • Obtains the approval of the sponsor for the transfer of his/her residence visa and sponsorship

5 • The non-existence of any UAE or GCC nationals registered at the competent authorities and who are searching in the UAE to occupy the same job to which an employee will be transferred.

The explanatory note also provides situations where employees can be transferred regardless of the categories in which they belong and regardless of the requirements stated above. Such situations are:

1 • Transfer from a company or establishment to another company or establishment owned by the same partners of the first one.

2 • If the transfer is due to the transfer of ownership or title of one company or establishment to another in the following cases:

a • The merger of two companies or the acquisition of one company of another whether the resulting company remained with the same trade name or not and regardless of the change to the shareholders of the same.

b • The division of one company into two companies for any reason, for example:

b1 • The division of one company owned by several partners into several companies each owned by one of the partners or more

b2 • The division of one company into several companies, after the death of the owner thereof, whereby each of the heirs owns one or more of the resulting companies.

b3 • The division of a company between partners as in b1 or between heirs as in the above men and the merger of resulting companies with companies already owned by such partners or heirs

b4 • The partial sale of one company to another where such sale includes all the requirements including human resources

It should be noted that once the labour card has been obtained on an employee's behalf, it is necessary for a residence permit application to be made, as explained in Chapter 2. The medical test, labour card and residence permit application should be made within a period of 60 days from the date the employee enters the country, failing which a fine of Dhs 100 will be payable for each subsequent day, until the necessary procedures have been fulfilled.

The Labour Law of the United Arab Emirates

The Labour Law of the United Arab Emirates is mainly contained in Federal Law No. 8 of 1980 on Regulating Labour Relations, as amended (the Labour Law). In addition, there are several Ministerial orders and Cabinet decisions which provide regulations pertaining to the Labour Law. These collectively cover all aspects regarding employer/employee relations in the UAE and are essential reading for any person wishing to set up a business in the UAE.

The Labour Law is applicable to all employees working in the UAE with the exception of those employed in public or government bodies, the armed forces, police and security services, private domestic help and those employed in the agricultural industry subject to certain conditions.

Note: There is at present a draft amendment to the labour law which has been subject to broad discussions at various levels in the country and is in the process of legislation through the Ministry of Justice and the National Assembly.

A brief synopsis of the present Labour Law follows:

Employment Contracts

Types of Employment Contracts

Under the Labour Law, an employment contract may either be for a specific period, that is, a fixed term contract or for an unlimited period. A fixed term contract must, as the name suggests, be for a fixed term with a certain commencement and completion date which must not exceed a period of four years. It may, however, subsequently be renewed should the parties so desire.

An unlimited term contract on the other hand, is essentially one that has a commencement date but no termination date. An employment contract is also considered unlimited in the following circumstances under Article 39 of the Labour Law:

- If it is not made in writing
- Its period is unspecified
- It is a fixed term contract executed in writing and the term has expired but the parties continue to act on its terms and conditions after the expiry without entering into a written agreement specifying a termination date
- The purpose of the employment is to complete work not estimated within a specified time frame or is by its nature renewable and the contract continues after the work is agreed upon.

Contents of Employment Contracts

An employment contract should be drawn up in at least two copies, one for the employer and the other for the employee. Legally, the only provisions which are required to be in an employment contract are the following:

- The wages payable
- The date the contract was signed
- The date the employment is to commence
- The nature of the contract (fixed term or limited)
- The location of the employment
- The duration of the employment (if it is a fixed term contract).

Any provisions in an employment contract which contravene the provisions of the Labour Law are considered null and void, unless they are more beneficial to the employee than the provisions stipulated under the Labour Law.

If the provisions in an employment contract are null and void, this does not legally invalidate the contract as a whole. Rather such provisions are severable from the contract and the remainder of its terms remain valid.

If an employment contract has been altered, it is necessary to file the amended or new version with the Ministry when the employee's labour card is renewed.

Probation Periods

It is common in Dubai for employees to be appointed for an initial probationary period although this is not a legal requirement for employment. A probationary period can be for a maximum period of six months. However, it is not possible to employ someone on probation more than once.

If an employee is working under a probationary period, he may be dismissed for any reason by his employer within or immediately upon the completion of the probationary period without receiving any notice or gratuity from the employer. When an employee has completed his probationary period successfully and continues employment, the probationary period, however, is counted towards his overall period of service.

Records and Files

According to the Labour Law, employers who employ five or more employees must maintain a record which contains various information regarding their employees. The Labour Law also stipulates the type of records which must be kept by those employing five or more employees and those employing fifteen or more employees as explained below.

Where there are five or more employees, the employer must :
a • Keep a file for every employee which includes the employee's name, profession, age,

nationality, place of residence, marital status, date of commencement of service, wage (and changes in pay scale), disciplinary measures, vocational illnesses and injuries and the termination date of service and reasons for leaving.

- b• Keep a leave card for every employee. This should be divided into three parts:
- c• Annual leave
- d• Sick leave and
- e• Other leave.

All leave taken by the employee should be entered on the leave card.

Where there are 15 or more employees, the employer must
- a• Keep a record of payroll, listing:
  - i   • The employees' names according to their recruitment date
  - ii • The daily, weekly or monthly wages
  - iii • Any allowances
  - iv • Any wage for piece work or commission
  - v • The length of service and
  - vi • The dates of leaving their employment.
- b• Keep a record of work injuries.
- c• Keep a display board (known as the Article of Association) at the place of work detailing working hours, weekly holidays, official holidays and the necessary precautions and measures to avoid work hazards and fire dangers. The Article of Association and any amendments thereto must be approved by the Labour Department.
- d• Keep records and documents relating to disciplinary codes and prominently display in the work place a penalties sheet detailing the measures that will be taken against those who violate regulations and conditions. The enforcement of penalties and any amendments to the penalties should be approved by the Ministry of Labour & Social Affairs.

The above records should be kept at the business's main offices or branches.

Wages

The Labour Law defines wages or remuneration as:

"All payments made to the employee on a yearly, monthly, weekly, daily, hourly, piece work, or production or commission basis in return for the work he performs under the employment contract, whether such payments are made in cash or in kind… and shall not include the cost of living allowance. It shall also include any grant given to the employee as a reward for his honesty or efficiency if such amounts are provided for in the employment contract or in the internal regulations of the establishment or have been granted by custom or common practice to such extent the employees of the establishment regard them as part of their remuneration and not as donations. "

The Labour Law further distinguishes between two types of wages: the basic wage and the total wage. The basic wage is simply the wage specified in the employment contract and is representative of an employee's wage excluding any benefits or allowances whatsoever. The total wage on the other hand includes the basic wage in addition to all and any allowance paid to an employee.

The legal significance between the two as mentioned earlier is that an employee's end of service benefits or gratuity, if applicable, is calculated according to the basic wage and not the total wage paid.

Wages must be paid during a working day at the place of work and in the national currency. Employees employed on a monthly or yearly wage must be paid at least once a month and all other employees must be paid at least once every fortnight. Employers should keep in mind that the non-payment of an employee's wages may constitute a ground for the employee to validly terminate his contract of employment.

There is as yet no minimum wage requirement in the UAE.

Working Hours

The maximum working hours permissible under the Labour Law for adult employees is eight hours per day or 48 hours per week. However, those employed in certain jobs such as hotel staff, guards, restaurants and in commercial establishments may work up to nine hours per day.

During the month of Ramadan, working hours are reduced by two hours.

Employees are not obliged to work for more than five consecutive hours without receiving a break which must be at least an hour long.

Overtime is calculated according to its duration and whether or not it falls on a Friday. If the work requires overtime, it must be paid and must be equivalent to the wage payable for ordinary working hours plus at least 25% of the employee's normal wage. Overtime payments for work between the hours of 9.00 pm and 4.00 am are equivalent to the ordinary wage plus at least 50% of that wage. As the legal weekly holiday for all employees is Friday, an employee required to work on a Friday is entitled to either a day off or his basic wage plus at least 50% of the basic wage. In addition, employees cannot be required to work on two successive Fridays.

Overtime should not exceed two hours per day, unless it is necessary to prevent substantial loss or a serious accident or to remove or reduce its effect.

It should be noted that the provisions of the Labour Law on working hours do not apply to the following :

1 • Persons in high positions of a managerial or supervisory nature, if such persons enjoy the same authority over employees as an employer (such as, senior managers, lawyers, accountants and other professionals).
2 • The crew of naval ships and maritime employees who enjoy special privileges, because of the nature of their work with the exception of dock workers engaged in loading and unloading and other related operations.

Leave

Under the Labour Law an employee is entitled to various types of leave. The general rule is that an employer must grant the employee the leave he is entitled to or pay him a sum in lieu of it. The leave an employee has, as of right, are discussed below.

National Holidays

Under Article 74 of the Labour Law, employees are entitled to an official holiday with full wage on the following occasions:

Dates of Holidays till 2006			
Hijrah New Year	1 Muharram 1424 4 March 2003	1 Muharram 1425 21 Feb 2004	1 Muharram 1426 10 Feb 2005	1 Muharram 1427 30 Jan 2006
Prophet's Birthday	12 Rabi'A. 1424 13 May 2003	12 Rabi'A. 1425 1 May 2004	12 Rabi'A. 1426 21 April 2005	12 Rabi'A. 1427 10 April 2006
Al Isra'wa Al Miraj	27 Rajab 1424 23 Sept 2003	27 Rajab 1425 11 Sept 2004	27 Rajab 1426 1 Sept 2005	27 Rajab 1427 21 Aug 2006
Eid Al Fitr	1 Shawwal 1424 25 Nov 2003	1 Shawwal 1425 13 Nov 2004	1 Shawwal 1426 3 Nov 2005	1 Shawwal 1427 23 Oct 2006
Arafat Day	9 Thu Hijah 1424 31 Jan 2004	9 Thu Hijah 1425 19 Jan 2005	9 Thu Hijah 1426 9 Jan 2006	9 Thu Hijah 1427 29 Dec 2006
Eid Al Adha	10 Thu Hijah 1424 1 Feb 2004	10 Thu Hijah 1425 20 Jan 2005	10 Thu Hijah 1426 10 Jan 2006	10 Thu Hijah 1427 30 Dec 2006

National Day which falls on 2nd December and the Gregorian New Year's Day 1st Jan are National Holidays as well. If it is necessary for an employee to work on any of the official holidays stipulated under the Labour Law or a rest day, the employee is entitled to full or partial pay, and he must be allowed an equal number of days off together with payment of 50% of his basic wage. If the employee does not receive the applicable days off, the employer must pay him 150% of his basic wage in lieu of those days.

The above dates are approximate as they vary from year to year. The newspapers announce the exact date the holiday will fall a few days in advance. It is incidentally up to firms in the private sector to choose whether or not they wish to grant their employees time off during the above public holidays.

Annual Leave

For every year of service an employee is entitled to an annual leave of not less than:
1 • two days for every month of service if the service is more than six months and less than one year or
2 • 30 (calendar) days annual leave if the period of service exceeds one year

Employers are entitled to determine the start of the annual leave and may if necessary divide it into a maximum of two parts. Official and weekly holidays, maternity and sick leave which fall during the annual leave constitute part of the annual leave. An employee is entitled to his total wage during the annual leave.

If an employee's services are terminated or he leaves work after giving adequate notice, he is entitled to his wage for the annual leave which he has not taken. At the end of service the employee is entitled to receive that portion of annual leave which corresponds to the fraction of the year spent in service.

Sick Leave

If an employee becomes ill, he must report his illness to the employer within a maximum of two days. The employer is in return obliged to take steps to ascertain the nature of the employee's illness. Where an employee has been employed for three continuous months (excluding any probation period), he is entitled to sick leave not exceeding 90 continuous or interrupted days for each year of his service. Under article 83 of the Labour Law, sick leave is payable on the following basis:

1• Full wage for the first 15 days
2• Half wage for the next 30 days
3• No wage for the following periods

If an employee's illness is entirely self-induced such as through alcohol or drug abuse, he is not entitled to receive wages during his sick leave. In addition, employers are entitled to dismiss employees who do not report to work after taking their sick leave entitlement.

The employee is, however, entitled to his gratuity in accordance with the rules of the Labour Law. The employee is not entitled to be paid for sick leave during his probationary period.

Maternity Leave

Women employees are entitled to 45 days maternity leave with full pay provided they have served a minimum of one year's continuous employment. The leave may be taken before and after confinement takes place. Where a shorter period of employment has been served, female employees are entitled to 45 days leave with half pay.

Once a female employee has exhausted her maternity leave, she may be absent from work for a total period of 100 consecutive (which includes the 45 days maternity leave) or non-consecutive days without pay, if such an absence is due to an illness preventing her from returning to work and is supported by a medical certificate.

During the 18 months after confinement, female employees are in addition entitled to two breaks lasting a maximum of half an hour each for nursing purposes.

Maternity leave is not deductible from other leave periods.

Other Leave Rules

In addition to the above leave entitlements, an employee is entitled to Haj or pilgrimage leave once during the course of his service. This is without pay and should not exceed a period of 30 days.

An employee is not allowed to work for another employer during any leave period. If an employer obtains evidence that the employee has been working for another employer during leave, the employer can dismiss the employee without notice. An employee otherwise should not be dismissed or given notice during the periods of leave referred to above.

Health and Safety of Employees

The Labour Law contains very detailed provisions on the health and safety of employees at work under Articles 91 to 101 (inclusive). All employers should be aware of these provisions, particularly those involved in the industrial sector.

Discipline

The Labour Law contains a comprehensive disciplinary code which should be observed by employers at all times. It includes the 'tools' or penalties an employer may use in disciplining his work force such as issuing warnings, imposing fines, suspending an employee from work and deducting from his remuneration, and the circumstances in which such penalties may be used. An example of these would be the provision which stipulates that the maximum fine an employer may impose on his employee is five days wages (which presumably is basic wages rather than total wages).

Termination of Employment

Part VII of the Labour Law deals with the termination of an employment contract which is dealt with in the following sections.

Lawful Termination

Under Article 113 of the Labour Law, a contract of employment may be terminated in any one of the following circumstances:

1 • If both parties agree, provided that the employee consents in writing;
2 • If the contract is a fixed term contract and the specified term has expired (unless the contact has been implicitly or explicitly renewed); or
3 • Where the parties have expressed an intention to terminate the contract and the contract is an unlimited term employment contract, provided the appropriate notice period has been given by either of the parties.

Termination by Employers Without Notice

Under Article 120 of the Labour Law, an employer may dismiss an employee without notice in any of the following circumstances:

1 • If the employee has assumed a personality or nationality other than his own or has produced false documents or certificates.
2 • If the employment contract provides for a probation period and the termination has occurred

during that period.

3 • If the employee makes a mistake which causes the employer to suffer substantial material loss, provided that the employer informs the Labour Department of the incident within 48 hours of discovering it.

4 • If the employee has violated instructions for work or work place safety, provided that:
    a • The instructions were written and displayed in a prominent place; and
    b • The employee was informed of them orally if the employee is illiterate.

5 • If the employee fails to carry out his basic duties as provided in the employment contract and has continued to do so despite receiving a written warning that his services will be terminated if he fails to rectify the situation.

6 • If the employee discloses a secret of the employer.

7 • If the employee is convicted of a crime involving honour, honesty or public morals.

8 • If the employee is found drunk or under the influence of drugs during working hours.

9 • If the employee commits a physical assault on his employer or manager or one of his colleagues during work.

10 • If the employee is absent from work, without a valid reason for more than 20 non-consecutive days in any year or for over seven days continuously.

If the duration of a labour contract is for a fixed term and the employer terminates it for any reason other than those indicated above, the employer will be liable to compensate the employee for such termination. The maximum amount of compensation payable is the employee's total wages for three months or the wages due for the remaining period of the contract, whichever is the lesser unless the contract provides otherwise.

Termination by Employees Without Notice

An employee may leave work without notice in any of the following cases:

1 • IIf the employer has not fulfilled his obligations towards the employee as provided for in the contract of employment or in the Labour Law.

2 • If the employee is assaulted by the employer or a representative of the employer.

In such cases, the employer will be liable to compensate the employee for any damages suffered by the employee as a result of the termination.

Termination with Notice

If the contract of employment is for an unlimited term, both the employer and the employee may terminate the employment contract for any legitimate reason (see below) provided they give 30 days notice. There are separate notice provisions in the Labour Law for employees who are employed on a daily basis as outlined below.

Term of Employment	Required Notice Period
6 months to 1 year	1 week
1 year +	2 weeks
5 years +	1 month

According to Article 118 of the Labour Law, the contract of employment will continue to be valid during the course of the notice period and the employee is required to continue working in return for his agreed wage. It is also unlawful for the parties to cancel or reduce the notice periods required under law.

If the employer or the employee fails to give the required period of notice prior to terminating the employment contract, the party in breach will be liable to pay the other compensation known as compensation in lieu of notice. This holds true even where such failure has caused no loss to the other party. Compensation in lieu of notice is calculated as the amount equal to the employee's last received wage for all or part of the notice period.

Termination of an employee's services will be considered arbitrary and improper if:

a • the reason for dismissal given by the employer does not relate to the employee's work
b • the dismissal is as a result of a complaint made by the employee to the labour authorities

or

c • the employee has taken the employer to court and proved his case to be genuine.

In addition to the above, an employer may not terminate the employee's services for health reasons before the employee has taken the period of sick leave he is entitled to and any agreement made to the contrary is null and void.

Post Termination

Restraint of Trade

If the nature of an employee's work allows him to gain knowledge of the employer's clients and/or trade secrets, the employment contract may provide that at the end of the contractual term the employee will not compete with the employer or take part in any business competing with that of the employer. However, for such a provision to be valid, the employee must be at least 21 years of age at the time of signing the contract and the provision must be limited in time, place and nature and should be limited to protect only the legal interests of the employer.

New Employment

If an expatriate employee under a fixed term employment contract terminates his employment for no valid reason before the end of the contractual term, the Labour Law provides that he shall not be allowed to seek further employment, even with the employer's consent, for a period of one year from the date of termination.

Notwithstanding the above, under Ministerial Order No. 13 of 1991 regarding the Organization of the Transfer of Sponsorships for Non-National Employees, non-national employees may transfer from one job to another and thus from one sponsorship to another (see Chapter 2) if they satisfy the following conditions:

a • They fall within one of the following categories:
  - Engineers
  - Doctors, pharmacists and nurses (male/ female) and pharmacist's assistants
  - Agricultural instructors
  - Qualified accountants and auditors, with a master's degree in accounting, CPA or chartered accountant certificate
  - Qualified administrative officials, with a master degree
  - Technicians operating on electronic equipment and laboratories
  - Drivers - licensed to drive heavy vehicles and buses
  - Programmers with a college degree in computer science

b • The new employment title is similar to the previous one

c • The employee holds a valid residence permit

d • The employee has spent at least one year in his previous employment

e • The employee has obtained the consent of his previous employer to transfer his sponsorship as well as the approval of the Ministry of Labour & Social Affairs

There are exceptions to the above conditions. For instance, those transferring from one branch to another of the same company or transferring as a result of the acquisition of the business they are working for to a new owner are not subject to the above rules. Thus, consideration of the labour laws is necessary when expatriate employees are contemplating new employment.

Repatriation of Expenses and References

The employer is responsible for the cost of repatriating an expatriate employee to the place of recruitment (or to any other place agreed upon) at the end of the contract of employment. If the employer fails to repatriate the employee, the authorities will do so at the cost and expense of the employer. However, if the employee is responsible for terminating the employment contract, he will have to bear the costs of his travel if he has the means to do so. On transfer of employment from one employer in the UAE to another employer in the UAE, the new employer rather than the previous employer will be responsible for the employee's repatriation costs.

Upon the termination of an employee's services, the employer must give the employee (if he so requests) a certificate detailing the date of commencement and termination of service, the expiry date, the total period of service, and the employee's last wage and bonuses received.

At the cancellation of an employee's visa all employees will receive a ban seal which prevents them from reentering UAE for 6 months from the date of departure. except for the following categories: Doctors, nurses, engineers, pharmacists, managers, programmers, lawyers & consultants.

Gratuity/ End of Service Benefits

The Basic Rule

When an employee completes a period of continuous service that is longer than one year, he is entitled to gratuity calculated as follows:

1 • 21 days' basic wages for every year of the first five years of service
2 • 30 days' basic wages for every year thereafter, provided that the gratuity does not exceed two years wages in total.

Gratuity is calculated according to the last basic wage paid to the employee and is payable on the termination or the expiry of the contract of employment. The employee will be entitled to gratuity for any fraction of a year of service provided he has completed at least one year of continuous service.

The amount of gratuity payable to an employee (if any) will depend on various factors including the employee's length of continuous employment, whether his contract of employment was for a fixed term or an unlimited term, and whether or not adequate notice was provided by the party terminating the employment.

Employees Who Resign

There are different gratuity rules applicable where an employee resigns from his employment under Article 137 of the Labour Law. Employees working under unlimited term contracts who resign are entitled to gratuity in accordance with the length of time they have spent in employment as follows (provided they give adequate notice):

Length of Continuous Employment	Gratuity Payable
1 to 3 years	One third of the amount provided as discussed above.
3 to 5 years	Two thirds of the amount as discussed above.
More than 5 years	Full gratuity

However, employees working under fixed term contracts and who resign are not entitled to gratuity pay unless their period of continuous service exceeds five years.

Employees Who are Dismissed Without Notice

Under Article 139 of the Labour Law, no gratuity is payable to the following employees:

a • Those dismissed for one of the reasons stated under Article 120 of the Labour Law, or those who leave their employment to avoid being dismissed for the reason in question
b • Those working under unlimited term contracts who terminate their employment voluntarily without providing the appropriate notice for reasons other than those stipulated under Article 121 of the Labour Law
c • Those working under fixed term employment contracts who terminate their employment contracts   voluntarily without giving the appropriate notice, and their period of continuous service is less than five years. In such cases they are liable to pay

their employers compensation amounting to a month and a half's basic wages or the wages for the remainder of the contract, whichever is less unless there is a provision in the contract of employment to the contrary.

Accidents at Work

The Labour Law contains detailed provisions relating to compensation for employees who suffer accidents or occupational diseases at work, in addition to an employer's obligations regarding injuries sustained by his employees during work.

Although the relevant rules will not be addressed in this book, it is necessary for employers to know that they should report directly to the Police and the Labour Department all incidents regarding any of their employees who suffer an accident or an occupational disease at work. The Police will investigate such matters and report back to the Labour Department. In some cases, the employer will be liable to pay the employee compensation for the medical treatment necessary to remedy the situation.

Chapter

Housing and Accomodation

Six

Hotels

▲ Hotels and apartment blocks lit up along the Creek

▲ The Jumeirah Beach Hotel - one of the fabulous hotels in Dubai.

There are over 400 hotels in Dubai, with many more planned, ranging from reasonably priced tourist hotels to luxury five and even seven star properties. Prices range from those costing under Dhs 100 to those with a published price of over Dhs 6,000 per night. Almost all the hotels in Dubai have bars, restaurants and fitness centres which are also open to non-guests. The peak season for hotels in Dubai is generally between September and May (inclusive). Hotel rooms are generally cheaper from May to August.

The Dubai Department of Tourism and Commerce Marketing (DTCM) maintains a hotel classification system, which gives an internationally recognised star rating system to hotels. The DTCM also operates an Internet reservation system for Dubai's hotels on their website. A comprehensive list of hotels together with telephone numbers, fax numbers, websites and e-mail addresses is included in the directory on the enclosed CD.

Serviced Apartments

▲ The Marriott Executive Apartments - linked by the longest bridge connecting two buildings in the world.

Serviced apartments are an economical alternative to hotels for prolonged business and tourist visits to Dubai. Indeed, many firms find it desirable to accommodate their expatriate managers and other senior employees in such complexes. This can be done on a daily/weekly/monthly or yearly basis and there are a number of agencies offering this service.

The advantages of serviced apartments are their low cost (in comparison with hotel rates), the freedom of living in a home and the availability of services such as cleaning, maintenance and room service. Most serviced apartments come fully furnished and bed linen is also provided. They vary from studio rooms to four bedroom apartments. The complexes in which most serviced apartments in Dubai are situated usually provide sports and leisure facilities. In addition, many hotels have serviced apartments within their complexes.

For more information on hotel apartments in Dubai, contact the One Stop Information Centre (04-2230000), Department of Tourism and Commerce Marketing.

A list of serviced apartment complexes in Dubai is also given in the directory, included on the CD.

Flats and Villas: Ownership & Leasing

Ownership of Property in Dubai

There is no specific Federal Land Law in the UAE. Instead each emirate has established its own specific land ownership policies through local orders and decrees and in accordance with its own economic and political circumstances.

Residential, commercial, agricultural and industrial land is currently all held in Dubai by UAE nationals, and in exceptional cases by other GCC nationals. A Dubai policy in the summer of 2002 announced freehold property ownership for people of all nationalities. Since then, buyers have been flocking to the various upscale developments and buying property in record times.

Such residential developments announced to date include the Jumeirah Beach Residence, The Palm Jumeirah, The Palm Jebel Ali, Jumeirah Islands, Jumeirah Lake Towers, Emirates Hills, Dubai Marina and Arabian Ranches. The list is growing. Recently commercial office space too has come onto the market.

The empowering Decree allowing foreign nationals ownership of freehold land, once enacted, will mark a departure from the restricted land ownership policy followed by the Government of Dubai to date.

It is not yet clear whether the open freehold ownership policy will be extended to further residential developments or indeed to industrial or agricultural real estate. These do appear to be one off projects and no general amendments to the Laws have yet been enacted.

Purchase prices in respect of new developments vary; the following chart provides information on a selection of some of the high quality villas and apartments available together with their location and purchase prices.

A selection of Properties available in Dubai (May 2003)

All the following properties are 20 minutes away from central Dubai in different directions.

Complex	Specifications	Purchase Price (Dhs)
Jumeirah Islands www.jumeirahislands.com	4 B/R Villas	1,900,000 – 2,400,000
Jumeirah Beach Residence www.jumeirahbeachresidence.com	Studio Apartments 1 B/R Apartments 2 B/R Apartments 3 B/R Apartments 4 B/R Apartments	275,000 – 299,000 415,000 – 449,000 550,000 – 599,000 699,000 949,000
The Palm Jumeirah www.thepalm.ae	1 B/R Apartments 2 B/R Apartments 3 B/R Apartments	660,000 – 685,000 800,000 – 1,150,000 1,150,000 – 1,275,000
The Palm Jebel Ali www.thepalm.ae	3 B/R Town Home Villas 4 B/R Town Home Villas 4 B/R Garden Home Villas 5-6 B/R Signature Home Villas Apartments	1,870,000 2,090,000 2,860,000 5,115,000 To be announced
Dubai Marina www.dubai-marina.com	Al Majara 1 B/R Suites Al Majara 2 B/R Suites Al Sahab 1 B/R Suites Al Sahab 2 B/R Suites	468,800 865,800 484,800 708,800
Emirates Hills Landscaped Plots of Land - www.emaar.com	12,000 sq ft – 40,000 sq ft.	98 – 150 per sq ft.

The Properties mentioned below have prices and specs as quoted by the builders. while all care has been taken to present accurate information, some of this may have changed subsequently.

Complex	Specifications	Purchase Price (Dhs)	
The Meadows www.emaar.com	3 B/R Villas 4 B/R Villas 5 B/R Villas 6 B/R Villas 7 B/R Villas	From 999,888 From 1,397,888 From 1,397,888 From 1,397,888 From 1,827,888	
The Springs www.emaar.com	3 B/R Villas 4 B/R Villas 5 B/R Villas	From 448,888 From 628,888 – 748,888 From 888,888	
The Greens www.thegreensategc.com	1 B/R Apartments 2 B/R Apartments 3 B/R Apartments	From 188,888 From 348,000 From 478,800	
Arabian Ranches www.arabianranches.com	3 B/R Villas & Townhouses 5 B/R Villas & Townhouses	998,000 – 1,300,000 1,400,000 – 2,500,000	
Gazelle www.emaar.com	3 B/R Villas 4 B/R Villas 5 B/R Villas	450,000 – 600,000 515,000 – 900,000 850,000 – 1,250,000	
Green Community www.unionproperties.com	to be announced for 99 year lease		

Leasing Property in Dubai: The Common Practice

Expatriates may rent or lease property in Dubai. Details of properties available for rent usually appear in the classified sections of the daily newspapers. Rents are always quoted for the year, unless otherwise stated. There are also relocation specialists who handle all relocating aspects ranging from housing matters to arranging schooling for children for both companies and individuals moving to Dubai from abroad.

There are currently no written standards or regulations regarding the leasing of property in Dubai. Property in Dubai is generally let on an annual basis. There are different payment systems depending on who the landlord is and whether or not the property is being let through estate agents, which is usually the case.

The tenant will normally be required to pay the full year's rent in advance by giving one current and up to three post-dated cheques. For properties in high demand, the landlord usually requires two cheques, the first payable on the signing of the tenancy contract and the second payable six months later.

To take out a lease personally you need to be a resident. The real estate agent will need a copy of your passport and visa, a no objection letter (NOC) from your company, a copy of your salary certificate and an initial signed rent cheque (plus up to three post-dated cheques covering the remaining period).

To rent through your company, you require a copy of the company trade licence, a passport copy of whoever is signing the rent cheque, along with the rent cheque.

Some of the deposits that are normally required when renting or leasing a property in Dubai.

Security Deposit

Some landlords require a security deposit against material damage that may be caused to the apartment or villa being rented and/or any appliances provided by the landlord of the property. This is refundable. Various factors determine the amount of the security deposit payable, such as the size of the property, its price and whether any appliances are being provided by the landlord. Generally, however, the deposits required for apartments range from Dhs 1,000 to Dhs 3,000 and are payable in advance. In the case of villas, the deposit required is normally between Dhs 3,000 and Dhs 10,000. In some cases, particularly when the property is luxurious and up-market, the landlord may require a security deposit of up to 10% of the property's annual rent.

Service Charges or Maintenance Fee

In the case of flats, some landlords request a non-refundable payment of 5% of the annual rent (one-off payment) as service or maintenance charges per annum. Other landlords include such charges and at times water and electricity charges in the rent itself.

DEWA Deposit

In addition to the security deposit, there is another (refundable) deposit payable in advance to the Dubai Electricity & Water Authority (DEWA). This deposit is adjusted towards any water and electricity bills which are outstanding at the end of the tenancy contract and is Dhs 2,000 for villas and Dhs 1,000 for apartments and fully refundable on cancellation of lease.

Estate Agent's Commission

If the property has been let through an agent, the agent's commission which is usually 5% of the annual rent and a one-time payment will also have to be paid on signing the tenancy contract.

Tenants should note that if they terminate the contract prematurely, the full rent becomes payable. Considering that it is virtually impossible to stop the payment of a cheque in Dubai, the tenant should select his residential property carefully. As soon as the tenancy contract has been signed and the cheques delivered, the tenant is fully bound to the tenancy contract for the full term of the agreement and to the payment of the estate agent's commission where applicable. It is possible to negotiate shorter terms with the real estate agents, but this will generally result in higher rents.

Municipality (Property) Tax

This is an annual payment of 5% of the rent of a property payable to the Dubai Municipality and is further detailed on page 216.

Depending on the location, standard and size of the flat or villa in Dubai, the average annual rentals tend to be approximately as follows:

APARTMENTS		VILLAS		
No of Bedrooms	Annual Rent (Dhs)	No of Bedrooms	Annual Rent (Dhs)	
1	25,000 - 40,000	2	50,000 - 80,000	
2	30,000 - 75,000	3	95,000 - 125,000	
3	55,000 - 75,000	4	100,000+	

Furnished properties are generally more expensive than unfurnished ones and properties in the Jumeirah area have higher rents than other areas.

Residential Areas In and Around Dubai

The main residential areas in Dubai are Satwa, Jumeirah, Bur Dubai, Karama, Umm Suqeim, Deira, Al Qusais, Al Garhoud, Rashidiya and Jebel Ali Village.

The more up-market areas for villas are Jumeirah and Umm Suqeim, with cheaper options in Satwa, Al Garhoud, Mirdif and Rashidiya. The most popular area for apartments tends to be Bur Dubai, behind the BurJuman Centre and along Sheikh Zayed Road, which is lined with modern skyscrapers. Less expensive options are available in Deira, the old Pakistani consulate area, Satwa and Karama.

▲ The Creek with the two residential areas of Bur Dubai and Deira on either side.

As mentioned, Jumeirah is one of the more expensive residential areas in Dubai and is located between Al Wasl Road (commonly called the Iranian Hospital Road) and the beachfront. This area is popular with expatriates with families particularly since schools based on the British, American and Baccalaureate curriculum are situated in Jumeirah. Most of the residential buildings in Jumeirah are villas, which are more expensive than other parts of Dubai. However, the odd bargain can still be found in Jumeirah too.

Situated well out of town towards Jebel Ali, Umm Suqeim has emerged as a very popular residential area for people who prefer to live away from the buzz of the city centre. Many villa developments have emerged in Umm Suqeim in recent years.

Jebel Ali Village is also popular among those working in the Jebel Ali Free Zone, Dubai Internet City and Dubai Media City as it is very conveniently located. It is approximately a 20-minute drive from Dubai city. Recently the village has been substantially expanded with the addition of a number of apartment buildings like The Gardens, where the prices for apartments are much cheaper.

The suburbs of Al Garhoud, Mirdif and Rashidiya have also grown in recent years, popular with expatriates, families and residents, as villas here are normally cheaper than in Jumeirah and Umm Suqeim.

A glance through the property section in the local newspapers will give you an idea about what is available where, and for how much.

Domestic Utilities   www.dewa.gov.ae

Rented premises will invariably have water, sewage and electrical services installed by the landlord of the property. If not, an electricity and water supply meter can be obtained by submitting the following documents to the Dubai Electricity & Water Authority (DEWA):

①
The completed prescribed application form as supplied by DEWA
②
Permission letter from Dubai Municipality (very old buildings only)
③
Completion certificate from Dubai Municipality (new buildings only)
④
Site plan copy from the owner of the building
⑤
No objection letter from the owner of the building
⑥
Original tenancy contract (and copy)
⑦
Passport copy (including the visa permit page) if the account is being registered in an individual's name or a copy of the company's trade licence if the account is being registered in a company's name
⑧
The security deposit (Dhs 2,000 for villas; Dhs 1,000 for apartments)
⑨
The consumer number which appears on the gate of a villa, where a villa is being rented or supplied by the management office in the case of a flat.

If the property is being let through a real estate agent, it is the agent's responsibility to offer assistance to the tenant in installing water and electricity in the property. The agent should also ensure that all the water and electricity bills have been paid by the previous tenant. We have already mentioned that a tenant is required to pay a refundable deposit to DEWA when renting a property. This deposit covers any outstanding water and electricity dues when the tenant terminates the tenancy contract.

Bills are sent monthly and must be paid within 14 days at any DEWA office, through various banks, or even on the Internet. Those offering this service are listed on the reverse of the bill. If services are disconnected, a reconnection fee is payable.

DEWA main office: next to Wafi City, Oud Metha (Tel: 04-3244444)

The electricity supply in Dubai is at 220/240 volts at 50 cycles. Socket type is identical to the three-point British system. Adaptors can be purchased at any grocery or hardware stores. Tap water is safe to drink, although most people prefer to consume bottled water, which is fairly inexpensive.

There is no main gas supply in Dubai, and gas cylinders are sold in the open market. There is no registration procedure for this, and there are numerous companies providing these.

Domestic Services

Maids can be employed on either a full time or part time basis. If a maid is employed on a full time basis, the employer will be responsible for sponsoring the maid, providing accommodation and paying for a return air ticket home at least once every two years, unless of course the maid is being obtained through an agency, in which case the agency will be responsible for these matters. It is only permissible under the law to hire a part-time maid if you go through an agency registered for this purpose. There are a number of agencies that offer domestic help on an hourly basis.

As domestic helps are exempt from the provisions of Federal Law No. 8 of 1980 on the Regulation of Labour Relations (the Labour Law), they do not have to obtain a labour card in order to be employed nor does the employer need to seek the approval of the Ministry for their employment. Therefore applications for the employment of domestic help are made directly to the immigration authorities on the prescribed application forms provided that the necessary requirements for obtaining an employment visa are met. Unlike normal residence permits, residence permits for maids or domestic help are for periods of one year rather than three years. It should be noted that maids or domestic help can only be employed by individuals resident in Dubai and not businesses. Such individuals will assume the role of the domestic helps sponsor for immigration purposes provided they satisfy the conditions stipulated under Article 23 of the Decree, namely:

❶
Have a monthly salary of at least Dhs 6,000.

❷
Pay an annual amount to the state treasury equal to the annual salary of the help. The help's monthly salary must be at least Dhs 400 in which case the amount payable is Dhs 4,800.

❸
The sponsor has not sponsored a domestic help or a housemaid for one year ending on the date the application is submitted.

❹
The help is not related to the sponsor.

❺
The sponsor resides in the country with his family.

Some embassies require to see the labour contract of a newly appointed maid. It is illegal to share a maid with another household.

Property Tax

All residential properties in Dubai are subject to an annual property tax payable to the Dubai Municipality. The amount of tax payable depends upon the employment status of the tenant. All professional, managerial and other senior employees are charged at the rate of 5% of the annual rent of their property, whereas junior employees are charged at a flat rate of Dhs 300.

Whilst it is the tenant's obligation to pay the property tax, the Dubai Municipality will often collect the tax from the tenant's employer at the time of annual renewal of the employer's Trade Licence.

▼ The spectacular development of the artificial island, The Palm Jumeira, between December 2001 and February 2003

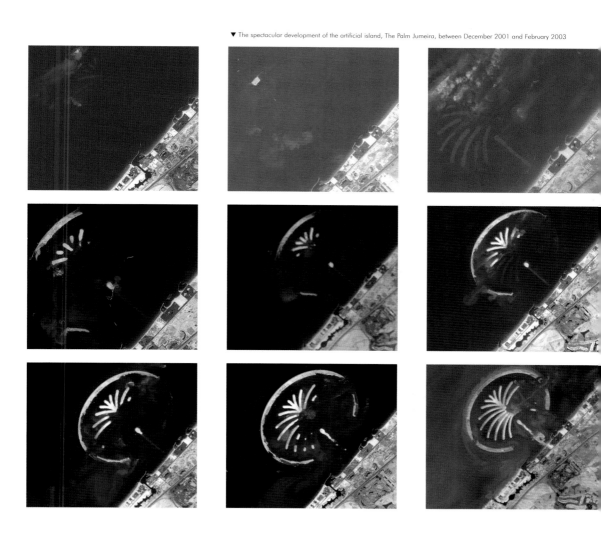

Chapter Seven

Health and Education

Health care in Dubai is very advanced and the services provided by both public and private medical establishments are of a high standard. Visitors to Dubai and residents should have little trouble in obtaining appropriate treatment if they need it, whether privately or from the government-managed hospitals. UAE nationals and expatriate residents are provided low-cost healthcare facilities at the government hospitals and clinics. There are also private hospitals and medical establishments in Dubai and the other emirates. All are required to display a price list in Arabic and English for patients.

▲ The Ministry of Health is located on the Trade Centre Road.

Emergency Treatment

Emergency health treatment is provided free of charge to everyone in Dubai, whether the person is a resident or not. It is not necessary to have a medical card for emergency treatment, although residents in Dubai who do not have a medical card may be charged for follow-up treatment.

General Practitioners

Dubai has a number of public and private hospitals, clinics and diagnostic centres. A list of these is provided in the directory on the CD included with this book.

Hospitals

www.dohms.gov.ae

The Dubai Department of Health & Medical Services, which was established in October 1970, operates four government-run hospitals: Rashid Hospital, Al Maktoum Hospital, Al Wasl Hospital and Dubai Hospital. Dubai Hospital has a number of specialist clinics and is regarded as one of the best medical centres in the Middle East. The Al Wasl Hospital is a specialised maternity and gynaecology hospital. In addition to these hospitals, the UAE Ministry of Health operates the Al Baraha Hospital in Dubai. The Iranian Hospital Dubai is financed by the Government of Iran.

▲ The Dubai Hospital - one of the government run hospitals.

In order to benefit from the subsidised services provided by the government hospitals, with the exception of emergency treatment, residents in Dubai must obtain a medical card as explained below. Contact telephone numbers and addresses of some public and private hospitals and clinics can be found listed on

▼ Dubai's premier aviation college

Chapter Eight

Transport

Road Transport

Dubai has taken great pains to produce a first class road network both in the city and to connect it with the other Emirates. Driving is on the right hand side of the road. This section outlines the different road transport mechanisms and facilities available, useful information about driving in Dubai, as well as the procedures for obtaining a driving licence.

The Dubai Traffic Police Interactive Voice Response line (04-2685555) or Website in (Arabic and English) tells you all you ever wanted to know about fines, speeding tickets, registering vehicles, applying for driving licenses, emergency numbers, suggestions, etc.

▲ One of the elaborate interchanges at the Dubai World Trade Centre.

Obtaining a Driving Licence

The rules relating to driving licences differ from Emirate to Emirate, as all the Emirates can form their own laws and procedures in this regard. However, in conjunction with the local laws, traffic regulations are also contained in a Federal Law, which is applicable to all Emirates.

Two types of driving licenses are issued in Dubai depending on the period of their validity. These are: (a) the temporary driving licence which is issued to visitors to the UAE who are not resident in Dubai, and who wish to drive outside the Emirate of Dubai and (b) the full or Dubai driving licence which every resident in Dubai wishing to drive must obtain. The procedures for obtaining full driving licences depend on the nationality of the applicant.

The Dubai Traffic Department allows licence holders of certain countries to transfer (or exchange) their valid licence to a Dubai licence without having to take a driving test. This is pursuant to the internal regulations of the Department as distinct from the Law and is therefore subject to change from time to time. The validity for this driving licence is 10 years.

The nationalities which are exempted from taking a driving test and can be issued a full driving licence on the presentation of the right documents and the necessary fee are listed below.

Australia	Austria	Bahrain	Belgium
Canada	Cyprus	Czech Republic	Denmark
Finland	France	Germany	Greece
Iceland	Ireland	Italy	Japan
Kuwait	Luxemborg	Netherlands	New Zealand
Norway	Oman	Poland	Portugal
Qatar	Saudi Arabia	Singapore	Slovakia
South Africa	South Korea	Spain	Sweden
Switzerland	Turkey	UK	USA

It should be noted here that some employees of the Government of Iran may exchange their licence for a Dubai driving licence. All other Iranian citizens do not come under this category.

→ Procedure to Apply for Driving Licences

Temporary Driving Licenses

Those entering the UAE on visit or tourist visas may drive in Dubai, provided they hold a valid driving license from their own countries. However, those who wish to drive outside Dubai may only do so if they hold a valid international driving licence or a temporary driving licence, which is issued by the Traffic Department in Dubai. A temporary driving licence can be obtained by all nationalities providing they hold a valid driving licence from their country and a valid visa.

Applications are made to the Dubai Traffic Police Department on the prescribed form along with the following documents:

❶
Passport (original and copy)
❷
Tourist, employment, residence or visit visa (copy)
❸
Foreign driving licence (original and copy)
❹
2 passport size photographs (6cm x 4cm)
❺
An application fee of Dhs 10
❻
If sponsored, then a No-Objection letter from the sponsor or company stamp on the application form.
If sponsored by an individual, sponsor's passport (copy).

However, UK citizens may drive for a period of 30 days without obtaining either a full or temporary driving licence in the UAE. Also nationals of all GCC countries may drive in Dubai with their own national driving licences.

Visitors to Dubai or those on an employment visa who are waiting for residence permit processing may drive private or rental vehicles if they first register and apply with the Dubai Traffic Police. A valid foreign driving licence (any) is needed to apply for a temporary licence.

Dubai residents who have lost their Dubai driving licence, or who have passed all driving tests but the permanent licence processing is being held up, may in the meantime apply for a temporary driving licence with the Traffic Police.

Full Dubai Driving Licences

Once an individual becomes a resident of Dubai, that is when he obtains a residence visa, he may only drive in Dubai on a full driving licence. Full driving licences are valid for a period of 10 years. The permitted driving age in Dubai is 18. The procedure for obtaining a full driving licence and whether the applicant is required to take a driving test vary according to the applicant's nationality.

If you have a valid exchangeable licence, as described above, you may transfer it to a Dubai licence the same day and you do not need to follow any other procedure.

For those resident in Dubai, but without a valid exchangeable licence, applications are to be made to the Dubai Traffic Police Department on the prescribed form (from any Traffic Police office or downloaded from the website: www.dxbtraffic.gov.ae.) along with the following documents:

❶
1 passport size photograph (6cm x 4cm)
❷
Completed application form.
❸
Passport (original and copy)
❹
If sponsored by an individual, sponsor's passport (original and copy)
❺
If sponsored by a company, valid trade licence (copy)
❻
No objection letter from the sponsor or
company stamp on the application form
❼
Eye test certificate
❽
Dhs 100 – application fee

The Dubai Traffic Police, Driving Licence Section is open from Saturday to Wednesday from 07:30 hrs to 14:30 hrs.

If you are not from one of the exempted countries, you are required to take a full driving test with the exception of nationals of Arab countries who can obtain a full driving licence by completing a scaled down driving test, provided they have held their national driving licences for at least three years. It should be noted that one may currently only apply for a full driving license in the emirate one is resident in. Thus residents of Dubai may not apply for driving licences in any other emirate.

Regardless of whether or not a driving test is required, all driving licence applicants must pass an eye test.

Traffic Offences & Fines in Dubai

The Dubai Traffic Police fine drivers for traffic infractions such as speeding, parking illegally, driving recklessly etc. Note that unless you are pulled over and fined on the spot, you will not know you have been fined, nor will you be aware of how many black points you have against your licence until you inquire with the Traffic Police.

Before renewing your vehicle registration, you will have to pay all outstanding fines. The simplest method to determine how much you owe in fines is to log on to www.dxbtraffic.gov.ae before visiting the Traffic Police. Enter your licence plate number (vehicle registration number) or your driving licence number. Ensure you bring the specified amount with you when you go to renew your registration.

No.	Violations	Charges	Points
	Violations		
1.	Driving a vehicle without a permit from the licensing authority	Dhs 200	3
2.	Driving a vehicle with an expired driving license	Dhs 100	1
3.	Driving a vehicle whose type is not in the license	Dhs 200	3
4.	Driving with a license from a foreign country	Dhs 150	2
5.	Driving a vehicle with an expired booklet	Dhs 100	1
6.	Not presenting driving license when requested	Dhs 100	1
7.	Not presenting booklet when requested	Dhs 100	1
8.	Driving a taxi without a permit	Dhs 100	2
9.	Exceeding speed limit (By Radar)	Dhs 200	1
10.	Driving recklessly and causing danger to public	Dhs 200	3
11.	Jumping red traffic signals	Dhs 500	5
12.	Disobeying traffic policeman's instructions	Dhs 200	1
13.	Absconding from traffic policeman	Dhs 200	2
14.	Refusal to give name/address to traffic policeman	Dhs 200	2
15.	Failing to observe traffic signs & instructions	Dhs 100	2
16.	Obstructing traffic	Dhs 100	1
17.	Not giving way to emergency/official vehicles	Dhs 200	2
18.	Not giving way to vehicles coming from left	Dhs 100	1

No.	Violations	Charges	Points
19.	Performing illegal turning manoeuvre	Dhs 100	2
20.	Overtaking on the right or dangerously	Dhs 150	3
21.	Not giving signals when turning or changing lane	Dhs 150	1
22.	Reversing in a dangerous manner	Dhs 100	1
23.	Violating 'No Entry' sign	Dhs 200	2
24.	Stopping vehicle on pedestrian zone without keeping a safe distance	Dhs 100	2
25.	Not keeping safe distance from other vehicles	Dhs 100	1
26.	Parking in 'No Parking' area	Dhs 150	1
27.	Parking on footpaths (pavements)	Dhs 150	1
28.	Parking beside parked vehicles	Dhs 150	2
29.	Parking the vehicle on the left side of the road	Dhs 150	2
30.	Parking which could endanger the pedestrians	Dhs 100	2
31.	Failure to take appropriate action when vehicle breaks down	Dhs 100	2
32.	Not making sure that the car is parked safely	Dhs 150	1
33.	Vehicle modified without permission	Dhs 400	3
34.	Use of vehicle for purposes other than designed for	Dhs 100	1
35.	Vehicle unfit to be driven (not road-worthy)	Dhs 150	1
36.	Driving a vehicle which is not road-worthy	Dhs 150	2
37.	Touting for passengers	Dhs 50	1
38.	Refusal to carry passengers in a taxi	Dhs 100	1
39.	Carrying more passengers than permitted	Dhs 50	2
40.	Not displaying approved tariffs in a public vehicle	Dhs 150	1
41.	Failure to adhere to authorised tariffs	Dhs 100	1
42.	Excess loading or load protruding more than 1.5 metres	Dhs 200	2
43.	Loading a vehicle in such a way so as to cause danger	Dhs 100	2
44.	Driving without number plates or with one number plate	Dhs 200	3
45.	Unclear number plates	Dhs 150	1
46.	Use of horn in restricted areas in a disturbing manner	Dhs 100	1
47.	Driving without wearing medical glasses or lenses	Dhs 100	1
48 .	Not wearing seat belt while driving	Dhs 100	3
49.	Not wearing helmet when riding a motorcycle	Dhs 200	2
50.	Driving a vehicle emitting excessive noise	Dhs 100	1
51.	Driving at night or in fog without using lights	Dhs 150	2

No.	Violations	Charges	Points
52.	Rear and side lights on trailer not provided	Dhs 150	2
53.	Placing signs on roads which may confuse drivers	Dhs 100	2
54.	Driving at speed below specified for minimum speed	Dhs 100	0
55.	Teaching driving without teaching permit	Dhs 200	3
56.	Teaching to drive without 'L' plate	Dhs 100	3
57.	Not staying in lane when must	Dhs 100	2
58.	Entering the road without making sure its safe	Dhs 200	1
59.	Sudden deviation of a vehicle	Dhs 150	1
60.	Differences between number plates for cab trailer	Dhs 100	1
61.	Driving in opposite direction to the flow of traffic	Dhs 200	3
62.	Not giving way to a following car	Dhs 100	2
63.	Dangerous overtaking by truck drivers	Dhs 400	4
64.	Overtaking where prohibited	Dhs 400	4
65.	Vehicles entering the road in dangerous manner	Dhs 400	4
66.	Towing a vehicle or boat or trailer improperly	Dhs 100	2
67.	Leakage or falling of materials from vehicle	Dhs 100	2
68.	Littering road from a vehicle	Dhs 100	2
69.	Use of rotating multicoloured lights	Dhs 100	2
70.	Modification to vehicle without permission	Dhs 100	1
71.	Failing to use internal lights in buses at nights	Dhs 100	1
72.	Not carrying driving license or registration booklet	Dhs 100	1
73.	Driving taxi with an expired sponsorship	Dhs 100	2
74.	Carrying passengers in a vehicle used for learning	Dhs 100	2
75.	Teaching driving beyond permitted time & place	Dhs 100	2
76.	Violating the rules of trade number plates	Dhs 100	2
77.	Teaching driving in a vehicle not permitted to do so	Dhs 100	3
78.	Unfit tyres for driving	Dhs 150	2
79.	Indicators &/or lights not functioning	Dhs 100	2
80.	Absence of red light at the rear of vehicle	Dhs 100	1
81.	Driving a vehicle which causes pollution	Dhs 100	1
82.	Not having vehicle inspected after modification	Dhs 300	2
83.	Leaving vehicle on the road with its engine running	Dhs 100	2
84.	Misuse of parking spaces	Dhs 100	3
85.	Not fixing reflectors to the rear of the vehicle	Dhs 100	2
86.	Fixing indecent materials on the car	Dhs 100	3

No.	Violations	Charges	Points
87.	Failure to write 'Heavy Vehicle Load' on its side	Dhs 100	3
88.	Failure to display excess permit	Dhs 100	1
89.	Failure to attach 'Taxi' sign in appropriate places	Dhs 100	1
90.	Not conforming to specified colour of taxi or 'L' plate	Dhs 100	1
91.	Not conforming to loading & unloading regulations	Dhs 100	1
92.	Opening left door of a taxi	Dhs 100	2
93.	Not wearing specified taxi driver's uniform or unclean one	Dhs 100	1
94.	Heavy vehicle without the vertical exhaust pipe	Dhs 200	2
95.	Uncovered load in trucks	Dhs 100	2
96.	Pedestrians crossing on roads or unmarked crossings	Dhs 50	0
97.	Driving heavy vehicle in prohibited areas	Dhs 100	2
98.	Not giving way to pedestrians	Dhs 100	1
99.	Failing to stop after causing an accident	Dhs 100	1
100.	Parking in front of water hydrants or handicapped zone	Dhs 100	1

Violations with detention		
No	Violation	Period of Detention
1.	Parking in NO PARKING area	Vehicle held in custody for 2 weeks
	For loading or unloading	or fine of Dhs 500
2.	Driving recklessly & causing danger to public	Vehicle held in custody
	Racing or chaotic driving	for two months
3.	Modification of vehicle without permission	Vehicle held in custody for 1 month or
	eg.Tinted glass	fine payment of Dhs 10,000
4.	Not conforming to loading and unloading	First Time - Vehicle held in custody for
	regulations	one month or Dhs 1000 fine
	eg: Taking in more passengers at stations	Second Time - Vehicle held in custody
		for 2 months or Dhs 2000 fine
		Third Time - Vehicle held in custody for
		3 months or Dhs 3000 fine
5.	Carrying more passengers than permitted	First Time - Vehicle held in custody for
	eg: Labour transport	1 week or Dhs 1000 fine.
		Second Time - Vehicle held in custody
		for 1 month or Dhs 1000 fine
		Third Time - Vehicle held in custody
		for 1 month

Source: www.dxbtraffic.gov.ae

Buying a car is easily done in Dubai. Nearly all the international manufacturers have distributors in Dubai and almost all banks provide financing at competitive interest rates, subject to their individual terms and conditions.

In addition, there are a number of second hand car dealers in Dubai who sell good quality cars at competitive prices. The classified sections of the newspapers in Dubai contain details of new and second hand cars on sale.

▲ The Used Car Complex at Al Awir

Alternatively, visit Dubai Municipality's Used Car-Complex at Al Awir, where all the cars have been checked by EPPCO's Tasjeel service.

Anyone in Dubai may purchase a car regardless of whether or not he/she is a resident in Dubai. However, in order to be allowed to actually drive the car in the UAE, it is necessary to register the car at the Traffic Department. Only those with valid residence visas can do so. Companies may only purchase cars if, among other things, they hold a valid trade licence issued by the Department of Economic Development.

Those purchasing a car through bank financing are normally required (by the bank) to hold a valid and full driving licence, a regular and adequate form of income like a salary and a no-objection letter from the employer where applicable to purchase a vehicle. As mentioned above, banks are quite efficient in firming up the financing process.

Car Registration

Once a car has been bought, it is necessary to register it with the Dubai Traffic Police in the Emirate, which has issued the applicant his residence visa. In order to obtain licence plates for the vehicle, the car must first be registered with the Traffic Police. There are no longer any restrictions on the number of cars anyone may register. If you have purchased a new vehicle from a dealer, the dealer will register the car for you. You do not need to test new vehicles for the first two years, though you must re-register it after one year. In some cases, second-hand car dealers will register the car for you.

Car registrations in Dubai require completing the prescribed application form and presenting it with the documents listed on the following page.

❶

The original passport (for inspection only) and a copy with residence visa
(with the exception of UAE nationals who hold a registered
driving licence or a motor vehicle)

❷

A copy of the sponsor's passport

❸

A no objection letter from the sponsor to register the vehicle

❹

A copy of the company's trade licence

❺

A no-objection letter from the sponsoring company

❻

The sale agreement signed at the Traffic Department by the vendor

❼

Proof of purchase agreement (original)

❽

Vehicle transfer or customs certificate (if applicable)

❾

Vehicle Insurance certificate (original, valid 13 months)

Vehicles older than 2 years must be tested on an annual basis. The first step in the vehicle registration process involves testing the car. All testing has been outsourced by the Traffic Police to EPPCO Tasjeel, www.eppcouae.com/retail/tasjeel. There are four testing stations in Dubai where you can have the vehicle tested, then registered with the Traffic Police.

Vehicles will only be registered if they are covered by at least third party car insurance. Car insurance premiums are quite high in the UAE compared with other countries. The insurers will need to know the year of manufacture and may need to inspect the vehicle. Take along a copy of your Dubai driving licence, passport copy and copy of the existing vehicle registration card.

Annual insurance policies are for a 13 month period (this covers a one month grace period that you are allowed when your registration expires). Rates depend on the age and model of your car and your previous insurance history.

Renting Cars

Self-drive rental cars are available in Dubai and most of the major rental agencies are present. For a non-UAE national to hire a car, he must produce either a valid international driving licence or a national driving licence issued in any of the following countries, providing the renter is also a national of the country:

Australia	Austria	Bahrain	Belgium
Canada	Cyprus	Czech Republic	Denmark
Finland	France	Germany	Greece
Iceland	Ireland	Italy	Japan
Kuwait	Luxemborg	The Netherlands	New Zealand
Norway	Oman	Poland	Portugal
Qatar	Saudi Arabia	Singapore	Slovakia
South Africa	South Korea	Spain	Sweden
Switzerland	Turkey	UK	USA

In all other cases, the rental agency will arrange a temporary driving licence as explained earlier. Most car rental businesses will require the renter's credit card or his passport as security against payment of any traffic fines incurred during the rental period.

A list of major rental agencies in Dubai is provided in the directory included on the CD.

Public Transport

For those wishing to utilise public transportation in Dubai there are various options available. Taxis, Buses and Water Taxis, more commonly known as the Abra, are the most popular modes of public transport in Dubai.

Taxis

▲ The Bur Dubai Taxi stand

Taxis in Dubai are fairly inexpensive (meters mostly start at Dhs 3.50) and are in abundance. Taxis can be hailed on most streets and the drivers are almost always able to understand instructions in English. The main taxi company in Dubai is Dubai Transport which maintains a large fleet of metered taxis equipped with radios. They may either be hailed off the street or ordered by telephone (04-2080808). Dubai Transport also operates metered taxis exclusively from Dubai International Airport.

There are also other taxi companies like Metro Taxi, Cars Taxi and National Taxi, all franchisees of Dubai Transport, which operate metered taxis. Some taxis in Dubai however, are not metered and so prospective passengers should negotiate fares in advance. Persons wishing to make longer journeys, including Inter-Emirates travel, can opt for the Central Taxi Stations in Deira and Bur Dubai. Women should note that when using a taxi in the UAE, they should refrain from taking the seat next to the driver.

Buses

Dubai is serviced by an efficient public bus service run by the Dubai Municipality, which operates a very inexpensive and reliable service around town. There is a bus timetable published by the Municipality (in Arabic and English), which contains the various routes available and their timings. Alternatively, there is a toll free number 800-4848 that one can call for enquiring about bus routes.

▲ A Dubai Transport Bus at the airport

Buses operate over 35 routes covering almost all areas of the City from Al Qusais in the north east to Jebel Ali in the southwest and some destinations out of the city. The main bus station in Deira is near the Gold Souq and in Bur Dubai along the Al Ghubaiba Road, near the Plaza Cinema. Buses run at regular intervals from 6am to around 11pm and fares are cheap at Dh 1-3 per journey. Fares are paid in cash to the driver upon boarding. One can also purchase monthly season-passes at nominal rates. Recently, the Municipality has introduced half-hourly luxury shuttle services to Deira and Bur Dubai from the Dubai International Airport for the convenience of those passengers wishing to utilize these services.

Abra

Another popular and cheaper mode of transport is the water taxi, known locally as the Abra, which crosses the creek between Bur Dubai and Deira. Using an Abra can be an enjoyable experience and costs Dhs1 for a round trip.

Abras are small motorised dhows that can seat 20 passengers. About 150 Abras ply on the two routes to and from 4 stations carrying about 15 million passengers annually, as per Dubai Municipality estimates. The cruise across the creek takes less than 10 minutes.

▲ The Abra ride across the Creek - quick and cost-effective.

Air Transport
www.dubaiairport.com

Dubai's location at the crossroads of Europe, Asia and Africa makes it a convenient stop-over for all of the major airlines flying to any of these continents. Most major cities have direct flights to Dubai, many with a choice of airlines.

The Dubai International Airport is rated one of the fastest growing airport in the Middle East, and also currently ranked fourth amongst the world's top international airports. Nearly 14 million passengers use the airport every year.

▲ The Dubai International Airport

An open sky policy has resulted in the Airport being served by some 90 airlines flying to over 120 destinations around the world and involving more than 105,000 aircraft movements annually. The Dubai Government, through the agency of the Department of Civil Aviation has devoted extensive efforts and resources to putting Dubai International Airport on the world map. An ambitious $540 million expansion programme (explained later) has transformed the already excellent airport into a state-of-the-art facility ready to meet the needs of passengers for the next 30 years. Work has already started on an even larger third terminal to service all Emirates flights.

www.ekgroup.com   Emirates Group

---

www.emirates.com   Emirates

The UAE's award winning national airline, Emirates, is based in Dubai. Launched in 1985, and already a world-class airline, Emirates is setting standards in every area with one of the most modern fleets.

Emirates is one of the fastest growing airlines in the world and has received more than 200 international awards for excellence in everything from Cargo to In-flight meals since launch in 1985.

The professional, friendly, multi-lingual cabin crew is drawn from some 80 nationalities and will do everything they can to make

▲ Dubai's famous Airline - Emirates.

you feel at home. All Emirates aircraft are equipped with a personal entertainment system in all classes.

With recent additions of new routes to Perth, Mauritius, Moscow and Cochin, Emirates now flies non-stop to over 60 destinations in 42 countries in Europe, the Middle East, the Far East, Africa, Asia and Australia. Plans are already afoot to fly non-stop to China and the United States of America.

Emirates Group companies now cover almost all major airline travel related areas with well established entities like Emirates Holidays, Galileo Emirates, Al Maha Resort, Arabian Adventures, Emirates SkyCargo, Skywards, Mercator, Emirates Abela Catering, Business Travel International and World of Events.

www.dnata.com   DNATA

First established by the Dubai Government in 1959 with a staff of five, to provide handling services at the newly opened Dubai International Airport, Dubai National Air Travel Agency (DNATA) is now one of the largest travel organizations in the Middle East. Through its various agencies and services, it covers the entire gamut of air traveller and air cargo customer requirements.

DNATA Agencies meet the demands of the air travelling public with a full range of wholesale and retail products distributed within Dubai and through partner travel agencies abroad.

DNATA Airport Services is the exclusive ground-handling agent at Dubai International Airport and through its DNATA Cargo arm, is the sole operator of Dubai Cargo Village and three satellite terminals.

DNATA Passenger Services is responsible for the safety, care and comfort of the passengers traveling via Dubai International Airport and is dedicated to ensuring their rapid, trouble-free progress through the necessary formalities. The adoption of the DMACS multi-access departure control system, which has greatly enhanced the speed and efficiency of check-in procedures, has made a notable contribution in achieving this objective.

Trained Passenger Services personnel are on hand to look after the old and infirm, disabled passengers and children traveling alone. Passengers with bulky purchases are also given special attention. First class passengers, and holders of DNATA Travel Card, are entitled to enjoy the luxurious facilities of the First Class Lounge.

Marhaba Services   www.marhabaservices.com

Marhaba services -"welcome" in Arabic – was first introduced by DNATA in 1991, as an exclusive "welcoming host" service for passengers traveling through Dubai International Airport. This service now contains four main features. The Meet and Greet; the Marhaba Lounge; Marhaba City Stop and Marhaba Express Check-in. All services are available to customers, while corporate organizations whose staff are regular users of the Airport, can take advantage of this Marhaba Service Corporate membership scheme.

The priorities of the DNATA Red Caps staff are the safety of aircraft, the welfare of passengers and the ensuring of on-schedule departure. Their particular role is the proactive anticipation of Airport problems through a continuous process of consultation, coordination and checking.

Dubai Duty Free   www.dubaidutyfree.com

The popular Dubai Duty Free shop at Dubai International Airport has won several awards for the quality of its services and the value for money that it provides. Various surveys have indicated the Dubai Duty Free's enormous popularity among visitors. By way of example, the readers of the International Airline Passengers Association Magazine (IAPA) voted Dubai Duty Free as the best duty free outlet world-wide. Since its creation in 1983, the Dubai Duty Free shop has continuously improved its services and the quality of the merchandise offered to customers. In 1989, Dubai Duty Free

offered passengers the chance to win a luxury car in its 'Finest Surprise' raffle draw and has since given away over 850 luxury cars. The outlet currently registers a turnover in the range of US$ 200 million.

Duty Free shops are located in both the arrival and departure halls, although the extent of the arrivals hall outlet is limited.

▲ Dubai Duty Free - with the 'Finest Surprise' on display

Dubai Airport Expansion

On May 1, 1998 the opening of Terminal 2 of the Dubai International Airport, completed at a cost of US $540 million, marked the end of the first phase of its current expansion programme. The second phase of the programme, which involves an expenditure of US$ 2.5 billion, has already begun with completion expected by 2006.

The main purpose of the project will be to increase the passenger-handling capacity of the Airport by the addition of a third Terminal and two new concourses, but several other existing facilities at the Airport are to be substantially developed too.

▲ The Interior of the the Sheikh Rashid Terminal.

The phase 2 buildings will incorporate the latest design concepts with an emphasis on passenger comfort and safety. Currently, the Airport already boasts a huge variety of facilities including:

A 100-room 5-star hotel on the upper two levels, offering high-quality accommodation

- Restaurants and dining facilities
- Health spa and swimming pool
- Fully-equipped business and conference center
- On the centre section of the concourse a new Dubai Duty Free shopping area nearly four times the size of the previous facility
- Airport fire stations
- A Dubai Duty Free warehouse
- An access road system to the new Terminal with parking for 2,300 cars
- Automated baggage handling systems for all inbound, outbound and transfer baggage
- State-of-the-art laser guided docking systems

Dubai Airport Free Zone   www.dafza.gov.ae

As discussed in Chapter 3, the Dubai Airport Free Zone which was launched in 1996, is a valuable addition to the many free zones currently operating in the UAE. Being an integral part of Dubai International Airport's expansion programme, Dubai Airport Free Zone is located on a 1.2 million square metre airport site and provides a supporting environment for a wide range of businesses, particularly those featuring import and export facilities. The Dubai Airport Free Zone offers extensive incentives to non-nationals, including 100% ownership of a business operating within the Zone.

▲ The Dubai Airport Free Zone

Dubai Cargo Village   www.dubaicargovillage.com

The emergence of Dubai as the transport hub of the Middle East has resulted in the rapid growth of air and sea transport activity over the years. Established in 1991, the Dubai Cargo Village handles all air cargo operations for Dubai International Airport. In 1995, the Dubai Cargo Village was expanded to handle 350,000 tonnes.

At present Dubai Cargo Village handles up to 675,000 tonnes of cargo per annum. However, as part of the Dubai International Airport expansion scheme, the capacity of Cargo Village is to be dramatically increased over the coming years. The expansion project will include storage facilities, offices, workshops, equipment stores and housing for personnel employed at the Cargo Village.

Dubai Airport VIP and Executive Facilities

Those who own their private or corporate jets may benefit from the exclusive services offered at Dubai International Airport for VIP travelers, which include a new passenger lounge, crew briefing and rest rooms, a dedicated check-in area and an operation centre.

▲ The VIP Lounge at the Airport

▲ The Conference Room at the International Airport

As discussed in Chapter 3, Dubai is served by world-class deep water ports for commercial vessels, namely Jebel Ali Port and Port Rashid. The Dubai Ports Authority (DPA), a government organisation formed in 1991, manages both ports. The ports are equipped with the very latest in loading equipment and have significant container terminals.

▲ Port Rashid

Dubai's ports have proved to be extremely popular with the world's shipping lines. Apart from their role as a regional centre, their facilities are used by many lines as a major east/west hub. Dubai is regarded as an ideal discharge point for cargo bound not only for the Middle East, but also for transshipment to North America, Africa, Europe and the Far East.

Port Rashid is located at latitude 25 degrees 16 north and longitude 55 degrees 16 east. Among the services offered by the port are bunkering, catering, crew change services, the supply of labourers for loading and unloading, fresh water supply services and ship repair and maintenance services. Port Rashid also operates storage areas, covered and open. Details of storage charge and port handling rates can be obtained from the DPA Port Tariff Bank. Port Rashid also operates a dedicated cruise ship terminal.

▲ The Jebel Ali Port

The Jebel Ali Port (JAP), which was officially inaugurated in 1979, is located 35 kilometres from Dubai city and lies at latitude 25 degrees north and longitude 55 degrees east. Renowned as the largest man-made harbour in the world and the largest in the Middle East, JAP offers extensive services. These include cold, covered and open storage services for cargo, a fleet of trucks for the transport of general cargo and container cargo both in the UAE and to GCC countries, maintenance and repair services for visiting vessels and a free storage area.

There are five shipbuilding and repair dockyards in Dubai, four of which (including one floating) are in the large dry dock complex operated by the Dubai Dry Docks Company (www.dubaidrydocks.gov.ae). The Dubai Ship Docking Yard (DSDY) at Al Jaddaf (www.jadafdubai.com) operates the other dry dock in Dubai. Originally established for the repair of dhows and fishing boats, the DSDY now offers a variety of services for a variety of vessels including cargo ships, leisure craft and oilfield-related vessels. In addition there is a large container repair workshop, which is situated near the container terminal in Port Rashid and provides a full repair/maintenance service in the free storage area.

▲ The Creek - a major waterway in Dubai

In addition to Dubai's ports, an important and historical aspect of commerce in Dubai is the Dubai Creek. The Creek has developed tremendously over the years and facilitates the loading and unloading of cargo carried by dhows and large vessels from areas like the Arabian Gulf, the Indian sub-continent and the East African ports.

Rail Transport

One of the plans before the Dubai Municipality is to introduce a rapid mass rail transit system in the near future. Relying on a comprehensive study about the increase in the number of commuters between 1997-2017, Dubai Municipality has chosen the Rail Rapid Transit System as a strategic alternative to traditional modes of transportation in Dubai.

The total cost of the project is expected to be Dhs 2.68 billion with construction due to start in 2003 with completion slated in four to six years from commencement.

The proposed project will have two lines - Red and Green, the total length of which will be 50 kilometres with 37 stations. The network will be part underground subway and part elevated/ground-level. The Red Line will stretch from the Sharjah border to Jebel Ali. The Green Line will stretch from Dubai International Airport to Al Ghubaiba, passing through Khalid bin Al Waleed Road. The main station is proposed to be in Al Ittihad Square in Bur Dubai.

▼ Proposed Metro Network

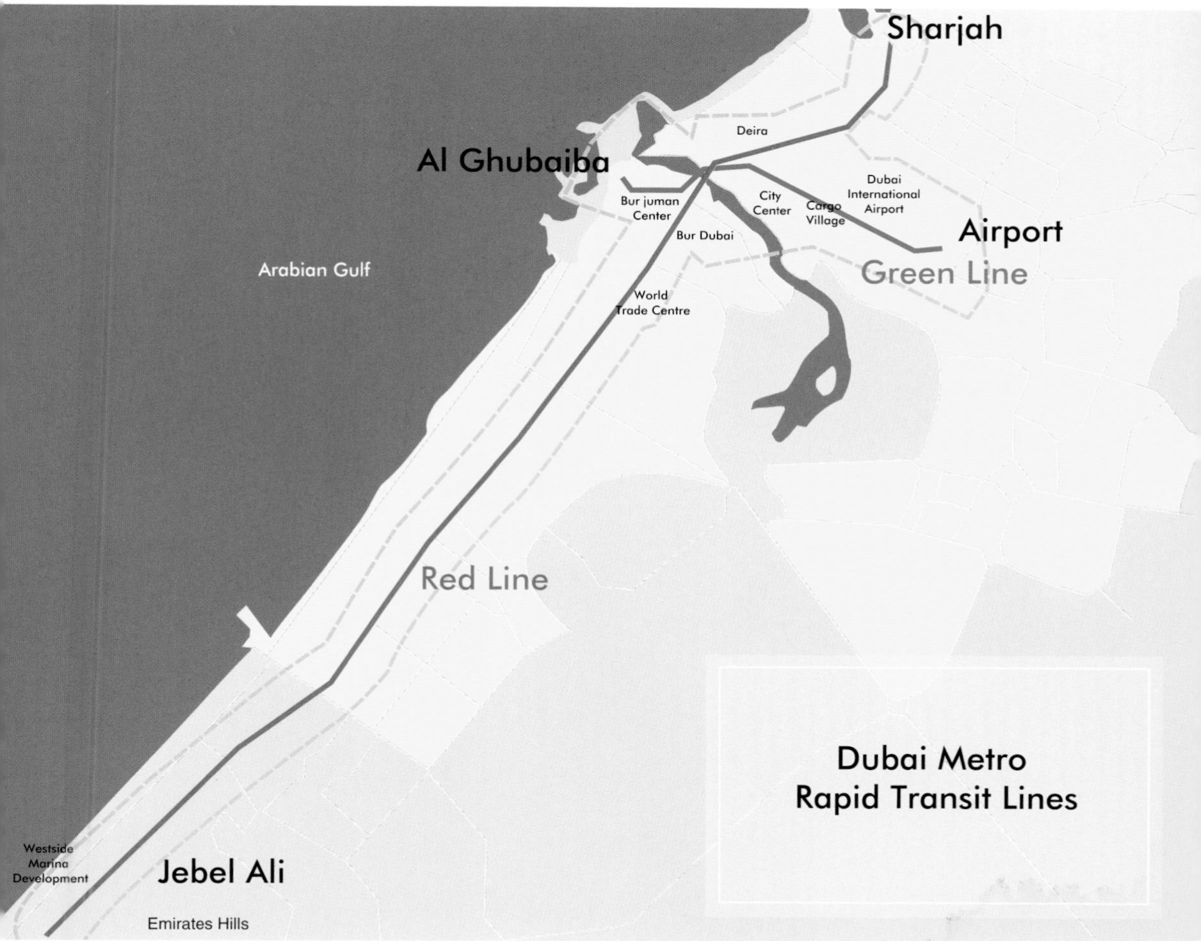

Sharjah

Al Ghubaiba

Deira

Bur juman
Center

City
Center

Cargo
Village

Dubai
International
Airport

Airport

Bur Dubai

Green Line

Arabian Gulf

World
Trade Centre

Red Line

Dubai Metro
Rapid Transit Lines

Westside
Marina
Development

Jebel Ali

Emirates Hills

Chapter Nine

Leisure Activities

Shopping

▲ The Al Ghurair Centre on Al Riqqa Road

▲ The City Centre Shopping Mall in Deira

Dubai has variously been described as a 'shopper's paradise' and the 'shopping capital' of the Middle East. Prices are reasonable and the variety of products available is enormous. As import duties are quite low and there are no local taxes levied on retail goods, many shoppers find that goods are often cheaper here than in their home countries. Visitors to Dubai will be surprised to find so many modern indoor air-conditioned shopping malls. If you want to shop in a more traditional setting, you can visit the many traditional market places, known as 'souks', which are scattered around the emirate.

Shoppers in Dubai, particularly when shopping in the various souks, should be prepared to bargain. Bargaining is a time-honoured tradition here. Shop-owners will often make substantial reductions in the price, especially for cash sales. Although the supermarkets and department stores tend to operate on a fixed price basis, many of the other retail outlets regard bargaining as an essential way of doing business. Shoppers should never be afraid to offer a merchant a price well below his initial asking price, especially in the souks.

Shopping hours in Dubai are from 9.00 am to 1.00 pm and from 4.00 pm till 10.00 pm Saturday to Thursday. On Fridays the shops open between 5.00 pm and 10.00 pm. Many of them remain closed for prayer between 11.30 am and 1.30 pm on Fridays. Shopping malls however stay open from 10.00 am to 10.00 pm on a straight shift. There are also a number of 24-hour supermarkets in Dubai.

▲ The new Mercato Mall in Jumeirah

If you have a problem with a product after purchase, usually faulty goods are more easily exchanged than refunded, so always keep receipts. Ask to see the manager if there is a problem. According to the UAE Civil and Commercial Code, a customer is entitled to recover the price paid on faulty goods. However, you would have to be prepared to take the shop to court. If you have a complaint about a purchased item, you can contact the Emirates Society for Consumer Protection (04-3945132).

Alternatively, the Consumer Protection division in the Department of Economic Development (04-2229922) will assist customers who have a problem.

As mentioned previously, there are many very modern, imaginatively designed and extravagant air-conditioned shopping malls in Dubai. Shopping malls contain virtually every kind of store from card shops and supermarkets to clothes emporia, specialist perfume and electronics shops. Apart from this, there are plenty of entertainment and refreshment facilities like multiplex cinemas and well endowed food courts.

During the annual Dubai Shopping Festival and Dubai Summer Surprises, the larger malls are venues for special events such as concerts, dance performances and magic shows. These performances quite often involve acts from all around the world. The malls also feature numerous raffles during these months, and the prize for the lucky winner is usually a luxury car.

Malls also tend to be more than just a place to buy things as they double up as meeting places for friends and family, thus creating a social buzz about them. A list of shopping centres is provided in the directory included on the CD.

Souks are the traditional Arabian market places. They are well-defined areas of town where the majority of shops are all engaged in selling similar products. The most famous souk in Dubai is the Gold Souk in Deira, located near the Hyatt Regency, where all the shops lining the narrow streets sell gold jewellery at very reasonable prices. There are, in addition, electronics souks in Deira and Bur Dubai, particularly on Al Fahidi Street in Bur Dubai, where electronic goods of all descriptions can be purchased at very reasonable prices.

▲ The Gold Souq in Deira

Other souks dealing in carpets, perfume, spices, and textiles are scattered around Dubai. All types of carpets ranging from expensive Persian carpets to reasonably priced rugs are in abundance particularly in the Deira Tower and many of the hotels and shopping malls. Cosmos Lane off Al Fahidi Street and many of the shopping malls sell all kinds of fabrics from across the globe. Perfume is a rich tradition of Arabic culture, and many souks and shopping malls house the traditional Arabic perfume (known as 'Oud') as well as most of the international brands.

Dubai also has a wealth of vegetable, fruit and fish markets. The fish market next to the Hyatt Regency in Deira, the Hamriya fruit and vegetable market opposite the Dubai Hospital and the fish market in Karama are some of the markets which sell fresh fish, fruit and vegetables.

Sports and Activities

Dubai has come to be regarded as the sporting capital of the Middle East. Recreational facilities are first class here, and a number of international sporting tournaments are staged each year wherein the world's best compete in sports such as sailing, powerboat racing, horse racing, golf, tennis, rugby, snooker and cricket. When the weather is cool, Dubai and the surrounding emirates are ideal for athletes and outdoor enthusiasts, making it hard to imagine that there is a sport or activity that isn't being practised at some point in the year. Traditional favourites are tennis, squash, golf, aerobics, rugby, cricket and hashing, while for the more adventurous, extreme pursuits such as skydiving, rock-climbing, mountain biking and caving are available too.

Water Sports

▲ Kite Surfing - the current craze off Jumeirah Beach

Dubai lies along the clear, warm waters of the Arabian Gulf, which makes it a real paradise for water-sports enthusiasts year-round. With its stunning beaches, clear water and world class water parks, it's no surprise that a variety of water sports are represented in the emirate.

With calm and shallow waters, Dubai is the ideal place for the scuba diver. The Arabian Gulf is also rich in coral reefs and tropical fish. There are a number of clubs and diving centres, which offer courses for both novices and beginners. The UAE is fortunate to have two coastlines; to the west, covering Abu Dhabi, Dubai and Sharjah, etc., and on the East Coast, covering Fujairah, Khor Fakkan, Dibba, etc. Most of the fascinating shipwrecks that can be visited by divers are found on the western coast, while the beautiful flora and fauna of coral reefs can be seen to the east.

If you like fishing, the season runs from September/October through to April. Fish that are common to the waters off Dubai include king mackerel, barracuda, tuna, trevally, bonito, kingfish, cobia and dorado or jacks. Beach or surf fishing is popular all along the coast of the UAE. Fishing charters, for deep sea fishing, can be tailor-made to your needs, depending on whether you want a full day trying for the challenging sailfish, or a half-day trawling or bottom fishing for the various species found in the Gulf.

Some of the most popular water sports in Dubai are water skiing, jet skiing and wake boarding, as the calm waters here are ideal for novices. A number of hotels and clubs organise courses and facilities for water skiers. Jet skis can often be seen parked at the first lagoon between Dubai and Sharjah, near Al Mamzar Beach Park, or near Al Garhoud Bridge, on the opposite side of the bridge to Dubai Creek Golf & Yacht Club. Most are available for hire at approximately Dhs 100 for a half-hour.

A new 1998 law limits jet skiers to within a 500 metre boundary from the shore, with the threat of legal action for exceeding this limit. This is due to the fatal accidents that have occurred in the past.

Since Dubai has a constant, predictable year round wind, combined with calm seas and warm weather, it also provides an ideal setting for the sailing enthusiast. Wind surfers can be rented at most of the marinas and beach clubs in Dubai and the sailing clubs in Dubai offer instruction and rentals.

Land Based Sports & Activities

In addition to the more common sports like tennis, squash, football and basketball, Dubai is popular for a variety of other sports and hosts a number of international competitions and tournaments annually.

The following events are most popular and regular fixtures on Dubai's sporting calendar: Dubai Desert Classic (Golf), Dubai Marathon, Dubai Raft Race, Dubai Rugby Sevens, Dubai Tennis Open, Dubai World Cup (Horse Racing) and the UAE Desert Challenge (cross country motor race).

www.dubaigolf.com   Golf

Dubai has excellent year-round facilities for playing golf, and has come to be known as the golf destination in the Gulf. The facilities include a range of fully grassed international courses, as well as sand courses and mixed courses.

Dubai Golf has a central reservation system for individual golfers and groups to book a round of the game. Their website has all the details or they can be contacted on 04-3475201.

The Emirates Hills 18-hole golf course, a signature Colin Montgomerie course, has been designed to reflect a Middle Eastern environment. Practice facilities include a golf academy, driving range, short game and putting practice areas, a skill-honing 9-hole par 3 course, plus a swing studio with state-of-the-art swing analysis software.

The Dubai Creek Golf & Yacht Club, which also contains a 115-berth marina in addition to other facilities, offers an 18-hole 6,956-yard par-72 course together with a floodlit 9-hole par-3 course. This used to be the venue of the Dubai Desert Classic on the PGA European Tour in 1999 and 2000 and is open to all on a 'pay as you play' basis.

The Dubai Golf & Racing Club, at Nad Al Sheba, offers another grass course which is a nine hole par-32 course situated in the centre of the race track, the home of the Dubai World Cup, the world's richest race meeting. This is the only floodlit 18-hole golf course in the UAE, with golf-playing possible until midnight all year. Coaching and courses are available including one called, 'learn golf in a week'.

The Dubai Country Club has the oldest golf course in the emirate, a sand rather than a green layout with both 9 and 18-hole courses.

▲ The Montgomerie Golf course by Emaar Properties

▲ The Dubai Creek Golf & Yacht Club

A club, which offers a perfect learning environment, is the Emirates Academy of Golf at the Emirates Golf Club. This club was the first grass course in the Middle East, and still sets very high standards. It has two 18-hole championship courses to choose from. This is the current venue of the widely renowned annual Dubai Desert Classic.

The Jebel Ali Golf Resort & Spa has a 9-hole par 36 course that offers golfers the opportunity to play while enjoying the panoramic views of the Arabian Gulf. It is located at the Jebel Ali Hotel.

The UAE Golf Association (www.ugagolf.com) is a non-profit organisation dedicated to supporting junior players and developing the national team.

Horse Riding

Horse riding has long been part of the Arabian tradition and many riding centres organise activities in Dubai. The horse racing season in Dubai runs from October to May during which regular weekly events take place at the race courses at Nad Al Sheba and Jebel Ali.

The ruling Maktoum family of Dubai are the patrons of horse racing, including endurance riding in Dubai and H.H. General Sheikh Mohammed bin Rashid Al Maktoum, who is famed throughout the world for promotion of and participation in endurance riding, has played a major part in placing the emirate firmly on the international racing map.

▲ A winning moment at the races.

The Dubai World Cup, (www.dubaiworldcup.com) the richest horse race in the world, is the highlight of Dubai's racing calendar and is held at the end of March each year. Among the equestrian clubs in Dubai are the Club Joumana, Emirates Riding Centre and Jebel Ali Equestrian Club.

Shooting

Shooting and archery are offered at the Jebel Ali Shooting Club, which is approximately half an hour's drive from Dubai city. The Club among other things offers simulated laser shooting, pistol, skeet and trap shooting. The Hatta Fort Hotel and Ras Al Khaimah Shooting Club also offer facilities and instruction.

Flying

The Dubai Flying Association was formed in 1987 and is a registered flying group of qualified pilots. The club is non-profit making, and aims to provide instructions to members at cost. Flying instruction is offered at Emirates Flying School, Fujairah Aviation Centre and Umm Al Quwain Aeroclub.

Wadi Bashing

▲ Wadi bashing in the Hajar Mountains

Wadi bashing is the exploration of stream beds which flow after the winter rains in the Hajar Mountains. Four-wheel drive vehicles are used and some of the most beautiful scenery in the world can be enjoyed. Many tour companies in Dubai organise trips into the desert wilderness.

Dune Driving

An unforgettable experience, dune driving as the name suggests, involves driving (four-wheel drives) on the dunes. Many tour operators provide organised desert safari tours which feature dune driving and a traditional Arabian barbecue in the desert.

Sand-Skiing/Boarding

Sand-skiing/boarding is a popular sport in Dubai and many of the tour operators provide trips to the desert dunes for this purpose. Basic instruction is also offered on how to stay up, how to fall and how to surf.

Camel Racing

Camel racing which takes place on Thursdays and Fridays (in the winter months) is a very popular sport among local people and can be a truly unforgettable experience. Many of the races take place under the patronage of the Ruling families of the UAE. The Nad Al Sheba Camel Race Track hosts various events annually. Morning races start very early, usually by 7:00 a.m., and the races are over by 8:30 a.m. Otherwise it's possible to watch the animals being trained at around 10:00 a.m. Admission is free.

Falconry

Falconry is one of the oldest sports in the region and is deeply imbedded in the tradition of the local people, although only a select few currently engage in it during their leisure times. It is the sport of the Sheikhs, and at one time falcons were used to catch wild prey, such as hare, so that the family would not have to kill any of their valuable livestock for meat. Some tour companies arrange falconry shows for their guests.

▲ Falconry is a favoured sport in the UAE.

Rugby

Rugby is a very popular sport particularly among the expatriates in the UAE. Dubai hosts the Dubai International Rugby Sevens around the month of December each year. This involves three tournaments over the span of two days. The tournaments attract international teams from all the major rugby playing nations.

Mountain Climbing

In Dubai, the rock-climbing enthusiast has only one option – the indoor climbing wall at Pharaohs Club in Wafi City, (www.waficity.com/sports). Classes run by professional instructors are available. The walls are varied with routes for climbing and bouldering, with crash mats for safety during low level climbs and top-ropes on all routes.

Excellent rock climbing options can be found outside of Dubai, especially in Ras Al Khaimah, Dibba, Hatta and the Al Ain/Buraimi region. Several areas are now being developed for sport climbing, and a growing number of climbs are being bolted for safety.

Activities

Dubai offers an excellent range of health clubs, beach clubs and sports facilities. Health clubs generally offer classes and personal training in keeping fit. Workout facilities include free weights and machines, swimming pools, steam and sauna. Beach clubs have the added bonus of beach access. Sports clubs generally have similar facilities as health clubs and also offer their members additional facilities like tennis, squash and/or golf.

A listing of the popular activities in Dubai can be found in the directory on the enclosed CD.

Nightlife

Dubai has a very vibrant nightlife. The bars in the hotels cater to a wide variety of tastes from traditional English pubs to American cocktail lounges. Most bars offer live music. In addition to the bars, there are a number of nightclubs and discotheques. Dubai's nightclubs generally get going at about 11:00 p.m. and go on until late. Even on weeknights, there is a good crowd and at the weekend many places are packed. Dubai also has an excellent selection of bars with a good variety of styles.

A listing of the most popular nightclubs and discothèques in Dubai can be found in the director, included on the CD.

Eating Out

Dubai boasts a huge variety of truly international restaurants, many of which are situated in the city's hotels and are therefore able to serve alcohol. Outside of the hotels there are a range of restaurants, fast food bars and cafes. Eating out in Dubai is fairly inexpensive. Service charges are usually included in bills, but if not, a 10% tip is generally appreciated. A listing of the most popular restaurants in Dubai can be found in the directory.

www.dubaicityguide.com/tourism/sightsee.htm, www.dubaitourism.co.ae   Places to Visit

Dubai and its surrounding areas contain numerous places of interest, which can be explored by residents and visitors alike. Places to visit include museums and heritage sites, parks and beaches, as well as tour and sightseeing opportunities. Some of these places are detailed below.

Sheikh Saeed's House

This ancient palace used to house the late ruler of Dubai, H.H. Sheikh Saeed bin Maktoum Al Maktoum (1912-1958), the grandfather of H.H. Sheikh Maktoum bin Rashid Al Maktoum (the current Ruler of Dubai). It has been fully restored and is now a museum open to visitors. It was strategically located at the mouth of Dubai Creek, but this carefully restored house-turned-museum is now situated close to the Bur Dubai side of Al Shindagha Tunnel. There are different sections of the house showing aspects of life in Dubai before the discovery of oil, as well as some rare photographs of Dubai.

Heritage & Diving Village

A traditional heritage village, located near the mouth of the Creek, has been created where potters and weavers display their crafts. Here the visitor can look back in time and experience some of Dubai's heritage. The Diving Village forms part of an ambitious plan to turn the entire Shindagha area into a cultural microcosm, recreating life in Dubai as it was in days gone by.

▼ The Dubai Museum

The Al Fahidi Fort (Dubai Museum)

The Al Fahidi Fort was first built in 1799 and was renovated into a museum in 1993. The Fort, which stands near the Ruler's Office in Bur Dubai, contains a number of archeological displays and offers a unique insight into the lives of the local people before the discovery of oil. It also houses artefacts from graves that date back to the third millennium BC. Everything in this museum is represented in an original and highly creative way.

The Jumeirah Mosque

Although there are many mosques in Dubai, none is as beautiful as the Jumeirah Mosque. This is a stunning example of modern Islamic architecture and is, perhaps, one of the most photographed sites in Dubai. The Sheikh Mohammed Centre for Cultural Understanding organises tours of this mosque on Sunday and Thursday mornings. These tours are conducted by a guide, who explains the process and procedure of prayer. The Centre can be contacted at 04-3536666.

The Bastakiya District

The Bastakiya district is one of the first areas to be originally settled in Dubai (around the nineteenth century). It displays the traditional courtyard houses and windtowers, which were used for cooling purposes before electricity was introduced here.

▲ A windtower in a culturally preserved area.

Burj Nahar

Built in 1870, Burj Nahar is one of the watchtowers, which guarded the city in the past and stands in the Deira district of Dubai.

Bait Al Wakeel

Situated near the Abra (traditional boat) landing at the Dubai Creek and built in 1934, Bait Al Wakeel is Dubai's first office building, which has now been renovated into a museum featuring Dubai's fishing and maritime traditions.

Palaces

Many visitors to Dubai find a drive past the beachfront palaces near Umm Suqeim to be a delightful experience. The modern Arabic architecture tends to stretch the imagination.

Hatta

Hatta, which is about an hour's drive from Dubai city, is one of UAE's popular mountainous and green attractions. The Hatta Fort Hotel which is the only mountain resort complex in Dubai is a beautiful resort which does wonders in terms of relaxation. The Hatta village is over 200 years old, and houses an old fort and spectacular wadi.

Al Maha Resort   www.al-maha.com

Al Maha Resort, which is the first ecotourism project in the UAE, consists of 27 standard suites and 2 royal suites. Part of the Emirates Group, it is located on a 3,300 acre site in the Dubai desert off

▲ A ride at the Wild Wadi Water Park

Al Ain motorway, and is approximately 45 minutes drive from the city. Ninety eight per cent of the site consists of a beautiful nature reserve.

www.wildwadi.com   The Wild Wadi

A water park in 12 acres of pure fun with 23 adrenalin pumping rides that leave you asking for more. It is situated between the Burj Al Arab and the Jumeriah Beach Hotel, a mere 20 minute drive from the city centre.

www.godolphin.com/prizes1   Godolphin Gallery

A great location for horse racing fans, the Godolphin Gallery features the ruling Maktoum family's private racing stable, and houses the world's finest collection of horse racing trophies.

www.goldanddiamondpark.com   Gold & Diamond Museum

Within the Gold & Diamond Park is the visitors' centre which includes a museum and a themed café. Exhibits include traditional Arabic jewellery giving their history, and there are guided tours of the manufacturing plant to see how jewellery is made.

Chapter Ten

Local Customs and Traditions

Religion

While Dubai is renowned for being a very open and liberal country, it should always be remembered that it is a Muslim country. Those wishing to live in Dubai should therefore acquire knowledge of the religious beliefs, customs and traditions of the people among whom they will be living and dealing with.

Islam

▲ The Jumeirah Mosque, a milestone in architectural splendour

Islam, the second largest religion in the world, is the official religion of the UAE. Islam literally means submission to the will of God. Its essence lies in the belief of its followers, the Muslims in an omnipotent, omnipresent, omniscient and monotheistic God, Allah, endorsed by the doctrine of unity and sovereignty.

Muslims believe that since the creation of the world, guidance on every aspect of life was revealed to humankind, through a series of prophets beginning with Adam, followed by Noah, Abraham, Moses, Jesus and many others in between. These divine missions culminated with the 'seal' of the prophets, Mohammad (570-632), and consequently the birth of Islam.

The Holy Quran and the Sunna, the Prophet Mohammed's teachings (which are the holy books of Islam) provide, among other things, a complete set of rules, which govern all aspects of human behavior. One of the sources of law in the UAE is the Sharia. Literally, Sharia means 'the way to a watering place' or the path to be followed. In western legal equivalence, it refers to Islamic law and is applicable to spiritual, material and temporal aspects of life.

Muslims pray five times a day. Prayer times are announced in the newspapers daily and are signalled by a call to prayer, which is broadcast by all mosques on loudspeakers. A full list of prayer times for the complete year can be obtained from the Ministry of Information & Culture. If a Muslim cannot attend a mosque or prayer room, he may pray in an area which is open to the public. Watching or walking in front of a Muslim while in the act of praying is considered impolite.

Though Islam is the official religion of the UAE, other religions are respected. Dubai has various Christian churches, such as the Evangelical Community Church, Holy Trinity Church, International Christian Church, St Mary's and St Francis de Assisi Churches (both Roman Catholic) and St. Thomas Orthodox Church. There are also two Hindu temples and a Sikh Gurudwara in Bur Dubai.

Ramadan

In Islam, Ramadan is the holy month and commemorates the revelation of the Holy Quran (the holy book of Islam). It is the time of year that Muslims fast and abstain from all food, drinks, cigarettes and unclean thoughts between dawn and dusk. In the evening, the fast is broken with the Iftar feast. Iftar timings are found in all the daily newspapers.

Social Customs

Shaking hands is an important social custom in the Arab world. As a sign of friendship, a handshake will generally take longer than it would in the West. It is also important to shake hands when leaving. However, it should be noted that some Muslim women do not shake hands with men. It is therefore wise to allow a Muslim woman to initiate a handshake.

▲ A traditional form of greeting in the Arab World

When meeting with an Arab, one is usually offered tea or coffee in addition to other refreshments, refusal of which may be considered insulting. Arabs are very proud of their reputation for great hospitality and may be offended if this hospitality is shunned. Eating or offering things should be done with the right hand rather than the left. Tea is usually served sweet and dark and normally in a small glass cup. A taste for this tea is easily acquired and it is surprisingly refreshing, particularly on hot summer days. Arabic coffee is usually served in a small cup too. If the meeting is at an Arabic home, one should normally remove one's shoes before entering. Sitting with one's soles pointing at someone else is considered impolite and insulting.

A person's clothing and general appearance is particularly important in Arab society. Office wear for men is lightweight trousers, shirt and tie. Jackets are only worn for important meetings and formal occasions. Ladies should wear a lightweight dress or long sleeved blouse and skirt. Away from the office, lightweight summer clothing is suitable for almost the entire year. The general dress code in Dubai is quite relaxed, although women should not wear clothing which is too revealing. Men should always wear a top in public. However, swimwear is acceptable at the poolside and on beaches.

In public, nationals choose to wear their traditional dress. For men this is the 'dishdash(a)' or 'khandura', a white full length shirt-dress, which is worn with a white or red checked headdress, known as a 'gutra'. This is secured with a black cord, 'agal'. For women, it is the 'abaya', a long loose black robe that covers their normal clothes along with a headscarf called the 'sheyla'.

Care should be taken when photographing in Dubai. It is best to avoid photographing Arab women, military buildings or installations and police stations.

It is advisable not to ask an Arab man about his wife, even if one knows him or her well. When exchanging pleasantries it is best to simply ask about the family.

It should also be noted that Dubai has a very young and cosmopolitan Arab population, with many individuals who have lived and traveled in the West. Many Arabs in Dubai (particularly the younger generation) are, therefore, unlikely to be too offended by minor breaches of social custom. Nonetheless, as with any foreign country, social and cultural norms should be respected if one is to enjoy and successfully conduct one's affairs.

Language

The official language of the country is Arabic, but English, Urdu and Hindi are widely spoken in Dubai. In addition, most of the road and shop signs, restaurant menus, etc., are in both English and Arabic. An attempt to speak basic Arabic will, however, be greatly appreciated. It is worth noting that written Arabic is different from spoken Arabic and although all Arabs can understand each other regardless of which country they come from, they do speak in diverse dialects.

We have set out below a number of common Arabic expressions (in the national dialect), which may be of use to non-Arabic speakers.

General	
Greeting	Assalam Alaikoom
Greeting (in reply)	Walaikoom Assalam
Hello	Marhaba
Hello (In reply)	Marhabtain
How are you	Keef halak
Fine, Praise be to God	Al Hamdu Lillah
Thank You	Shukran
Welcome	Marhaba
Goodbye	Ma'a Salama
Yes	Naam
No	La
What is your name	Shoo Ismak/Ismik (male/female)
My name is	Ismi
Please	Min Fadlak/ Fadlik (male/female)
I am sorry	Mut 'assef
Enough	Bas
Finished	Khallass
Hurry	Yalla Besora
Go away	Rooh
Good	Zain
Bad	Muzain
God willing	Insha Allah
Wait a moment	Stanna Shway
Let's go/come on	Yallah

Numbers	
One	Wahad
Two	Ithnain
Three	Thalatha
Four	Arba'a
Five	Khamsa
Six	Sitta
Seven	Saba'a
Eight	Thamania
Nine	Tissa'a
Ten	Ashra

Relating to taxis	
Straight On	Seeda
Slow Down	Shway Shway
Left	Yasaar
Right	Yameen
Stop	Kuf
Roundabout	Duwaar
Restaurant	Mata'am
Hotel	Funduk
Airport	Mataar

Alcohol

Alcoholic beverages are available in all the bars and restaurants in Dubai's four and five star hotels and sports clubs. However, they should not be consumed in other public places. If you wish to buy alcohol for consumption at home, you will need a special liquor licence to buy from an authorised liquor shop. You do not need a liquor licence to consume alcohol in a licenced hotel or club.

It should be noted that it is a criminal offence to sell and buy alcohol without obtaining the necessary permission or licence. The licence allows an individual to spend a limited amount on alcohol per month. This amount is based on one's monthly salary. The minimum monthly salary required is generally Dhs 3,500.

Only non-Muslims with a valid residence visa may obtain an alcohol licence. For married couples, only husbands may apply.

→ Procedure to get an Alchohol licence

An alcohol licence for individual use can be obtained by submitting an application on the prescribed form in both English and Arabic to the Dubai Police Headquarters. Your employer must submit the application form signed and stamped together with the following documents.

❶

Passport (and spouse's passport, if applicable) together with a photocopy containing valid residence permit

❷

Two passport size photographs with the name written on the reverse

❸

Copy of the employment contract (stating salary)

❹

Copy of tenancy agreement

❺

The appropriate licence fee (currently Dhs 105)

Business Etiquette

Foreign investment along with the expatriate population in Dubai has grown rapidly, and business customs here are generally the same as they are in the West. However, the foreign businessman should bear in mind a few points when doing business in Dubai.

• Always be on time. However, be prepared to accept delays or even postponements of meetings at short notice. Patience is a virtue and everyone is expected to wait no matter how important they are. This is purely a matter of local custom, and the product of a much slower lifestyle.

• Business meetings tend to be less formal. At an initial meeting there may be others in the room. The host may often be interrupted by staff or other visitors. It should be noted that the purpose of such a meeting is to arrange for a further private meeting.

• In any meeting or telephone conversation, a period of small talk is expected before the purpose of the meeting or call is discussed.

• Business cards should be printed in both English and Arabic. All brochures and leaflets should ideally be glossy, full of photographs and should also be printed in both English and Arabic.

• Respect confidentiality as Dubai is a very small community and word can get around very fast. It is therefore very important that all business discussions are kept in the strictest confidence. Breaches of confidence are not appreciated.

• Verbal agreements are binding and so the negotiator must be careful not to commit himself. It should be remembered that bargaining is very important. An Arab will take great pride in obtaining a good deal. This is not, however, an excuse to overcharge at the outset. There must be a reason for every price reduction so as to avoid suspicion of overpricing. Given the nature of Arab courtesy, a proposal is unlikely to be rejected outright at a meeting. An indication that a purchase may take place may be nothing more than polite interest in the product.

▼ The handshake - the preferred gesture for friendship

ADR	Alternative Dispute Resolution
CCL	Commercial Companies Law
DAFZA	Dubai Airport Free Zone Authority
DCA	Dubai Department of Civil Aviation
DCCI	Dubai Chamber of Commerce & Industry
DCV	Dubai Cargo Village
DDF	Dubai Duty Free
DDIA	Dubai Development & Investment Authority
DED	Dubai Department of Economic Development
DEWA	Dubai Electricity & Water Authority
DFM	Dubai Financial Market
DFSA	Duty Free Storage Area
DGDP	Dubai Gold & Diamond Park
DHCC	Dubai Healthcare City
Dhs	Dirham or the Arab Emirate Dirham (AED), the UAE Currency
DIA	Dubai International Airport
DIC	Dubai Internet City
DICC	Dubai International Convention Centre
DIMC	Dubai International Marine Club
DIP	Dubai Investments Park
DMC	Dubai Media City
DNATA	Dubai National Air Travel Agency
DNR	Department of Naturalization & Residency
DOHMS	Dubai Department of Health & Medical Services
DPA	Dubai Ports Authority
DQA	Dubai Quality Award
DSDY	Dubai Ship Docking Yard
DSF	Dubai Shopping Festival

DSS	Dubai Summer Surprises
DTCM	Dubai Department of Tourism & Commerce Marketing
DUCAMZ	Dubai Cars and Automotive Zone
DWTC	Dubai World Trade Centre
Etisalat	Emirates Telecommunications Corporation
FZ LLC	Free Zone Limited Liability Company
FZCO	Free Zone Company
FZE	Free Zone Establishment
GCC	Gulf Co-operation Council
GSM	Global System for Mobile Communications
H.H.	His Highness
IPTA	Inter Port Transfer Authority
JAFZA	Jebel Ali Free Zone Authority
LLC	Limited Liability Company
MOH	Ministry of Health
NOC	No Objection Certificate
OAPEC	Organisation of Arab Petroleum Exporting Companies
OFC	Operation Fitness Certificate
OPEC	Organisation of Petroleum Exporting Companies
PCFC	Ports, Customs and Free Zone Corporation
PJSC	Public Joint Stock Company
PLS	Partnership Limited with Shares
TECOM	Dubai Technology, E-Commerce & Media Free Zone Authority
UAE	United Arab Emirates
WTO	World Trade Organisation

Chapter 5 Employment Issues

Chapter 6 Housing and Accomodation

Chapter 7 Health and Education

We would like to thank the following individuals and organisations for their assistance and contribution of photographs to this edition of 'Setting Up in Dubai'.

Cover: Dubai Development & Investment Authority
Back: Dubai International Financial Centre, Nakheel Properties / Hill & Knowlton, Dubai Ports Authority

• **Page 2** Sheikh Zayed bin Sultan Al Nahyan – Mohammed Hamid Durrani • **Page 2** Early View of the Creek – DTCM • **Page 3** Oil Field – Khalidia Palace Hotel • **Page 4** DIFC Gate – Dubai International Financial Centre • **Page 4** Burj Dubai – Emaar Properties • **Page 5** Sheikh Rashid Terminal – Dept. of Civil Aviation • **Page 5** Jebel Ali Port – Dubai Ports Authority • **Page 6** Burj Al Arab - Dubai Development and Investment Authority • **Page 16** Ruler's Pictures – Ruler's Court • **Page 21** Justice Scales - Dubai Development and Investment Authority • **Page 34** Population - Dubai World Trade Centre • **Page 37 & 39** Post Office & Boxes – Emirates Post • **Page 48** WTC Exhibition Halls - Dept. of Tourism & Commerce Marketing • **Page 49** DICC - Dubai World Trade Centre • **Page 49** Grand Hyatt – Grand Hyatt • **Page 50** Passport Control-DCA• **Page 77** Customs centres – Dubai Customs • **Page 83** Al Aweer Customs Centre – Dubai Customs • **Page 89** DCCI – Dubai Municipality • **Page 95** Dubai Quality Award – Dubai Quality Award Secretariat • **Page 96** Dubai Shopping Festival - DDIA • **Page 97** Dubai Municipality – Dubai Municipality • **Page 104** DTCM – Dubai Municipality • **Page 109** DIFC - DIFC • **Page 110** DDIA Offices – Dubai Municipality • **Page 111** TECOM – www.dubaiinternetcity.com • **Page 112** JAFZ – DPA • **Page 113 & 242** DAFZ - DDIA • **Page 114** Dubai Cargo Village - DCA • **Page 115** World Trade Centre – Dubai Municipality • **Page 115** Dubai Investments Park - Dubai Investments Park • **Page 208** Creek – Dubai Municipality • **Page 208** Jumeirah Beach Hotel – Dubai Municipality • **Page 208** Marriott Executive Apartments – Union Properties / Tamra C2 • **Page 210** Jumeirah Islands – Nakheel Properties / Hill & Knowlton • Page 210 Jumeirah Beach Residence – Estithmaar Realty / Bates Pangulf • **Page 210** The Palm Jumeirah & The Palm Jebel Ali – Nakheel Properties / Hill & Knowlton • **Page 210 & Page 211** Dubai Marina, Emirates Hills, The Meadows, The Springs, The Greens, Arabian Ranches & Gazelle – Emaar Properties • **Page 211** Green Community – Union Properties / Tamra C2 • **Page 214** Creek – Dubai Municipality • **Page 217** – The Palm Jumeirah – Nakheel Properties / Hill & Knowlton • **Page 222** Dubai Healthcare City – Dubai Healthcare City • **Page 224** Knowledge Village – Knowledge Village • **Page 228** Trade Centre Interchange – Dubai Municipality • **Page 235** Al Awir Used Car Complex – Dubai Municipality • **Page 238** Abra – Dubai Municipality • **Page 239** – Dubai International Airport - DDIA • **Page 241** Dubai Duty Free – Dubai Duty Free • **Page 241** Interior of Sheikh Rashid Terminal - DCA • **Page 242** Airport Facilities - DCA • **Page 243** Port Rashid - DPA • **Page 243** Jebel Ali Port - JAFZA • **Page 244** Creek – Dubai Municipality • **Page 245** Proposed Rail Route – based on a Dubai Metro Map - Khaleej Times • **Page 248** Al Ghurair City – Al Ghurair City • **Page 248** Deira City Centre – Deira City Centre • **Page 248** Mercato Mall – Mercato Mall • **Page 249** Gold Souk – DTCM • **Page 252** The Montgomerie – Emaar Properties • **Page 253** Wadi Bashing - DTCM • **Page 257** Wild Wadi – www.jumeirahinternational.com •

Other publications by Essam Al Tamimi

United Arab Emirates, Court of Cassation Judgements, 1989-1997
- Richard Price and Essam Al Tamimi

The workings, attitudes, and jurisprudence of the United Arab Emirates Courts often remain an area of mystery to businesspeople. But the cases decided there bear major relevance and interest for all entities doing business in and with the United Arab Emirates and their legal advisors.

Any serious practitioner or academic in the field of Middle Eastern law needs a window onto this important forum. United Arab Emirates Court of Cassation Judgments 1989-1997 provides, for the first time in any language, summaries of recent key decisions of the Courts of Cassation (Supreme Courts) of Dubai and Abu Dhabi in the United Arab Emirates. These decisions address: questions of jurisdiction, conflict of laws, banking, insurance, maritime law, arbitration, and commerce in general.

Price: $ 133.00
ISBN: 9041110054

- Hardcover: 344 pages
- Publisher: Kluwer Law International (March 1999)

Practical Guide to Litigation and Arbitration in the United Arab Emirtaes
- Essam Al Tamimi

A detailed guide to litigation and arbitration in the United Arab Emirates based on Federal laws, laws specific to the individual Emirates, judgments delivered by the Court of Cassation and International Conventions to which the United Arab Emirates is a member.

- Hardcover 179 Pages, First Edition 2003
- Publisher: Kluwer Law International, Arab and Islamic Laws Series Volume 26

ISBN 90 411 2221 4

Know of someone who needs 'Business Investor' information about Dubai?

Give them a copy of 'Setting Up in Dubai'.

☐ Yes! I want _____ copies of 'Setting Up in Dubai' at Dhs 79.00 each.
Shipping charges (within UAE only).
Dhs 10 per copy. Each additional copy, add Dhs 5. Allow a week for delivery after receipt of form.

☐ Yes! I am interested in having a seminar conducted about Setting Up in Dubai. Please send me information.

My cheque/money order for _____ is enclosed.
or Please charge my Card

☐ Visa   ☐ Master Card   ☐ American Express

Card No ☐☐☐☐ ☐☐☐☐ ☐☐☐☐ ☐☐☐☐

Expiry Date ☐☐☐☐

Account Holder _____

Cardholder's signature _____

_____

Contact Details

Please use block letters

Organisation _____

Address _____

_____

_____

E Mail _____

Payable to

Cross Border Legal Publishing FZ LLC
PO Box 502129, Dubai, UAE.
info@crossborder.ae
Tel: 00971 4 3903520
Fax: 00971 4 3908219